PRINCE2 Agile™

AXELOS.com

Published by TSO (The Stationery Office), part of Williams Lea, and available from:

Online
www.tsoshop.co.uk

Mail, Telephone, Fax & E-mail
TSO
PO Box 29, Norwich, NR3 1GN
Telephone orders/General enquiries: 0870 600 5522
Fax orders: 0870 600 5533
E-mail: customer.services@tso.co.uk
Textphone 0870 240 3701

TSO@Blackwell and other Accredited Agents

First published 2015

ISBN 9780113314676

Printed in the United Kingdom for The Stationery Office
Material is FSC certified and produced using ECF pulp, sourced from fully sustainable forests.

P002701029   6/15

Contents

List of figures   vi

List of images   vii

List of tables   viii

Foreword   ix

About AXELOS   x

Acknowledgements   xi

Contents summary   xiii

PART I INTRODUCTION AND OVERVIEWS   1

1   PRINCE2 Agile introduction   3

1.1   What is PRINCE2 Agile?   5

1.2   PRINCE2 Agile is for projects only   5

2   An overview of agile   7

2.1   Introduction   9

2.2   Agile basics   10

**3   The rationale for blending PRINCE2
       and agile**   15

3.1   Who is PRINCE2 Agile for?   18

3.2   Which communities will benefit from
       PRINCE2 Agile?   18

3.3   When and where can I apply
       PRINCE2 Agile?   19

3.4   Course of action for each community in
       each situation   20

3.5   What does PRINCE2 Agile consist of?   20

3.6   Important points about PRINCE2 Agile
       and this manual   21

3.7   Beware of prejudice!   22

4   The PRINCE2 journey when using agile   23

4.1   Pre-project and the initiation stage   25

4.2   Subsequent delivery stages   27

4.3   Final delivery stage   29

5   An overview of PRINCE2   31

5.1   The structure of PRINCE2   34

5.2   The principles   34

5.3   The themes   36

5.4   The processes   36

5.5   The project environment   36

6   What to fix and what to flex?   37

6.1   The concept of flexing what is delivered   39

6.2   Why is there a need to work this way?

6.3   The rationale behind flexing what is
       being delivered   40

6.4   The five targets in more detail   40

6.5   Chapter summary   43

**PART II PRINCE2 AGILE GUIDANCE,
TAILORING AND TECHNIQUES**   45

7   Agile and the PRINCE2 principles   47

7.1   The PRINCE2 principles   49

7.2   The general view of agile with respect
       to the PRINCE2 principles   49

7.3   Guidance on applying the PRINCE2
       principles   49

7.4   PRINCE2 Agile behaviours   51

7.5   PRINCE2 principles summary   53

8   Agile and the PRINCE2 themes   55

8.1   The PRINCE2 themes   57

8.2   Some themes are more prominent
       than others   57

8.3   Summary of tailoring guidance for the
       PRINCE2 themes   58

9   Business Case theme   61

9.1   The PRINCE2 approach to the
       Business Case theme   63

9.2   The general view of agile with respect
       to the Business Case theme   63

9.3   PRINCE2 Agile guidance for the
       Business Case theme   64

9.4   Agile concepts and techniques   65

9.5   Business Case theme summary   68

10   Organization theme   71

10.1 The PRINCE2 approach to the
       Organization theme   73

10.2 The general view of agile with respect
       to the Organization theme   75

10.3 PRINCE2 Agile guidance for the
       Organization theme   76

10.4 Different concepts regarding roles
       between PRINCE2 and agile   76

10.5 Agile concepts and techniques   83

10.6 Organization theme summary   90

11	**Quality theme**	**91**
11.1	The PRINCE2 approach to the Quality theme	93
11.2	The general view of agile with respect to the Quality theme	94
11.3	PRINCE2 Agile guidance for the Quality theme	94
11.4	Agile concepts and techniques	97
11.5	Quality theme summary	97
12	**Plans theme**	**99**
12.1	The PRINCE2 approach to the Plans theme	101
12.2	The general view of agile with respect to the Plans theme	101
12.3	PRINCE2 Agile guidance for the Plans theme	102
12.4	Agile concepts and techniques	106
12.5	Plans theme summary	108
13	**Risk theme**	**109**
13.1	The PRINCE2 approach to the Risk theme	111
13.2	The general view of agile with respect to the Risk theme	112
13.3	PRINCE2 Agile guidance for the Risk theme	113
13.4	Agile concepts and techniques	114
13.5	Risk theme summary	114
14	**Change theme**	**117**
14.1	The PRINCE2 approach to the Change theme	119
14.2	The general view of agile with respect to the Change theme	119
14.3	PRINCE2 Agile guidance for the Change theme	120
14.4	Agile concepts and techniques	122
14.5	Change theme summary	123
15	**Progress theme**	**125**
15.1	The PRINCE2 approach to the Progress theme	127
15.2	The general view of agile with respect to the Progress theme	127
15.3	PRINCE2 Agile guidance for the Progress theme	128
15.4	Agile concepts and techniques	129
15.5	Progress theme summary	133
16	**Agile and the PRINCE2 processes**	**135**
16.1	The PRINCE2 processes	137
16.2	Tailoring guidance for the PRINCE2 processes	138
17	**Starting up a Project; Initiating a Project**	**141**
17.1	PRINCE2 guidance on Starting up a Project and Initiating a Project	143
17.2	Agile ways of working that may already exist	145
17.3	PRINCE2 Agile guidance on Starting up a Project and Initiating a Project	145
17.4	Agile concepts and techniques	149
17.5	Summary	151
18	**Directing a Project**	**153**
18.1	PRINCE2 guidance on Directing a Project	155
18.2	Agile ways of working that may already exist	156
18.3	PRINCE2 Agile guidance on Directing a Project	156
18.4	Summary	157
19	**Controlling a Stage**	**159**
19.1	PRINCE2 guidance on Controlling a Stage	161
19.2	Agile ways of working that may already exist	162
19.3	PRINCE2 Agile guidance on Controlling a Stage	162
19.4	Agile concepts and techniques	166
19.5	Summary	168
20	**Managing Product Delivery**	**171**
20.1	PRINCE2 guidance on Managing Product Delivery	173
20.2	Agile ways of working that may already exist	174
20.3	PRINCE2 Agile guidance for Managing Product Delivery	174
20.4	Agile concepts and techniques	176
20.5	Summary	187
21	**Managing a Stage Boundary**	**189**
21.1	PRINCE2 guidance on Managing a Stage Boundary	191

21.2 Agile ways of working that may
     already exist   192
21.3 PRINCE2 Agile guidance on Managing
     a Stage Boundary   192
21.4 Summary   194
22   Closing a Project   195
22.1 PRINCE2 guidance on Closing a Project 197
22.2 Agile ways of working that may
     already exist   198
22.3 PRINCE2 Agile guidance on Closing
     a Project   198
22.4 Agile concepts and techniques   200
22.5 Summary   201
23   Summary of tailoring guidance for the
     PRINCE2 products   203
23.1 Baseline products   205
23.2 Record products   207
23.3 Report products   207

PART III AREAS OF PARTICULAR FOCUS
FOR PRINCE2 AGILE   209
24   The Agilometer   211
24.1 Purpose   213
24.2 When to assess suitability   213
24.3 How suitability is assessed
     (the Agilometer)   213
24.4 Responding to the assessment   214
24.5 Monitoring the assessment   216
24.6 Evolving the Agilometer   216
24.7 The Agilometer slider definitions   216
25   Requirements   219
25.1 Purpose   221
25.2 Requirements definition   222
25.3 Defining product descriptions   222
25.4 Requirements decomposition
     and granularity   222
25.5 Requirements prioritization   223
25.6 Agile concepts and techniques   228
26   Rich communication   233
26.1 Purpose   235
26.2 Forms of communication   235

26.3 The PRINCE2 Agile approach to
     communication   235
26.4 Agile concepts and techniques   238
27   Frequent releases   241
27.1 Purpose   243
27.2 Releasing early and frequently   243
27.3 Summary   245
28   Creating contracts when
     using agile   247
28.1 Traditional contracts   249
28.2 Primary considerations when structuring
     an agile contract   249
28.3 Guidance on how to structure an
     agile contract   250
28.4 The role of the supplier in an
     outcome-based contract   252
28.5 Summary   252
APPENDICES   253
A   Product description outlines   255
B   Roles and responsibilities   277
C   Health check – PRINCE2 Agile version   283
D   Product-based-planning example   287
E   The fundamental values and principles
     of agile (including the Agile Manifesto) 295
F   Transitioning to agile, and what
     constitutes success?   301
G   Advice for a project manager using agile 305
H   The definitive guide to Scrum   311
Glossary   323
Index   337

List of figures

Figure 1.1   The difference between project work and BAU work   6

Figure 2.1   The Agile Manifesto   9

Figure 2.2   The contrast between Waterfall and agile phases   10

Figure 2.3   A basic 'backlog' and 'sprint' structure for delivering software   11

Figure 2.4   Sprints may exist within a wider context   11

Figure 3.1   Blending PRINCE2 and agile together   17

Figure 3.2   Tailoring PRINCE2 by blending in the agile ingredients   20

Figure 4.1   The life of a PRINCE2 project   25

Figure 5.1   Project management   33

Figure 5.2   The structure of PRINCE2   34

Figure 6.1   Applying tolerances to the six aspects of a project   39

Figure 6.2   On balance, what is more important to the customer?   44

Figure 7.1   PRINCE2 Agile behaviours   49

Figure 7.2   How a behaviour dashboard may look if a project manager is reporting to a project board   53

Figure 9.1   The development path of the business case   63

Figure 10.1   The three project interests   73

Figure 10.2   Project management team structure   74

Figure 10.3   Integrating the team manager role into an agile delivery team   78

Figure 10.4   An example of an organizational set-up for a project with one team   81

Figure 10.5   An example of an organizational set-up for a project with many teams   82

Figure 11.1   The quality audit trail   93

Figure 12.1   PRINCE2's planning levels   101

Figure 12.2   Timeboxed versus flow-based working   103

Figure 12.3   Different planning levels, horizons and formats   104

Figure 12.4   Painting a wall – comparing effort with complexity   108

Figure 13.1   The risk management procedure   112

Figure 13.2   An informal risk register may be appropriate in certain situations   113

Figure 14.1   Requirements change can happen to the baseline or to the detail   120

Figure 14.2   The feedback loop   122

Figure 15.1   Burn-down and burn-up charts   129

Figure 15.2   An example of how an information radiator might look   132

Figure 16.1   The PRINCE2 processes   137

Figure 16.2   The PRINCE2 processes and management products   139

Figure 16.3   How releases and sprints typically relate to a PRINCE2 stage   139

Figure 16.4   How typical agile processes would relate to the PRINCE2 process model   140

Figure 17.1   Overview of Starting up a Project   143

Figure 17.2   Overview of Initiating a Project   144

Figure 17.3   The Cynefin framework   149

Figure 18.1   Overview of Directing a Project   155

Figure 19.1   Overview of Controlling a Stage   161

Figure 19.2   A Glad! Sad! Mad! board   167

Figure 20.1   Overview of Managing Product Delivery   173

Figure 20.2   An example of how a Kanban board might look   177

Figure 20.3   An example of how a Kanban ticket might look   178

Figure 20.4   A cumulative flow diagram   181

Figure 20.5   A simple view of how to calculate WIP and lead (or cycle) time   182

Figure 20.6   The effect of delaying the delivery of a product   182

Figure 20.7   A Kanban card is used to signal that stock needs to be replenished   183

Figure 20.8   The build–measure–learn feedback loop from Lean Startup   185

Figure 21.1   Overview of Managing a Stage Boundary   191

Figure 22.1   Overview of Closing a Project   197

Figure 24.1   The Agilometer   214

Figure 25.1 Possible requirements decomposition and equivalent terminology 222
Figure 25.2 'MoSCoWing' a pen 225
Figure 25.3 A good user story and a poor one 230
Figure 26.1 Factors that may improve the quality and speed of communication 237
Figure D.1 Product breakdown structure in the form of a hierarchy chart 291
Figure D.2 Product breakdown structure in the form of a mindmap 291

List of images

Image 3.1 An agile fighter aircraft 22
Image 8.1 Merging fixed with flexible ways of working 57
Image 15.1 An example of a team board 131
Image 23.1 Adapting and reworking the PRINCE2 products 208
Image 25.1 List your priorities 227
Image 26.1 Agile makes extensive use of workshops 238

List of tables

Table 1.1   The different characteristics of a project and BAU work   5

Table 2.1   The most well-known agile methods and approaches   12

Table 2.2   Typical agile behaviours, concepts and techniques   13

Table 3.1   The communities on which PRINCE2 Agile is focused   18

Table 3.2   The situations for which PRINCE2 Agile is suitable   19

Table 3.3   The relationship between each community and each situation with respect to PRINCE2 Agile   19

Table 3.4   Summary of the key points in Chapter 3   22

Table 5.1   The PRINCE2 themes   35

Table 6.1   How PRINCE2 Agile views tolerances for the six aspects of a project: fix or flex?   40

Table 6.2   The five targets behind flexing what is delivered   41

Table 7.1   Overview of the guidance when applying PRINCE2 principles in an agile context   50

Table 7.2   Relevant agile guidance on PRINCE2 Agile behaviours   53

Table 8.1   Things to consider when tailoring the PRINCE2 themes to PRINCE2 Agile   58

Table 10.1   Combining PRINCE2 roles with agile roles   76

Table 10.2   Mapping the responsibilities of a PRINCE2 team manager to the common agile roles   77

Table 10.3   Integrating the project manager with the delivery team – options to consider   78

Table 10.4   Guidance on the PRINCE2 roles and possible agile mappings   84

Table 11.1   How to use some of the product description components to provide flexibility   95

Table 11.2   Common agile terms that relate to quality   96

Table 11.3   Relevant agile guidance for the Quality theme   97

Table 12.1   Estimation approaches that may be used at each PRINCE2 plan level   105

Table 12.2   Using ratios along with T-shirt sizes   107

Table 13.1   Agile concepts and techniques relevant to risk management   115

Table 16.1   Key to abbreviations in Figures 16.2 to 16.4   138

Table 16.2   Key to the PRINCE2 management products   138

Table 17.1   PRINCE2 Agile activities for start up and initiation   147

Table 17.2   Relevant agile guidance for Starting up a Project and Initiating a Project   148

Table 18.1   Relevant agile guidance for Directing a Project   156

Table 19.1   PRINCE2 Agile activities for Controlling a Stage   164

Table 19.2   Relevant agile guidance for Controlling a Stage   165

Table 20.1   PRINCE2 Agile activities for Managing Product Delivery   175

Table 20.2   Relevant agile guidance for Managing Product Delivery   176

Table 21.1   PRINCE2 Agile activities for Managing a Stage Boundary   193

Table 21.2   Relevant agile guidance for Managing a Stage Boundary   194

Table 22.1   PRINCE2 Agile activities for Closing a Project   199

Table 22.2   Relevant agile guidance for Closing a Project   200

Table 23.1   Tailoring baseline products   205

Table 23.2   Tailoring record products   207

Table 23.3   Tailoring report products   208

Table 25.1   Requirements and equivalent terms   221

Table 25.2   Typical levels of requirements decomposition   223

Table 25.3   MoSCoW priorities   224

Table 26.1   Possible workshop techniques   239

Table 28.1   Sliding-scale incentives   251

Table 28.2   Levels of trust and incentives   251

Table B.1   PRINCE2 roles   279

Table B.2   PRINCE2 Agile delivery roles   280

Foreword

PRINCE2® is extensively used in more than 150 countries around the world and its take-up grows daily. It is widely considered as the leading method in project management, with thousands of organizations already benefiting from its pioneering and trusted approach. In conjunction with this, there has been a growth in agile delivery approaches as they allow organizations to be more responsive to change. As the use of agile continues to flourish, the need for specific guidance on how to use PRINCE2 in an agile context has grown accordingly.

We at AXELOS Global Best Practice help to make organizations more effective because we work with practitioners collaboratively to ensure that the guidance continues to meet their needs. PRINCE2 Agile is a result of this collaborative relationship.

I believe that PRINCE2 Agile represents an evolution of PRINCE2, being the first extension module to the PRINCE2 method. This guidance is an example of how PRINCE2 can be tailored to your organization in an agile way.

How does the new product relate to the wider PPM portfolio? PRINCE2 Agile will also be of interest to programme managers, with Managing Successful Programmes (MSP®) knowledge, who need to understand not only how a programme relates to projects, but also how projects relate to the delivery mechanism. The majority of the guidance and course material will be new to those familiar with PRINCE2 and will look at the interactions between PRINCE2 and agile, and how each can be adapted to accommodate the other.

I am confident that this new product, along with the associated accredited training and qualification scheme, will help current and aspiring PRINCE2 project managers to successfully deliver their projects in an agile world. I also recommend this guidance to all organizations looking to get the best from combining PRINCE2 project management with agile delivery approaches, as it demonstrates how to optimize the marriage of these two approaches.

Peter Hepworth
CEO
AXELOS Global Best Practice

About AXELOS

PUBLICATIONS

AXELOS publishes a comprehensive range of guidance, including:

- *Managing Successful Projects with PRINCE2*
- *Directing Successful Projects with PRINCE2*
- *Managing Successful Programmes* (MSP®)
- *Management of Portfolios* (MoP®)
- *Portfolio, Programme and Project Offices* (P3O®)
- *Management of Risk* (M_o_R®)
- *Management of Value* (MoV®)
- Portfolio, Programme and Project Management Maturity Model (P3M3®)
- IT service management publications (ITIL®)
- *Cyber Resilience Best Practices* (Resilia™).

Full details of the range of materials published under the AXELOS Global Best Practice banner, including *PRINCE2 Agile,* can be found at:

https://www.axelos.com/best-practice-solutions

If you would like to inform AXELOS of any changes that may be required to *PRINCE2 Agile* or any other AXELOS publication, please log them at:

https://www.axelos.com/best-practice-feedback

CONTACT INFORMATION

Full details on how to contact AXELOS can be found at:

https://www.axelos.com

For further information on qualifications and training accreditation, please visit:

https://www.axelos.com/qualifications

https://www.axelos.com/training-organization-benefits

For all other enquiries, please email:

Ask@AXELOS.com

Acknowledgements

AXELOS Ltd is grateful to everyone who has contributed to the development of this guidance and in particular would like to thank the following:

AUTHOR

Keith Richards

Keith is the founder and director of agilekrc, a company that has specialized in bringing the benefits of agile and Lean to organizations since the late 1990s.

Keith has more than 30 years' experience in IT and project management. He was a trainer in PRINCE2 for nearly a decade and is an accredited PRINCE2 practitioner. He is also an accredited DSDM advanced practitioner and trainer, and an IAF-accredited facilitator.

In 2006 he became the technical director of the DSDM Consortium and in the following year led the team that created DSDM Atern, a project-focused agile framework. Specializing in the pioneering approach of combining agile with PRINCE2, he authored the book *Agile Project Management: Running PRINCE2 projects with DSDM Atern* (TSO, 2007).

In 2010 Keith was involved in the development of Agile Project Management (AgilePM), a ground-breaking new training course and agile qualification from APMG. He was presented with the 'Most Valuable Agile Player' award at the UK Agile Awards in 2011, in recognition of a decade of thought leadership, delivery and innovation.

In 2014 Keith was selected by AXELOS to be the lead author for *PRINCE2 Agile*, which involved an international collaboration of more than 40 people of varied experience from different backgrounds across the whole spectrum of project management and agile.

MENTOR

Lawrence Cooper

Larry Cooper, BSc, MA, is a portfolio/project manager and strategic adviser in the public and private sectors in Canada and the USA, and holds close to 25 industry certifications in agile, project management and ITIL. He has contributed to books, magazines and industry-leading websites, and achieved the top ITIL download for his White Paper 'Implementing ITIL using the PMBOK in Four Easy Steps' on www.forbes.com

Involved in the training industry since 2007, he has developed more than 30 courses on ITIL, project management, agile, and value management. He has been invited to speak at numerous conferences and symposia for the PMI, BAWorld and the *it*SMF. Most recently, he presented global webinars with BrightTalk on topics ranging from DevOps and ITSM, to the future of agile in organizations. Larry is an executive on the board of directors for PMI Ottawa and was AXELOS's North American mentor for *PRINCE2 Agile*. Larry and Jen Stone are also authors of a White Paper for AXELOS entitled 'Next Generation Agile'.

ADVISERS AND COLLABORATORS

The author team had advice and guidance from many collaborators and thought leaders, including:

David J. Anderson, David J. Anderson & Associates; Brian Askew, independent business/IT management consultant; Gabrielle Benefield, Evolve Beyond; Robert Buttrick, Project Workout Ltd; Phillip de Caux, C&J Clark International Ltd; Joe French, Consonance Project Management; Carl Grice, Keynetix; Julie Hendry, Cow Consulting Ltd; Tom Holsøe, Kammeradvokaten; Liz Keogh, Lunivore; Matthew Perkins, Mars Inc.; Troy Plant, Davisbase Consulting; Rob Smith, IndigoBlue; Dave Snowden, Cognitive Edge; Jennifer Stone, BSSNexus Global Inc. (Canada, USA); Kelly Walters, P2A; Dave Watson, Mars Inc.; Geoff Watts, Inspect & Adapt Ltd; James Yoxall, Indigo Blue.

Thanks are also due for the support given by:

Maree Butler, agilekrc; Mike Cohn, Mountain Goat Software; Tom Gilb; David Hinde, Orgtopia; Jude Irvine, agilekrc; Dan North, independent consultant; Erik Petersen, Emprove; David Putman, Value Driven Software; Amy Richards, UCLH; Ranjit Sidhu, ChangeQuest.

REVIEWERS

Appreciation is due to the following for the time and effort put into reviewers' drafts of the book:

Harminder Ahluwalia, SPOCE, Consulting 2U; Mike Burrows, David J Anderson & Associates Ltd; James Cannings, MMT Digital; Steven Denier, be.Projectized; Jonas Högstrand, Metier; Dan Martland, Capita; Tim Matthew, Capita; Andy Murray, Outperform UK Ltd; Nader K Rad, Management Plaza; Darren Radford, Aspire; Scott Spence, CC Learning; Steve Tait, Capita; Dot Tudor, TCC Ltd.

Contents summary

This manual provides the definitive explanation of PRINCE2 Agile. AXELOS examinations relating to PRINCE2 Agile will be based on this manual.

PRINCE2 Agile comprises:

- **Part I Introduction and overviews** What is PRINCE2 Agile? What is the rationale behind it? Who is it for? Overviews of PRINCE2 and agile in general. The fundamental concepts that PRINCE2 Agile is built upon. Understanding the project context and flexing what is delivered.

  - **Chapter 1 PRINCE2 Agile introduction** Introduces PRINCE2 Agile and compares the characteristics of projects and business as usual.
  - **Chapter 2 An overview of agile** Introduces agile and describes some of the basic agile ideas.
  - **Chapter 3 The rationale for blending PRINCE2 and agile** Identifies different PRINCE2 Agile communities of interest and how they will benefit from the guidance.
  - **Chapter 4 The PRINCE2 journey when using agile** Provides an overview of what a PRINCE2 Agile project will look like.
  - **Chapter 5 An overview of PRINCE2** Summarizes the elements of PRINCE2 covering the principles, themes, processes and the project environment.
  - **Chapter 6 What to fix and what to flex?** Looks at the flexibility of the six project characteristics and the five project targets that influence what can be flexed.

- **Part II PRINCE2 Agile guidance, tailoring and techniques** Detailed information of how PRINCE2 Agile tailors the PRINCE2 principles, themes, processes, products and roles. What considerations need to be made when using agile, and what specific behaviours and techniques should be applied at any particular point.

  - **Chapter 7 Agile and the PRINCE2 principles** Shows that using agile is completely compatible with the PRINCE2 principles and identifies behaviours for successful PRINCE2 Agile projects.
  - **Chapter 8 Agile and the PRINCE2 themes** Examines how the PRINCE2 themes are adapted for agile working.
  - **Chapter 9 Business Case theme** Explains how agile concepts, such as value, work with a PRINCE2 business case.
  - **Chapter 10 Organization theme** Describes the working relationships between PRINCE2 governance roles and agile team roles for different project structures.
  - **Chapter 11 Quality theme** Discusses the relationship between quality and scope in a PRINCE2 Agile project.
  - **Chapter 12 Plans theme** Brings together the PRINCE2 approach to planning with the collaborative and interactive techniques used in agile.
  - **Chapter 13 Risk theme** Explains how the agile behaviours work with PRINCE2 risk management.
  - **Chapter 14 Change theme** Describes how PRINCE2 management of change works with agile techniques for managing change during development and delivery.
  - **Chapter 15 Progress theme** Covers agile techniques for managing progress within the overall project progress theme.
  - **Chapter 16 Agile and the PRINCE2 processes** Introduces how agile activities fit in the key PRINCE2 processes.
  - **Chapter 17 Starting up a Project; Initiating a Project** Identifies the agile techniques that can be used in the PRINCE2 Starting Up and Initiating a Project stages.
  - **Chapter 18 Directing a Project** Emphasizes the benefits of empowering the project manager and delivery teams so that decisions can be made quickly.
  - **Chapter 19 Controlling a Stage** Describes the relationship between the project manager and delivery team and the use of agile review techniques.

- **Chapter 20 Managing Product Delivery** Covers a wide range of agile concepts and techniques that support product delivery, such as Kanban, Lean Startup and minimum viable product (MVP), as well as the relationship between the project manager and delivery team manager.
- **Chapter 21 Managing a Stage Boundary** Describes how agile concepts such as frequent delivery can provide the assurance that the project board looks for at the end of a stage.
- **Chapter 22 Closing a Project** Shows that the agile incremental delivery way of working is compatible with a clean project closure process in PRINCE2.
- **Chapter 23 Summary of tailoring guidance for the PRINCE2 products** Provides commentary on how agile information flows impact the PRINCE2 management products.

- **Part III Areas of particular focus for PRINCE2 Agile** Detailed guidance on specific areas that need to have prominence due to the nature of the agile way of working, along with discussion of specific techniques that can support this.
  - **Chapter 24 The Agilometer** Explains how to assess the agile environment in order to tailor PRINCE2 in the most effective way.
  - **Chapter 25 Requirements** Describes how to define and prioritize requirements in terms that are compatible with agile ways of working.
  - **Chapter 26 Rich communication** Emphasizes the value of good communications for agile working and effective project delivery.
  - **Chapter 27 Frequent releases** Shows how project plans and release plans should account for the important agile concept of frequent releases.
  - **Chapter 28 Creating contracts when using agile** Explores options to resolve possible conflicts between a traditional supply contract and agile delivery, covering concepts such as MVP and statement of work.

- **Appendices, glossary and index** Further supporting information that may be required, including the relevant PRINCE2 product description outlines, general agile values and a PRINCE2 Agile health check. Also included are the PRINCE2 product-based planning example, transitioning to agile, advice to a project manager using agile, and the definitive guide to Scrum.

CONVENTIONS USED IN THIS GUIDE

PRINCE2 content

This publication includes text, tables and figures taken directly from PRINCE2 guidance (*Managing Successful Projects with PRINCE2* and *Directing Successful Projects with PRINCE2*), with some minor amendments to accommodate the agile approach. This reproduced text is identified as having a light shaded background.

Capitalization

In addition to standard capitalization of proper nouns, names of PRINCE2 processes and themes are given upper-case initials in the text to distinguish them, along with particular recognized terms such as 'Waterfall' and 'Lean'. Most other terms for roles, products etc. are treated as normal everyday nouns and have lower-case initials. The term 'agile' appears in lower case throughout this publication, unless it is linked to PRINCE2 (as in 'PRINCE2 Agile').

Glossary terms

Please note that certain terms are emboldened in the main text. This is to signify their inclusion in the glossary. They are emboldened on first mention only.

PART I

INTRODUCTION AND OVERVIEWS

1

PRINCE2 Agile introduction

This chapter covers:

- What PRINCE2 Agile is for
- PRINCE2 Agile is for projects only
- Projects and business as usual

1 PRINCE2 Agile introduction

1.1 WHAT IS PRINCE2 AGILE?

PRINCE2 Agile describes how to configure and tune PRINCE2 so that PRINCE2 can be used in the most effective way when combining it with agile behaviours, concepts, frameworks and techniques.

1.2 PRINCE2 AGILE IS FOR PROJECTS ONLY

PRINCE2 and PRINCE2 Agile are only suitable for use on **projects**, whereas agile can be used for projects and routine ongoing work as well. Throughout this manual, routine ongoing work is referred to as 'business as usual' (BAU) and covers such areas as ongoing product development, product maintenance and continual improvement.

The distinction between project work and BAU work (see Table 1.1 and Figure 1.1) is important because some of the agile ways of working need to be applied differently in each situation. Therefore, when carrying out a piece of work it is important to understand the type of work being undertaken, to ensure that it is addressed in the appropriate way and that agile is used appropriately.

1.2.1 What does BAU look like?

BAU work would typically be repeatable routine tasks that can be carried out by people with the appropriate technical skills without needing to be managed by a **project manager**. An example of this would be where modifications or enhancements need to be made to an existing product and the timescales are relatively short. There would usually be a long list of these tasks arriving regularly throughout the lifespan of the product. There may be an established team dedicated to this work.

1.2.2 What does a project look like?

A project is a temporary situation, where a team is assembled to address a specific problem, opportunity or change that is sufficiently difficult that it cannot be handled as BAU. It may even be a collection of BAU items handled collectively. An example of a project would be where a new product or service is being created – there may be a need to engage many stakeholders and a significant amount of uncertainty exists. The project team may be based in different locations, the team personnel may change, the project may last a long time and it may be part of a wider programme of work. Importantly, it needs to be managed by a project manager.

Table 1.1 The different characteristics of a project and BAU work

Project characteristics	BAU characteristics
Temporary	Ongoing
Team is created	Stable team
Difficult	Routine
A degree of uncertainty	A degree of certainty

Tip

AXELOS's *Managing Successful Programmes* (MSP) provides best-practice guidance for managing related projects and activities in programmes of work that deliver business benefits through new capabilities.

Figure 1.1 illustrates the different characteristics of project work in comparison with BAU work. A project has defined **stage**s for upfront work before any delivery activity commences. It also has layers of project management and project direction to ensure the correct output is ultimately arrived at. By the end of a project, at which point the project team disbands (or moves to other work), the product created will have gone into operational use, and from then on it may be maintained and enhanced in a BAU environment.

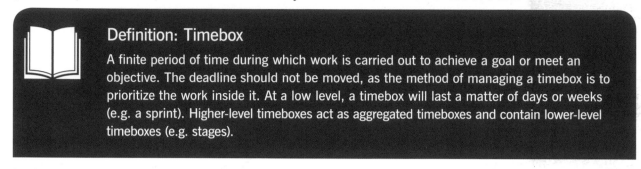

Definition: Timebox

A finite period of time during which work is carried out to achieve a goal or meet an objective. The deadline should not be moved, as the method of managing a timebox is to prioritize the work inside it. At a low level, a timebox will last a matter of days or weeks (e.g. a sprint). Higher-level timeboxes act as aggregated timeboxes and contain lower-level timeboxes (e.g. stages).

In a BAU environment, the list of work is prioritized in some form and may be batched into **timebox**es. As the work is completed the existing product evolves, continually, over time.

Although PRINCE2 Agile is only suitable for projects, it uses a wide range of agile behaviours, concepts, frameworks and techniques that are also used in a BAU environment.

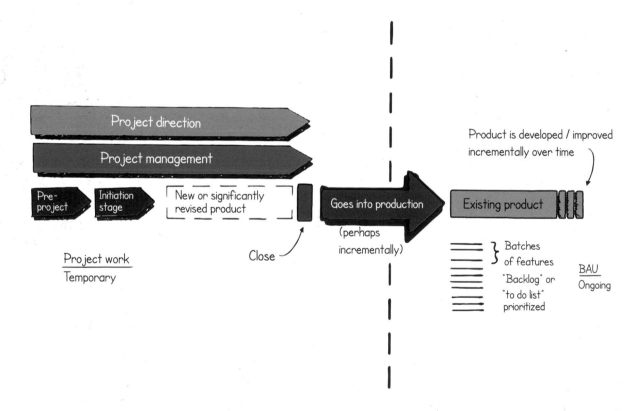

Figure 1.1 The difference between project work and BAU work

Note: PRINCE2 Agile can be used to the left-hand side of the dotted line only (i.e. for projects). Agile can be used on both sides (i.e. used on projects and for BAU).

2

An overview of agile

This chapter covers:

- Some history behind agile and what it is today
- Agile basics including the frameworks, behaviours, concepts and techniques

2 An overview of agile

2.1 INTRODUCTION

The term 'agile' is very broad and is viewed in many different ways throughout the agile community. There is a set of well-known frameworks referred to as 'agile methods' and there are also well-known behaviours, concepts and techniques that are recognized as characterizing the agile way of working. But there is no single definition of agile that accurately encapsulates them all, although the Agile Manifesto (see Figure 2.1) comes the closest to achieving this.

2.1.1 Some history

The term 'agile' was created in 2001 (www.agilemanifesto.org) when a group of 'independent thinkers around software development' came together to talk about an alternative to the heavyweight, document-driven processes that existed at the time. Known as the '**Waterfall methodology**' (see Figure 2.2), these old-fashioned processes comprised a sequence of technical phases that were slow and struggled to respond to changing **requirement**s, particularly when they were mired in too much detail from the start.

The group was already working in ways that later become described as agile; an output from this meeting was the Manifesto for agile Software Development, or the 'Agile Manifesto' as it is more commonly known, and its impact and success have been quite dramatic. The Agile Manifesto is summarized in Figure 2.1; it also contains 12 principles which are listed in Appendix E.1. It is important to appreciate the intent of the final two lines of the Agile Manifesto: it is a case of relative importance of the values, and not a case of 'good' or 'bad'.

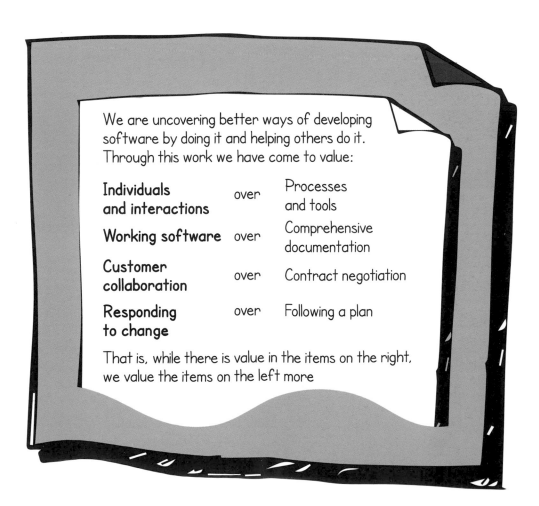

Figure 2.1 The Agile Manifesto

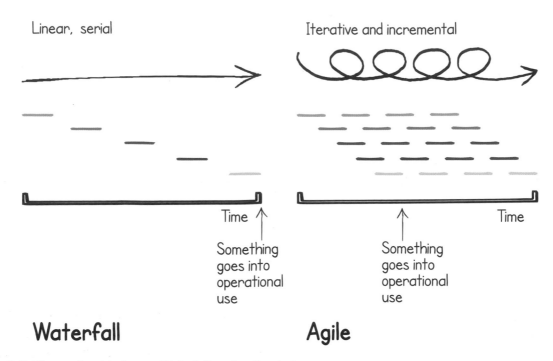

Figure 2.2 The contrast between Waterfall and agile phases

The reason for agile becoming so popular was that it helped to address the new demands being placed on how software was delivered. Software needed to be produced more frequently whilst at the same time being of the appropriate **level of quality** to meet the demands of new technologies, the internet and the digital era. In contrast to the Waterfall way of working, agile phases are smaller and more iterative and incremental (see Figure 2.2).

By definition, the Agile Manifesto only applies to developing software, and most of its underlying principles appear to suggest that this is in the context of the continual timeboxed development of a software product. Although it was created as a way to develop software, it has since been recognized as a successful approach beyond software development, and many people use the Agile Manifesto, replacing the word 'software' with 'products' or 'solutions'.

2.1.2 Agile today

Agile has come a long way since 2001 and is no longer just 'an IT thing'. It now includes situations that are large scale, complex in nature and happening in a wide array of contexts far beyond software development.

Nowadays, most if not all organizations are aware of the term agile, and every organization should have a strategy in place to adopt it to some degree. For many years it was seen as a niche area; it is now mainstream and is used by organizations that are large and small, old and new, public sector and private sector.

2.2 AGILE BASICS

When combining PRINCE2 with agile it is important to know what agile is, otherwise an inconsistent view of the basics of agile will make combining the two difficult (e.g. if someone in an organization thinks that agile can only be used on the IT part of a project, whereas someone else thinks it can be applied across the whole project, then this will present a problem).

A basic view of agile could generally be seen as one or more of the following (see Figure 2.3):

● Using a timeboxed and iterative approach to delivering software
● Using a collection of techniques such as daily **stand-up meeting**s, **sprint**s and user stories
● Using the Scrum framework (see Table 2.1).

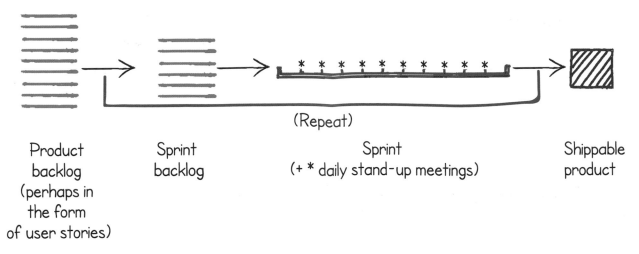

Figure 2.3 A basic 'backlog' and 'sprint' structure for delivering software

This is a very common structure used when working in an agile way for developing software. In simple terms, new **feature**s for a product are held in a prioritized list called the product **backlog**. The list may be made up of user stories, which are structured in a way that describes who wants the feature and why. The team that will build the features decides on what items from the top of the product backlog they can create in a timeframe of typically two to four weeks (which is known as a sprint). The work that the team think they can achieve during the sprint is held in a list called a sprint backlog. Each day throughout the sprint, a meeting is held to assess progress. At the end of a sprint new features should have been created and they may go into operational use. The output (i.e. the new features) is reviewed along with the way the team worked to achieve that output.

> ### Definition: Release
>
> A general term used to describe a collection of features that will be moved into (or near to) operational use (or the act of doing this). In PRINCE2 Agile, a release is typically a container for more than one low-level timebox (e.g. a sprint) but this is not necessarily the case as the act of releasing features into operational use may happen more regularly (e.g. after each sprint or several times during a sprint). The term 'deployment' is sometimes used in agile and has a similar meaning, although it is not used in PRINCE2 Agile.

This basic structure may exist within an overall approach that includes a **vision**, a **product roadmap** (which is a plan of how a product will evolve) and a series of **release**s (see Figure 2.4)

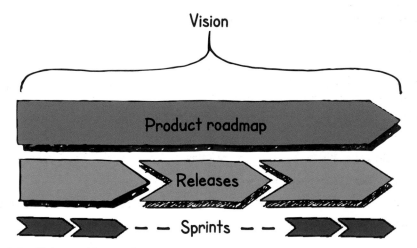

Figure 2.4 Sprints may exist within a wider context

The two examples represented in Figures 2.3 and 2.4 provide a typical view of agile, although it is somewhat limited. A more comprehensive view would include:

● IT and non-IT situations

● Large and small projects as well as routine 'business as usual' (BAU) tasks

● **Flow-based** working as well as timeboxing.

Further to this there also needs to be a wider mind-set and a collection of behaviours that enable the agile way of working to thrive.

Definition: Flow-based working

This approach avoids the use of partitioning work into timeboxes and manages work by using a queue. Work is then continually pulled into the system (which may itself be a high-level timebox) and moves through various work states until it is done.

Table 2.1 The most well-known agile methods and approaches

Term	Brief description
ASD (Adaptive Software Development)	(IT only). Iterative development process (Highsmith, 2000).
Crystal	(IT only). Iterative development method (Cockburn, 2001).
DAD (Disciplined Agile Delivery)	(IT only). An enterprise-wide scalable process framework described as 'a process decision framework that is a people-first, learning-oriented hybrid agile approach to IT solution delivery', that has 'a risk-value delivery lifecycle, is goal-driven, is enterprise aware and is scalable.' See http://www.disciplinedagiledelivery.com
DevOps	(IT only). A collaborative approach between development and operations aimed at creating a product or service where the two types of work and even the teams merge as much as possible.
DSDM (Dynamic Systems Development Method)/AgilePM	An agile project framework that focuses on the iterative delivery of business systems through the use of timeboxing and continual business involvement. It has a defined process and corresponding set of products, a set of roles that operate at all levels of a project, eight guiding principles and a collection of key techniques that can be used throughout a project.
FDD (feature-driven development)	(IT only). Iterative software development process focusing on features.
Kanban	A way to improve flow and provoke system improvement through visualization and controlling **work in progress**.
Lean	An approach that focuses on improving processes by maximizing **value** through eliminating waste (such as wasted time and wasted effort).
Lean Startup	Originally an approach to creating and managing start-up companies, but now applied to any business, to help them deliver products to customers quickly.
SAFe (Scaled Agile Framework)	(IT only). Large-scale application of agile across an organization. PRINCE2 and PRINCE2 Agile could be used in SAFe where a piece of work is of a sufficient size or level of difficulty that it should be run as a project.
Scrum	An iterative timeboxed approach to product delivery that is described as 'a framework within which people can address complex adaptive problems, while productively and creatively delivering products of the highest possible value' (see Appendix H).
XP (eXtreme Programming)	(IT only). Iterative software engineering practice that can be used on its own but often exists in tandem with Scrum or Kanban, where XP covers the creation of the software and Scrum or Kanban is used as an overarching framework to control the work.

> **Tip**
> PRINCE2 Agile regards agile as a family of behaviours, concepts, frameworks and techniques.

2.2.1 Agile frameworks

There is a family of frameworks (also referred to as methods or approaches) that are generally recognized as being agile. However, some are only applicable to IT situations. A summary of the most well known is shown in Table 2.1.

2.2.2 Agile behaviours, concepts and techniques

Along with the agile frameworks there are a variety of behaviours, concepts and techniques that are seen as being part of the agile way of working. Examples are shown in Table 2.2 (some of which are defined in the glossary) but the table only provides a few illustrative examples of what is seen as agile. It is not a complete list and it is not necessary to be strict on the exact terms used (e.g. whether or not something is a technique or a behaviour).

Table 2.2 Typical agile behaviours, concepts and techniques

Term	Examples	Similar terms
Behaviours	Being collaborative, self-organizing, customer-focused, empowered, trusting not blaming.	Principles, values, mind-set
Concepts	Prioritizing what is delivered, working iteratively and incrementally, not delivering everything, time-focused, 'inspect and adapt'. **Kaizen.** Limiting work in progress (WIP).	Fundamentals
Techniques	**Burn charts**, user stories, **retrospectives**, timeboxing, measuring flow.	Practices, tools

PRINCE2 and PRINCE2 Agile do not favour one agile approach over any other (this is sometimes referred to as being 'agile agnostic'), and with due care and consideration, they can engage with agile in all of its many forms to provide a holistic project management approach that can be tailored to suit a wide variety of conditions and working environments.

ACKNOWLEDGEMENTS AND FURTHER READING

Alistair Cockburn (2001). *Agile Software Development: Software Through People.* Addison Wesley.

J.A. Highsmith (2000). *Adaptive Software Development: A Collaborative Approach to Managing Complex Systems.* Dorset House, New York.

3

The rationale for blending PRINCE2 and agile

This chapter covers:

- Who PRINCE2 Agile is for and who will benefit from it?

- When and where to apply PRINCE2 Agile

- What PRINCE2 Agile consists of

3 The rationale for blending PRINCE2 and agile

PRINCE2 is the most commonly used project management approach in the world, and it is increasingly being used in conjunction with agile. As more organizations adopt agile, the need for specific guidance on how to use PRINCE2 in an agile context has grown accordingly.

In simple terms, PRINCE2 and agile each have their own strengths and when combined they complement each other and create a holistic approach to managing projects in an agile way.

The strength of PRINCE2 lies in the areas of project direction and project management. However, it provides little focus on the field of product delivery.

Conversely, agile has a very strong focus on product delivery but relatively little on project direction and project management (see Figure 3.1).

Therefore, when PRINCE2 and agile are combined, all three areas in Figure 3.1 are addressed.

It is essential to see this combination as a blend and a mixture as opposed to PRINCE2 and agile working in parallel. Those directing and managing a project in an agile context need to adopt agile disciplines and behaviours. Equally, those using agile to deliver need to integrate seamlessly with the PRINCE2 ethos of staying in control by empowering people and ensuring that the project remains viable.

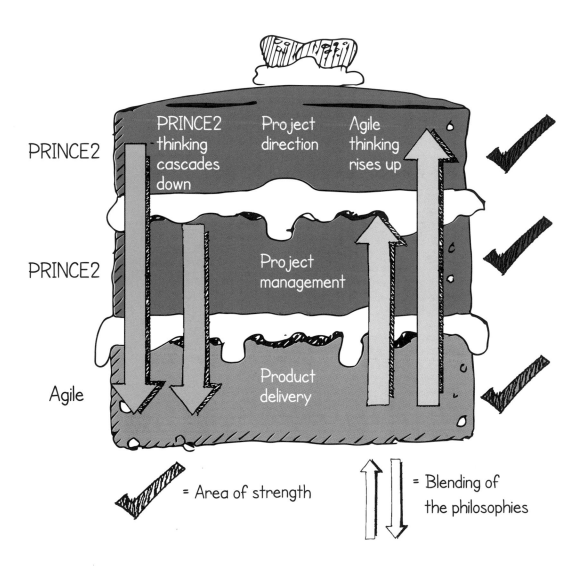

Figure 3.1 Blending PRINCE2 and agile together

Historically, the majority of the applications of agile related to ongoing product development, and this would typically be in an IT context. However, the use of agile has now gone beyond IT and is being used in more challenging situations. Therefore, as the need for agile to work in a project context increases, the established and internationally recognized methods for project management have needed to provide guidance on how they work with agile.

PRINCE2 Agile provides guidance for tailoring PRINCE2 to work in the most effective way in an agile context.

3.1 WHO IS PRINCE2 AGILE FOR?

The primary purpose of this guidance is to help and support the existing PRINCE2 community and in particular PRINCE2 practitioners. Anyone directing or managing a PRINCE2 project who is using agile will benefit from this guidance. Anyone involved with, or impacted by, a PRINCE2 project that is using agile will also benefit from this guidance (e.g. **project support**, **quality assurance**).

Organizations and individuals outside the PRINCE2 community can also benefit from this guidance in one of the following ways:

● Those who currently have experience with agile may want to become familiar with, and perhaps ultimately adopt, an internationally recognized standard for project management along with their existing agile capability.

● Those who are relatively new to agile may want to become familiar with, and perhaps ultimately adopt, an internationally recognized standard for project management as they evolve their agile capability.

PRINCE2 Agile is not a substitute for PRINCE2. However, for those outside the PRINCE2 community, *PRINCE2 Agile* may provide additional guidance to help them adopt PRINCE2 for all of their projects, irrespective of whether or not they involve agile.

3.2 WHICH COMMUNITIES WILL BENEFIT FROM PRINCE2 AGILE?

PRINCE2 Agile is aimed at the communities shown in Table 3.1.

Table 3.1 The communities on which PRINCE2 Agile is focused

Focus of PRINCE2 Agile	Community	Description	Possible goals
Primary	PRINCE2 wanting to go agile	PRINCE2 organizations, departments or individuals who wish to adopt agile.	They wish to integrate agile into their existing PRINCE2 working practices in order to benefit from the advantages of this way of working.
Primary	PRINCE2 encountering agile	PRINCE2 organizations, departments or individuals who are encountering other organizations, departments or individuals using agile in some form.	They wish to understand what agile is and how it works so that they can tailor PRINCE2 appropriately and integrate with it.
Primary	PRINCE2 practising agile	PRINCE2 organizations, departments or individuals who are practising agile in some form.	They wish to adopt a formal standard for using agile in a PRINCE2 context.
Secondary	Agile wanting to adopt PRINCE2	Organizations, departments or individuals who have some agile experience and wish to adopt PRINCE2.	They wish to adopt an industry standard approach to project management and project governance to complement their existing agile working practices.
Possible area of focus	Mature agile	Organizations, departments or individuals who have adopted agile and have reached high levels of maturity for both BAU and project work.	They wish to become familiar with PRINCE2 Agile in order to add to their existing body of knowledge.

3.3 WHEN AND WHERE CAN I APPLY PRINCE2 AGILE?

PRINCE2 Agile provides governance and project management controls that are suitable for some situations but not others as shown in Table 3.2.

Table 3.2 The situations for which PRINCE2 Agile is suitable

Situation	Description	Suitability of PRINCE2 Agile
Agile is not used for projects, or is at a basic level	Either agile is not used for projects, or an agile way of working exists and is evolving with a limited level of maturity in terms of processes and behaviours (e.g. how formalized and documented they are and how predominant they are).	Suitable for organizations, departments and the individuals working within them.
Agile is used for business as usual (BAU)	An agile way of working exists for use with ongoing routine development of an existing product. Most, if not all, work is handled this way.	Not suitable for organizations and departments. However, it is suitable to support and enhance this style of working (i.e. product delivery) in a project context, as some work may be better suited to being managed as a project. Additionally, it may help individuals' career progression.
A mature level of agile is used for projects and BAU	An agile way of working exists that is taking place in a mature agile environment where processes are formalized and repeatable and agile behaviours are predominant.	Suitable for projects, but may be of limited use. Could be of use to support information to enhance an existing body of knowledge. Organizations, departments and individuals who are conversant with PRINCE2 Agile will be suitable for this situation as they will understand it quickly and integrate with it easily, albeit using different terminology.

Table 3.3 The relationship between each community and each situation with respect to PRINCE2 Agile

Community	Situation		
	Agile is not used for projects, or is at a basic level	Agile is used for BAU	A mature level of agile is used for projects and BAU
PRINCE2 wanting to go agile, or encountering, or practising agile	Use PRINCE2 Agile.	Should some of the BAU work be handled as a project? If so, use PRINCE2 Agile for this.	Potentially, PRINCE2 Agile may be of use, although the existing agile process may suffice. See note 1.
Agile wanting to adopt PRINCE2	Use PRINCE2 Agile.	Should some of the BAU work be handled as a project? If so, use PRINCE2 Agile for this.	Potentially PRINCE2 Agile may be of use although the existing agile process may suffice. See note 2.

Notes:

1. Mapping of similar terms may be of benefit (e.g. product board may be an equivalent to project sponsor).

2. A situation where a mature level of agile is used for projects may potentially benefit from using PRINCE2 Agile, unless it is felt that the existing governance and project management controls are sufficient. Using PRINCE2 Agile may be appropriate if a more challenging piece of work is being undertaken or a project involves a customer, supplier or another part of the organization that is using PRINCE2 or PRINCE2 Agile. In any of these cases PRINCE2 Agile could be adopted, or similar terms could be mapped between the different approaches.

3.4 COURSE OF ACTION FOR EACH COMMUNITY IN EACH SITUATION

Table 3.3 outlines the most appropriate course of action that the communities listed in Table 3.1 would need to take in terms of using PRINCE2 Agile, when faced with the situations described in Table 3.2.

3.5 WHAT DOES PRINCE2 AGILE CONSIST OF?

PRINCE2 comprises an integrated set of principles, themes and processes that are tailored to the specific needs of a project (see Figure 3.2).

PRINCE2 Agile provides guidance on tailoring PRINCE2 in an agile context and covers:

● How to tailor the principles, themes and processes

● How to produce the PRINCE2 management products

● How to map the common agile roles to the PRINCE2 project management team structure

● How to incorporate the fundamental agile behaviours, concepts and techniques into PRINCE2

● What areas are of particular significance when using agile and need specific focus.

This applies to all levels of a PRINCE2 project – i.e. project direction, project management and product delivery.

Agile encapsulates a wide collection of frameworks, and PRINCE2 Agile incorporates and references several of them. A few of these methods and approaches receive particular attention in PRINCE2 Agile because they are seen as very popular or good practice. They are Scrum, Kanban and Lean Startup (see Table 2.1 for a brief description).

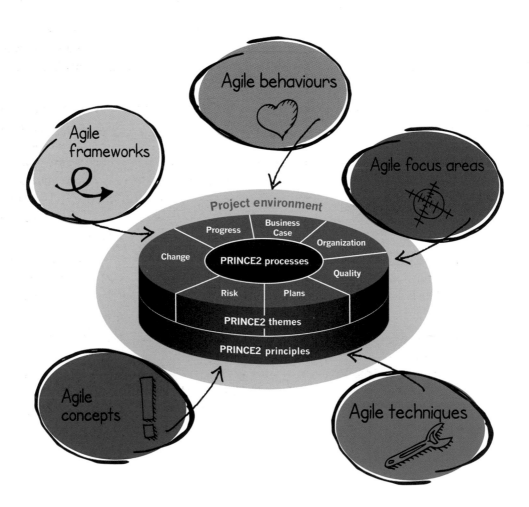

Figure 3.2 Tailoring PRINCE2 by blending in the agile ingredients

3.6 IMPORTANT POINTS ABOUT PRINCE2 AGILE AND THIS MANUAL

PRINCE2 has been used and implemented in a wide variety of situations and has evolved significantly since it was first published in 1996. Agile has had a similar journey, but also comes in many different forms.

In order to correctly understand PRINCE2 Agile and this manual, the reader must be aware of the following eight guidance points which are intended to provide clarity where there is potential for ambiguity, and accuracy where there may be misconceptions. These points are summarized in Table 3.4 for quick reference.

1. All references to PRINCE2 refer to the edition created in 2009 (*Managing Successful Projects with PRINCE2*). This version is already enabled to work with agile; it just needs to be tailored to suit any given project. Configuring PRINCE2 in the most effective way for agile is a matter of where to put emphasis and where to add further levels of detailed guidance. Nothing needs to be removed or significantly changed, as this is achieved through blending agile into PRINCE2 and tuning PRINCE2 appropriately.

2. PRINCE2 allows for any style of working, such as with environments that involve high levels of informality, collaboration and trust. It should be understood that PRINCE2 should not be thought of as a 'traditional project management approach' in the stereotypical sense of being predominantly 'Waterfall', 'big design up front', 'bureaucratic' and using a 'command and control' culture. PRINCE2 does not suggest that a project should be run in this way, and much of its guidance is to the contrary.

3. Most of the heritage and thinking behind agile has come from IT and software development, but PRINCE2 Agile does not assume an IT context – although it can be used in an IT context, it is not an IT framework or an IT method.

4. Many agile approaches and frameworks are created solely for IT situations – for example, eXtreme Programming (XP) and the Scaled Agile Framework (SAFe). PRINCE2 Agile will only make passing reference to IT-only frameworks (see Table 2.1 for brief descriptions).

5. The most well-known agile framework is Scrum, and PRINCE2 Agile is written with the view that although Scrum can rightly be described as being 'agile', the converse is not the case: it is not true to describe agile as 'using the Scrum framework'. Other frameworks exist and a framework is only part of the agile way of working.

6. Although agile appears in many forms, the use of the Scrum framework and (to a lesser extent) the Kanban framework (either separately or in combination) make up the vast majority of what agile practitioners use. There are many other frameworks and approaches but when this manual uses expressions such as 'commonly used in agile' or 'widely used in agile' it will usually be referring to either of these two frameworks. It is important to note that Scrum and Kanban are not project management frameworks, and a project manager role is not defined in either. On their own, and in isolation, they cannot be used to manage a project. They can, however, be used on a project as part of an approach to delivering products, as long as they are contained within a wider project management framework such as PRINCE2.

7. The term 'agile' when used on its own in this manual refers to a general family of behaviours, concepts, frameworks and techniques that is widely accepted throughout the agile community as being part of the agile way of working. The terms 'behaviours, concepts, frameworks, and techniques' also encapsulate other similar terms such as methods, principles, values, mind-sets and approaches.

8. PRINCE2 Agile does not see working in an agile way as a binary condition (i.e. you either are or you are not working in an agile way). It always sees agile as a question of how much (or how little) it can be used according to the situation that exists. To illustrate this point, *PRINCE2 Agile* does not refer to 'agile projects' as this would infer that some projects are agile, whereas others are not. *PRINCE2 Agile* is written with the view that agile behaviours, concepts, frameworks and techniques can be applied to any project.

Table 3.4 Summary of the key points in Chapter 3

	Key point
1	PRINCE2 (2009 version) is already enabled for use with agile.
2	PRINCE2 is suitable for any style of project and is not a 'traditional' project management approach as is typically contrasted to agile.
3	PRINCE2 Agile is for any project and not just for IT projects.
4	'IT-only' frameworks and techniques are mentioned in PRINCE2 Agile but not extensively.
5	There is much more to agile than the Scrum framework. Agile is not Scrum.
6	The most 'commonly used' agile approaches are Scrum and Kanban, but they are not suitable for managing a project in isolation. However, they can be effectively used in a project context.
7	The term 'agile' (in this manual) refers to a family of behaviours, concepts, frameworks and techniques.
8	Using agile on a project is not a question of 'yes or no': it is about 'how much'.

3.7 BEWARE OF PREJUDICE!

It would be understandable to think that bringing more control and governance into the agile domain could prove counter-productive. However, PRINCE2 Agile represents a marriage that is based on the opposite view – that control and governance allow agile to be used in more situations such as those involving multiple teams or complex environments.

A fighter aircraft is built with a deliberately unstable airframe. This instability gives it agility and allows it to change direction easily and adapt quickly to situations. However, to do this still requires control and governance!

This personifies PRINCE2 Agile.

Image 3.1 An agile fighter aircraft

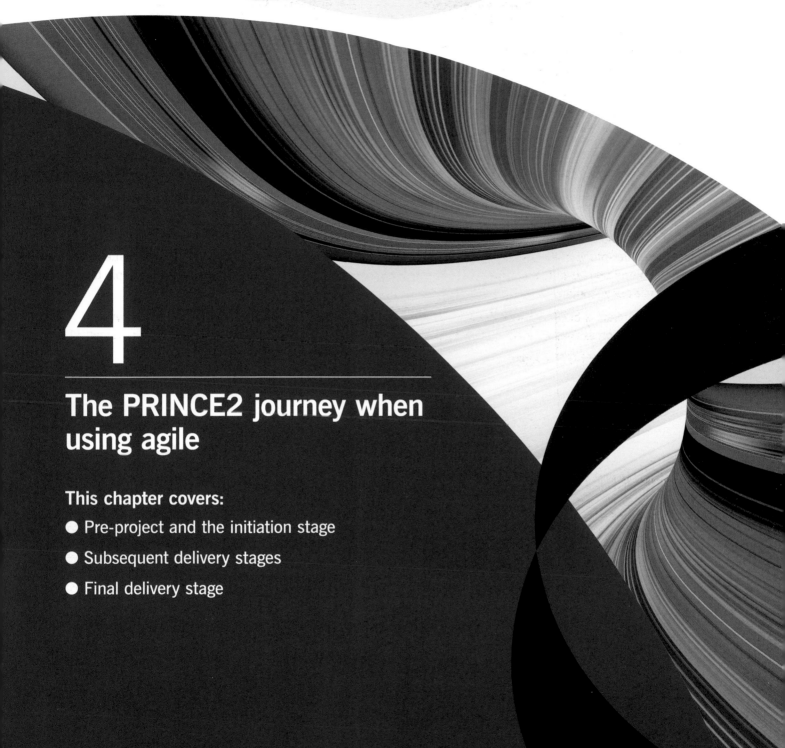

4

The PRINCE2 journey when using agile

This chapter covers:

- Pre-project and the initiation stage
- Subsequent delivery stages
- Final delivery stage

4 The PRINCE2 journey when using agile

This chapter acts as a brief summary of how PRINCE2 would typically look when working in an agile way. The best way to tailor PRINCE2 depends on the project context, and the purpose of this chapter is to illustrate examples that would be common in many situations; however, many other alternatives exist. The chapter illustrates *a* way but not *the* way.

PRINCE2 provides a process model for managing a project (see Figure 4.1). The processes can easily be scaled and tailored to suit the requirements of all types of project. They consist of a set of activities that are required to direct, manage and deliver a project.

4.1 PRE-PROJECT AND THE INITIATION STAGE

4.1.1 Pre-project

In the beginning, someone has an idea or a need. This may result from new business objectives, responding to competitive pressures, changes in legislation, or a recommendation in a report or an audit. The trigger for the project could be almost anything. In PRINCE2, this trigger is called a project mandate. The project mandate is provided by the commissioning organization (corporate or programme management) and can vary in form from a verbal instruction to a well-defined and justified project definition.

Prior to the activity to scope the project appropriately, it is important to verify that the project is worthwhile and viable. Such activities are covered by the process Starting up a Project, which culminates in the production of a **project brief** and a **stage plan** for project initiation.

The project board reviews the project brief and decides whether to initiate the project, and states the levels of authority to be delegated to the project manager for the initiation stage.

4.1.2 Initiation stage

Once there is a decision to go ahead with the project, it needs to be planned in sufficient detail. Funding needs to be obtained and controls should be defined to ensure that the project proceeds in accordance with the wishes of those people paying for the project and those who will make use of what the project delivers. The planning, establishment of the project management strategies and controls, development of a robust **business case**, and a means of reviewing **benefits** are covered by the Initiating a Project process. Also, during the initiation stage, the Managing a Stage Boundary process is used to plan the next stage.

The initiation stage culminates in the production of the **project initiation documentation**, which is reviewed by the project board to decide whether to authorize the project. As the contents of the project initiation documentation are likely to change throughout the project, this version of the project initiation documentation is preserved as input for later performance reviews.

4.1.3 How pre-project and the initiation stage would typically look when using agile

4.1.3.1 Plan, monitor and control

● Project-level planning focuses on sets of features and intended releases.
● There is strong engagement from all levels of the project management team in the planning and estimation activities.

Figure 4.1 The life of a PRINCE2 project

- Stage-level planning is carried out collaboratively with the customer in order to most accurately meet their needs and achieve the most benefit.

- Plans are timeboxed in some form – this could be in the form of a specific time interval (e.g. two-weekly) or it could be flow-based over a longer period – and these plans would be created at a time (i.e. 'just in time') and a level of detail that is appropriate to allow for uncertainties.

Definition: Feature

A generic term that is widely used to describe something a product does, or the way in which a product does something. A feature can be at any level of detail (e.g. it is waterproof, it makes a tone when switched off) and can be related to a specific requirement, user story or epic. Another similar term is 'function'.

4.1.3.2 Behaviour

- The use of self-organizing teams and people-centric values such as empowerment may be explicitly defined as part of the project approach.

- Mandating or recommending the use of specific agile approaches such as Scrum and/or Kanban may be explicitly defined as part of the project approach.

- The project initiation documentation may have been created collaboratively in a **workshop** in order to disseminate information to the project team quickly and more accurately and with a high level of engagement and ownership.

4.1.3.3 Process

- Information on what constitutes a **minimum viable product** (MVP) is defined (see section 20.4.2.5).

- The trigger for the project may have come from a product roadmap.

- There may be an indication of the appropriate use of agile for the project.

4.1.3.4 Products

- The **project product description** is likely to have been defined to show which requirements are mandatory and which are not.

- The project product description purpose is likely to be outcome-based (focusing on the delivery of value) as opposed to the delivery of a specific solution.

- **Product description**s have initially been captured using user stories (or as **epic**s), although it will be expected that more will be discovered throughout this phase and beyond.

- The business case is defined in a flexible way to allow for the amount of what is being delivered (and its value) to change to a degree during the project.

- The **benefits review plan** focuses on how to deliver value regularly and as early as possible. This will involve describing what products will be delivered when, and what value will be enabled.

- The project initiation documentation is likely to be a less formal document, as some of the **baseline** information is visible in the form of an **information radiator** (see section 15.4.2).

- The project initiation documentation will be less detailed in certain sections (e.g. product descriptions), since the solution is not necessarily defined at the start. It is a living document that evolves, although it will still need to be baselined.

- The **communication management strategy** will have been created using the concept of 'minimum viability' where communication approaches, and particularly documentation, are assessed on the basis of the minimum acceptable level that does not compromise the quality level of the final product.
- See also explanations of tailoring the project brief and project initiation documentation in section 23.1.

Definition: User story

A tool used to write a requirement in the form of who, what and why.

Definition: Epic

A high-level definition of a requirement that has not yet been sufficiently refined or understood. Eventually, an epic will be refined and broken down into several user stories/requirements.

Definition: Information radiator

A general term used to describe the use of walls or boards containing information that can be readily accessed by people working on the project. It can contain any information, although it would typically show such things as work to do and how work is progressing.

4.2 SUBSEQUENT DELIVERY STAGES

The project board delegates day-to-day control to the project manager on a stage-by-stage basis. The project manager needs to assign work to be done, ensure that the outputs of such work (products) meet relevant specifications, and gain suitable approval where appropriate. The project manager also needs to ensure that progress is in line with the approved plan and that the forecasts for the project's performance targets are within agreed **tolerance**s. The project manager ensures that a set of project records (daily log, lessons log, issue register, **risk register**, quality register and **configuration item records**) are maintained to assist with progress control. The project manager informs the project board of progress through regular **highlight report**s. The activities to control each stage are covered by the Controlling a Stage process.

In the Managing Product Delivery process, the **team manager**(s) or team members execute assigned **work packages** (that will deliver one or more products) and keep the project manager appraised of progress via **checkpoint report**s.

4.2.1 How subsequent delivery stages would typically look when using agile

4.2.1.1 Plan, monitor and control

- Work assignment throughout the stage is carried out collaboratively and in conjunction with the customer in order to address the customer's needs. This is likely to take the form of the delivery teams collectively selecting their own work (and collaboratively creating customer-focused work packages) as part of the agile concept of self-organization. The focus would be to work iteratively and deliver incrementally.
- High levels of trust and **transparency** mean that work packages are defined informally even though they represent a vital component when using PRINCE2 with agile.
- Self-organizing teams are responding rapidly to change, although this will be within well-understood boundaries in order to ensure the accuracy of the products being delivered.
- Progress is being measured by work completed and is visualized on a burn chart.

- Progress is supported by the use of reviews and demonstrations ('**demo**s') by the project management team and the delivery teams in association with the customer.
- Tracking of time and cost still takes place but it is less prominent than the tracking of features and/or work completed. This is because time and cost are more predictable due to working with fixed timescales and stable teams.
- Scope and **quality criteria** are the primary focus of any tolerances used.

Definition: Burn chart

A technique for showing progress (e.g. such as with a timebox) where work that is completed and work still to be done are shown with one or more lines: this is updated regularly/daily.

4.2.1.2 Behaviour

During Managing a Stage Boundary the key baseline information that needs to be updated focuses on what has been delivered, the benefits realized and the level of change taking place.

4.2.1.3 Process

If an **exception** arises it is most likely to have occurred due to the amount being delivered being forecast to go outside the agreed tolerance level, as opposed to other aspects being forecast to exceed tolerance, such as time and cost.

4.2.1.4 Products

- **Quality tolerance**s in product descriptions are written in such a way as to allow for change without compromising the product's purpose (e.g. there are levels of tolerance that can be prioritized).
- There is less formality for logs at both the project management and delivery levels (particularly the latter) – a **risk log** may exist on a whiteboard, or an **issue** could be shown as a sticky note on a **Kanban board**.

Definition: Kanban board

A tool used in Kanban to visually display the work in the system (or timebox). It is usually made up of a series of columns and possibly rows where work items move from left to right as they move through various states in order to be completed.

- Highlight reporting is low-tech and primarily focuses on how much is being delivered – this could take the form of an information radiator where information is pulled by the project board without the need for the project manager to report at an agreed frequency.
- Checkpoint reports are likely to be informal and appear on an information radiator where information is pulled – or they could be replaced altogether by stand-up meetings if the delivery teams were happy for the project manager to be in attendance.

Definition: Stand-up meeting

A short meeting to assess progress. Typically lasting 15 minutes or less, they involve describing work that has been done, work still to be done and any problems being encountered.

4.3 FINAL DELIVERY STAGE

As a project is a temporary undertaking, during the final stage (once the project manager has gained approval for all of the project's products) it is time to decommission the project. The project board needs to be satisfied that the recipients of the project's products are in a position to own and use them on an ongoing basis. Should this be the case, the products can be transitioned into operational use and the project can close. The project documentation should be tidied up and archived, the project should be assessed for performance against its original plan and the resources assigned to the project need to be released. The closure activities include planning post-project benefits reviews to take place for those benefits that can only be assessed after the products have been in use (and therefore after the project has closed). The activities to decommission a project are covered by the Closing a Project process.

4.3.1 How the final delivery stage would typically look when using agile

4.3.1.1 Plan, monitor and control

When formal checks are made against the project baseline defined in the project initiation documentation, the key aspects that are assessed include the amount that was delivered, what extra was delivered and what was removed. This will have been happening continually throughout the project as the teams work iteratively and respond to feedback.

4.3.1.2 Behaviour

- Some of the products that the project intended to deliver may not have been created and may have been replaced by others that were not part of the original plan. This will have been communicated throughout the project and will not come as a surprise to the project board when they authorize project closure.
- The customer is already in ownership of several products that have transitioned into operational use and is now realizing benefits.
- Tidying up and archiving is a routine task by this point, as it has been taking place regularly throughout the project; its value is known to everyone and it is not seen as simply a bureaucratic task.

4.3.1.3 Process

- Closing and decommissioning a project is not a significant event as it is a case of 'tidying up' and finishing off many activities to do with lessons, archiving and handover which have already been started because by this point several releases have taken place.
- Project closure involves (or is held as) a retrospective.
- There is an assessment of how appropriate the use of agile turned out to be to help with guidance on the use of agile for future projects.
- Outstanding work still exists on backlogs of some kind (e.g. a release backlog), and this is then moved to other backlogs (e.g. an existing BAU backlog), discarded or archived.

Definition: Retrospective
A regular event that looks at how the process of doing work can be improved. In keeping with the agile concept of 'inspect and adapt' these events help teams to continually improve their working practices, little by little, over time.

4.3.1.4 Products

Lessons may be handed to project support informally, or project support may have been included in retrospectives if the teams were happy for them to be in attendance.

Definition: Backlog

A list of new features for a product. The list may be made up of user stories which are structured in a way that describes who wants the features and why.

5

An overview of PRINCE2

This chapter covers:

- The structure of PRINCE2 and its processes
- Principles and themes
- The project environment

5   An overview of PRINCE2

Much of the material in this chapter is drawn from *Managing Successful Projects with PRINCE2* and *Directing Successful Projects with PRINCE2*, although in many cases the wording and order of presentation have been adapted to suit this guide.

Definition: Project

A project is a temporary organization that is created for the purpose of delivering one or more business products according to an agreed business case.

PRINCE2 should only be used for managing projects. The 'temporary organization' needs to be big enough or complex enough to justify producing a business case and setting up project management controls. If the work can be managed simply as a 'line management' task, using PRINCE2 could create an inappropriate management overhead.

Definition: Programme

A programme is a temporary flexible organization structure created to coordinate, direct and oversee the implementation of a set of related projects and activities in order to deliver outcomes and benefits relating to an organization's strategic objectives. A programme may have a life that spans several years.

Definition: Project management

Project management is the planning, delegating, monitoring and control of all aspects of the project and the motivation of those involved, to achieve the project objectives within the expected performance targets for time, cost, quality, scope, benefits and risks (see Figure 5.1).

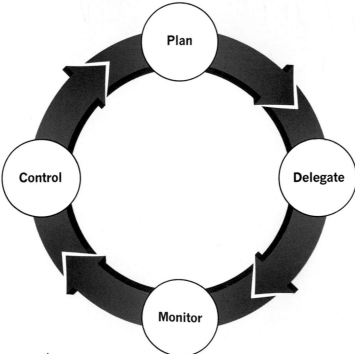

Figure 5.1 Project management

5.1 THE STRUCTURE OF PRINCE2

The PRINCE2 method addresses project management with four integrated elements of principles, themes, processes and the project environment (see Figure 5.2).

- Principles are the guiding obligation of good practice enshrined in PRINCE2.
- The themes provide guidance on how the activities are to be performed.
- The processes give a model for how the project will be managed.

5.2 THE PRINCIPLES

The seven PRINCE2 principles are the guiding obligations for good practice that a project should follow if it is using PRINCE2. They are:

- A PRINCE2 project has continued business justification.
- PRINCE2 project teams learn from previous experience (lessons are sought, recorded and acted upon throughout the life of the project).
- A PRINCE2 project has defined and agreed roles and responsibilities within an organization structure that engages the business, user and supplier stakeholder interests.
- A PRINCE2 project is planned, monitored and controlled on a stage-by-stage basis (management by stages).
- A PRINCE2 project has defined tolerances for each project objective to establish limits of delegated authority (management by exception).
- A PRINCE2 project focuses on the definition and delivery of products, in particular their scope and quality requirements.
- PRINCE2 is tailored to suit the project's environment, size, complexity, importance, capability and **risk**.

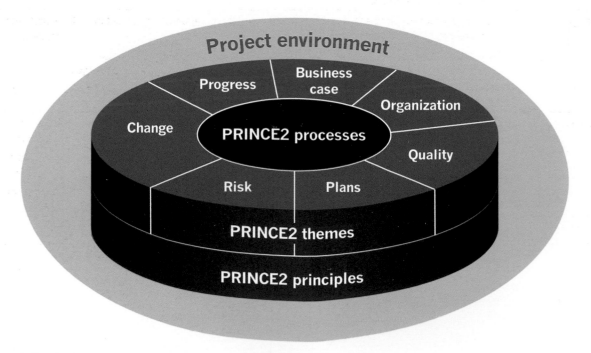

Figure 5.2 The structure of PRINCE2

Table 5.1　The PRINCE2 themes

Theme	Purpose and description	Answers
Business Case	The purpose of the Business Case theme is to establish mechanisms to judge whether the project is (and remains) desirable, viable and achievable as a means to support decision-making in its (continued) investment. The project starts with an idea which is considered to have potential value for the organization concerned. This theme addresses how the idea is developed into a viable investment proposition for the organization and how project management maintains the focus on the organization's objectives throughout the project.	Why?
Organization	The purpose of the Organization theme is to define and establish the project's structure of accountability and responsibilities. The organization sponsoring the project needs to allocate the work to managers who will be responsible for it and steer it through to completion. Projects are cross-functional so the normal line function structures are not suitable. This theme describes the roles and responsibilities in the temporary PRINCE2 project management team required to manage the project effectively.	Who?
Quality	The purpose of the Quality theme is to define and implement the means by which the project will verify products that are fit for purpose. The initial idea will only be understood as a broad outline. This theme explains how the outline is developed so that all participants understand the quality attributes of the products to be delivered – and then how project management will ensure that these requirements are subsequently delivered.	What?
Plans	The purpose of the Plans theme is to facilitate communication and control by defining the means of delivering the products. PRINCE2 projects proceed on the basis of a series of approved plans. This theme complements the Quality theme by describing the steps required to develop plans and the PRINCE2 techniques that should be applied. In PRINCE2 the plans are matched to the needs of the personnel at various levels of the organization. They are the focus for communication and control throughout the project.	How? How much? When?
Risk	The purpose of the Risk theme is to identify, assess and control uncertainty and as a result, improve the ability of the project to succeed. Projects typically entail more risk than stable operational activity. This theme addresses how project management manages the uncertainties in plans and in the wider project environment.	What if?
Change	The purpose of the Change theme is to identify, assess and control any potential and approved changes to the baseline. This theme describes how project management assesses and acts upon issues which have a potential impact on any of the baseline aspects of the project (its plans and completed products). Issues may be unanticipated general problems, requests for change or instances of quality failure.	What's the impact?
Progress	The purpose of the Progress theme is to establish mechanisms to monitor and compare actual achievements against those planned; provide a forecast for the project objectives and the project's continual viability; and control any unacceptable deviations. This theme addresses the ongoing viability of the plans. The theme explains the decision-making process for approving plans, the monitoring of actual performance and the escalation process if events do not go according to plan. Ultimately, the Progress theme determines whether and how the project should proceed.	Where are we now? Where are we going? Should we carry on?

5.3 THE THEMES

The PRINCE2 themes describe aspects of project management that must be addressed continually (see Table 5.1).

In summary, the set of PRINCE2 themes describe:

● How baselines are established (in the Business Case and Plans themes). The baselines cover all six project performance targets – benefits, risks, scope, quality, cost and time – and act as key reference points for subsequent monitoring and control.

● How the project management team monitors and controls the work as the project progresses (in the Progress, Quality, Change and Risk themes).

The Organization theme underpins the other themes with a secure structure of roles, clarifying accountability and offering clear paths for delegation and escalation.

5.4 THE PROCESSES

PRINCE2 provides a process model for managing a project. The processes can easily be scaled and tailored to suit the requirements of all types of project. They consist of a set of activities that are required to direct, manage and deliver a project.

5.5 THE PROJECT ENVIRONMENT

PRINCE2 can be used on projects irrespective of project scale, complexity, geography, culture etc. PRINCE2 can also be used whether the project is part of a programme or being managed as a stand-alone initiative. This reflects the principle that PRINCE2 must be tailored to suit the particular project context.

PRINCE2 Agile is an example of such tailoring designed to suit a context when a project is taking place in an agile environment.

6

What to fix and what to flex?

This chapter covers:

- Flexing what is delivered and why it may be necessary
- Tolerances and the six project variables
- The five targets for flexible delivery

6 What to fix and what to flex?

Of the many ideas, concepts and techniques that exist within PRINCE2 Agile, one of the most important is that it focuses on flexing what is being delivered, as opposed to focusing on flexing time and cost or flexing time and resources.

However, it is not enough just to understand *how* to flex what is delivered; it is essential to understand *why*.

Historically, the competing **constraints** on a project have often been shown graphically as a shape such as a triangle with constraints of time, cost, quality etc. pulling against each other. PRINCE2 does not have such a limited view of the variables on a project, as it identifies six 'aspects' that need to be controlled and managed: time, cost, quality, scope, risk and benefit.

PRINCE2 does not place emphasis on any of these aspects over and above the others. It sees them as equally significant and to be managed according to the needs of a particular project.

However, PRINCE2 Agile does define what to emphasize by giving guidance on the use of tolerance levels (i.e. permissible deviations from what is planned) for the six aspects in terms of which should be fixed and which ones should vary (or flex) (see Table 6.1).

In PRINCE2, tolerance is the permissible deviation above and below what has been planned, with respect to the six aspects of a project (i.e. time, cost, quality, scope, risk and benefit). Whenever any of these tolerances are forecast to be exceeded an exception will occur. It's not that fixed aspects can never flex, but they have tolerances set to zero and would be subject to management by exception if these were expected to be exceeded.

6.1 THE CONCEPT OF FLEXING WHAT IS DELIVERED

PRINCE2 Agile is built upon the concept of flexing what is delivered. This can also be described as prioritizing what is delivered. This, for many, may require a fundamental shift in how a project is executed. It is not a nuance or a 'different flavour': it represents a significant change in how people think and act when they are working on a project.

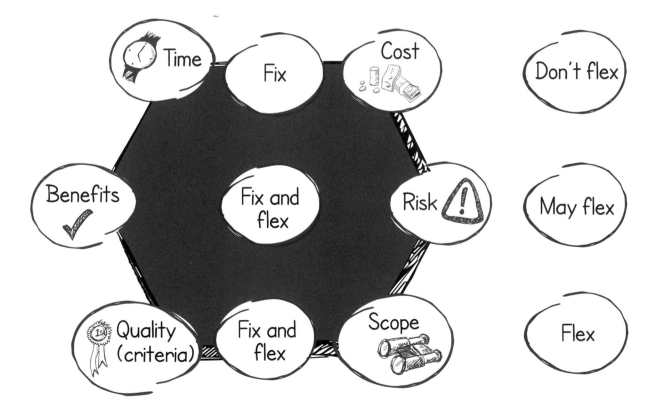

Figure 6.1 Applying tolerances to the six aspects of a project

Table 6.1 How PRINCE2 Agile views tolerances for the six aspects of a project: fix or flex?

Aspect	Tolerance guidance	Summary
Time	Zero tolerance for extra time on all levels of plan	Fix
Cost	Zero tolerance for extra cost on all levels of plan	Fix
Quality	Not all **acceptance criteria** and quality criteria are of equal importance, so they can be prioritized.	Fix and flex
	Project product description	
	Zero tolerance for the customer's quality expectations and acceptance criteria that are essential.	
	Tolerance may be used for the customer's quality expectations and acceptance criteria that are desirable but not essential.	
	Product descriptions (in general)	
	Zero tolerance for the quality criteria that are essential.	
	Tolerance may be used for the quality criteria that are desirable but not essential.	
Scope	Not everything the project aims to create is of equal importance, so they can be prioritized.	Fix and flex
	Zero tolerance for products that are essential.	
	Tolerance may be used for products that are desirable but not essential.	
Risk	Tolerance to be defined according to the needs of the project board and project manager as this depends on the specific situation.	Fix or flex
Benefit	Zero tolerance for the level that is defined as 'minimum viability' in the business case.	Fix or flex
	Tolerance may be used above the level that is defined as 'minimum viability' in the business case.	

6.2 WHY IS THERE A NEED TO WORK THIS WAY?

The internet and the dramatic increase in the use of technology have created a paradigm shift in terms of how quickly people want things such as information and products.

These needs have created a shift over many years from the desire for completeness to the desire for timeliness. Projects and products do not exist in isolation. One example of this is where a company may be creating a product that is competing against several other similar products in a marketplace. In this situation, is it more important to have the best product in the marketplace or to produce the first product in the marketplace? In truth, both points are important, but the agile mind-set is to deliver early, regularly and incrementally, thereby increasing customer confidence and reducing the risk of delivering the wrong thing.

This means that any approaches to project management that are Waterfall-based are not appropriate as they do not explicitly provide the mechanisms for flexing what is being delivered in a timeboxed way.

6.3 THE RATIONALE BEHIND FLEXING WHAT IS BEING DELIVERED

The rationale behind flexing what is being delivered is not straightforward and it can take time to understand the thinking behind it. It may even be the case that the theory is only understood when delivery is seen in practice. Either way, the need to understand this concept fully is essential for the correct use of PRINCE2 Agile.

The thinking behind being flexible with what is delivered is based around five targets, which when taken together provide a compelling case for moving to this way of working. These five targets are described in Table 6.2.

6.4 THE FIVE TARGETS IN MORE DETAIL

As previously mentioned, it is very important to understand the thinking behind flexing what is being delivered and not just do it 'because that's what the manual says'. The following sections outline the deeper and more specific reasons why PRINCE2 Agile involves basing the way a team thinks and acts on a different paradigm from that on which projects have traditionally been based.

Table 6.2 The five targets behind flexing what is delivered

	Target	Description
1	Be on time and hit deadlines	Being on time and hitting deadlines has many very significant advantages.
2	Protect the level of quality	Ensuring that the level of quality is protected and regarded as vital is of paramount importance to a project. This will lead to a lower cost of ownership throughout the lifetime of the final product.
3	Embrace change	Embracing change by seeing it not only as inevitable but also as a positive influence on a project allows for a more accurate final product.
4	Keep teams stable: do not add people to a team in order to try to go faster	Keeping a team stable over the short term removes the temptation to add people to a team in order to catch up with work when in reality it is more likely to have little or no effect.
5	Accept that the customer doesn't need everything	Accepting the premise that not everything defined in the initial stages of a project must be delivered is wise. It inevitably turns out that many things do not add enough value to warrant delaying the project because of them.

6.4.1 Being on time and hitting deadlines

For any project or piece of work being on time is naturally seen as desirable, but the advantages that meeting deadlines creates may not all be obvious; when the many upsides of this are taken together, it creates something that should be seen as essential as opposed to just desirable.

Some of these advantages can include:

- Delivering early realization of benefits, and these can be planned around
- Helping with planning (e.g. dependencies within a project or between projects, capacity and resources at the portfolio and programme level)
- Giving confidence (e.g. with progress)
- There may be no choice (e.g. external market forces or regulatory considerations)
- Reducing the likelihood of cost overruns (assuming that resources are fixed)
- Improving reputation (e.g. with the customer).

'Being on time and hitting deadlines' applies to any timescale – short-term (e.g. a two-week sprint), medium-term (e.g. a two-month stage) or long-term (a six-month project).

6.4.2 Protecting the level of quality

Any framework for projects or product delivery strives to ensure that the appropriate level of quality is achieved. However, in practice does the level of quality suffer (or is at risk of suffering) due to the very nature of the approach being used? For example, when using a traditional Waterfall lifecycle that is broken down into 'technical' phases such as analyse, design, build, test and implement (NB: PRINCE2 is built around 'management stages' and not 'technical stages'), there is a risk that frequently materializes of the earlier phases overrunning, leading to later phases becoming compressed in order to deliver on time. The most common example of this is where quality checking or testing is reduced in order to meet deadlines.

Tip
Technical phases (such as analyse, design, build, test and implement) take many forms and can cover such terms as requirements, planning, deployment, integration, acceptance and construction.

There is a likelihood that this leads to 'short-term gain but long-term pain' (e.g. a product goes into operational use on time but it contains errors that were missed during quality checking and testing, and several products need to be recalled).

Tip

Acceptance criteria is a term that is commonly used in agile to assess whether a user story has been completed. It is the equivalent to quality criteria in PRINCE2.

The concept of flexing what is being delivered ensures that the emphasis is on delivering less scope or using lower-priority quality criteria, as opposed to compromising the overall quality level of the final product (as described by the customer's quality expectations and the associated acceptance criteria).

Compromising the quality level of anything delivered during a project can take many forms but results from such situations as:

● Reduced testing
● Incomplete documentation
● Sub-optimal design
● Lack of appropriate training (e.g. for end-users, customers, support teams)
● Non-compliance with standards.

The result of any compromise to the level of quality can have damaging long-term effects in terms of the total cost of ownership of the final product as it may suffer from:

● Reduced usability
● Significant support requirements
● Degraded performance
● Lack of engagement with the user community.

Therefore, this should be avoided. PRINCE2 Agile protects the level of quality and ensures that deadlines are met by reducing the amount delivered by the project but not reducing activities that ensure that the quality level is met.

6.4.3 Embracing change

Change is inevitable when working on anything difficult so it is best to expect it and prepare for it. Change can take the form of a new idea that has not previously been thought of or a misunderstanding where an assumption proves to be incorrect. Change should be seen as positive because a more accurate final product is likely to be produced.

It is important to distinguish between minor change (e.g. to the detail) and major change (e.g. to the project baseline) because only the former can be handled dynamically and with little overhead. This illustrates the importance of setting the project baseline in the project initiation documentation at the correct level (e.g. avoiding unnecessary detail early on).

Definition: Trading (or swapping)

The act of handling change by replacing one or more requirements (or features or user stories) with others of a similar size in terms of effort.

Minor change can be handled by flexing what is being delivered through prioritization and **trading** (or swapping), whereas major change would usually require more formal change control processes and may even necessitate going into exception and/or stopping the project if the business case is no longer viable.

6.4.4 Keeping teams stable: avoid adding new team members

If a project falls behind schedule a traditional response would be to consider the option of increasing the number of people involved in order to speed up progress. In some circumstances where the work being undertaken is reasonably straightforward, this can solve the problem. However, when the work is more challenging it probably won't – particularly in the short term. This is the primary reason why the tolerance for cost is set to zero.

Although this has an impact in any situation, the agile way of working is particularly impacted by the changing of personnel because agile utilizes such things as informal communication and self-organizing whilst scheduling work into short timeframes (e.g. a two-week timebox). Therefore, changing team members or adding to the team can have a far more detrimental effect than normal for reasons such as:

● Time is spent bringing new team members up to speed.

● The number of communication lines in the team grows exponentially.

● There is an opportunity cost incurred to the areas providing the new people.

● The **team dynamics** change and need to be re-established.

The impact of changing a team's dynamics is usually underestimated and can sometimes be the most counter-productive side-effect of the four.

Definition: Team dynamics

The interpersonal interactions between the individuals on a team. This relates to the culture and attitudes of the people in the team and needs to be managed carefully: it can be a very positive and powerful force when it is working well, but it can be destructive when it breaks down.

It is important to understand that team members may need to change throughout the life of a project as the needs of a project change, but this concept of avoiding the use of extra people to improve progress applies primarily to the short term – for example four weeks or less, such as within a sprint.

6.4.5 Do we need everything we have asked for?

Usually no, although the customer may not realize this at the start of a project. This point can be easily demonstrated by looking at products we frequently use and analysing how many of the functions and features we rarely or never use. A washing machine is perhaps a good example of this in that it would normally contain many functions and features as well as a wide range of spin speeds, temperature settings and programmes, yet it would be unusual to find many people who used more than just a few of the options available. Most people would use two programmes at most.

The importance of this concept lies in the PRINCE2 Agile belief that the features of the product are the safest and most sensible area to compromise on (i.e. to use as **contingency**). A project using PRINCE2 Agile doesn't set out with the intention of not delivering everything, but it does aim to hit deadlines and protect the level of quality by reducing what is delivered accordingly. This in turn can result in the early delivery of a minimum viable product (MVP), and in general terms the project delivers what the customer really wants (or needs) more quickly.

6.5 CHAPTER SUMMARY

It is important to understand all of the five targets that underpin the thinking behind flexing what is being delivered. The five targets do not operate in isolation: they are interwoven and together they provide a lot of the reasoning behind the agile way of working.

It could be said that flexing what is being delivered represents an 'alternative deal' to the way people have traditionally worked. In its simplest form this new arrangement asks the customer a question: namely, 'If you want your project delivered on time, the level of quality protected and changes at the detailed level to be handled dynamically and at no extra cost ... are you happy to forgo some of your lower-priority requirements or lower-priority acceptance/quality criteria, if necessary?' (see Figure 6.2).

Getting an appropriate balance of what is essential and what is not essential becomes important when working this way. If the balance is not conducive to flexing what is being delivered (e.g. there is very little that can be described as not essential) then this creates a risk to this way of working and in extreme situations (e.g. where practically everything is essential), it may make the use of agile on a project inadvisable.

A lot of the understanding of agile falls into place when the thinking behind flexing what is being delivered is understood correctly. One of the reasons that agile is often misunderstood or hard to understand at times is that these concepts are a mixture of common sense (e.g. being on time) and ideas that are counterintuitive (e.g. seeing change in a positive light).

In order for a customer to understand that this is for their benefit, they need to see the holistic view that is supported by flexing what is being delivered. If this is not achieved then the customer may feel that flexing will not deliver everything they want. It would be unlikely that this will be seen as an attractive proposition.

Tip
To deliver more, deliver less!

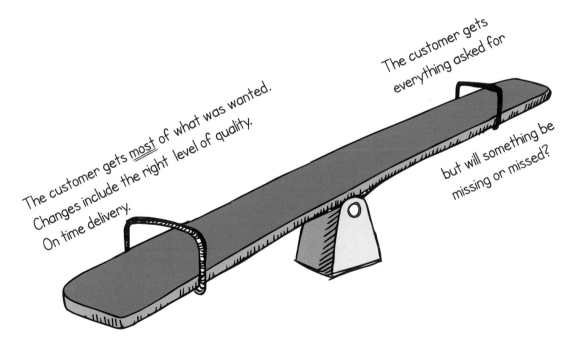

Figure 6.2 On balance, what is more important to the customer?

PART II

PRINCE2 AGILE GUIDANCE, TAILORING AND TECHNIQUES

7

Agile and the PRINCE2 principles

This chapter covers:

- A general view of agile and the PRINCE2 principles

- Guidance on applying the PRINCE2 principles

- PRINCE2 Agile behaviours

7 Agile and the PRINCE2 principles

7.1 THE PRINCE2 PRINCIPLES

The principles on which PRINCE2 is based originate from lessons learned from projects both good and bad. They provide a framework of good practice for those people involved in a project. If a project does not adhere to these principles, it is not being managed using PRINCE2, because the principles are the basis of what defines a PRINCE2 project.

The seven PRINCE2 principles are listed in section 5.2.

It is the adoption of these principles that characterizes whether a project is using PRINCE2, not the adoption of processes and documents alone. The principles facilitate good use of PRINCE2 by ensuring that the method is not applied in an overly prescriptive way or in name only, but applied in a way that is sufficient to contribute to the success of the project.

7.2 THE GENERAL VIEW OF AGILE WITH RESPECT TO THE PRINCE2 PRINCIPLES

Agile has a very strong focus on such things as principles. The Agile Manifesto and the agile frameworks and methods (see Appendix E) all promote a set of principles in some form, although the exact wording used to describe the fundamental mind-set, attitudes and ethos does vary and includes or is sometimes replaced by such terms as 'values', 'behaviours' and 'philosophy'.

PRINCE2 principles do not conflict with any of the agile principles. They are complementary to the agile way of working. Some of the PRINCE2 principles could be described as 'very much agile' such as continued business justification, learn from experience, focus on products and **manage by exception** – the latter being synonymous with giving people autonomy and empowerment.

7.3 GUIDANCE ON APPLYING THE PRINCE2 PRINCIPLES

PRINCE2 is principles-based and all seven of the principles are applicable when combining PRINCE2 with agile. Table 7.1 provides an overview of the guidance when applying the principles and some further considerations to bear in mind.

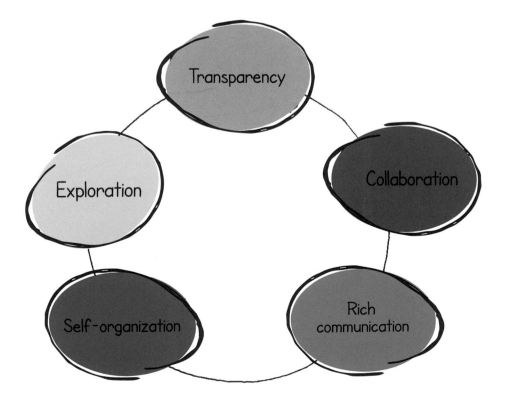

Figure 7.1 PRINCE2 Agile behaviours

Table 7.1 Overview of the guidance when applying PRINCE2 principles in an agile context

PRINCE2 principle	Overview of the guidance and further considerations	Example
Continued business justification	Agile often uses the term 'value' instead of 'benefit' (see section 9.4 for a detailed discussion of this). The rationale behind creating a minimum viable product (MVP) needs to be understood, and attention should be paid to it throughout the project by the project management team (for more information, see the Business Case theme covered in Chapter 9, and also section 20.4.2).	An MVP for an online service may comprise a simple landing page describing the service. If an insufficient number of visitors show interest in the service then there is no point providing it.
Learn from experience	Many agile concepts support this principle and as many of them as appropriate should be used in order to provide the techniques for continual learning. Examples of this include shortening the feedback loop to the customer, continual customer involvement, inspect and adapt, retrospectives and Kaizen.	A retrospective may conclude that using three-week sprints will be more productive than two-week sprints.
Defined roles and responsibilities	Additional agile roles will apply at the delivery level and they should be mapped and merged carefully to the PRINCE2 roles (for more information, see the Organization theme, which is covered in Chapter 10).	A new project involves three teams from the customer area who all have differing needs from those of the project. Each of the teams will need to be clear who is fulfilling the project-level roles (e.g. **senior user**) and the delivery-level roles (e.g. **product owner**).
Manage by stages	Significant timeboxes such as releases should be carefully planned to integrate with, and fit into, management stages. In situations of high uncertainty (e.g. creating something very innovative) many short stages can be used to ensure that control is maintained and a fail fast/learn fast environment exists.	A very expensive and unconventional marketing campaign is being delivered incrementally for a new perfume, which will take several months. The stage boundaries may only be two weeks apart to ensure that if the project does not turn out to be viable, the money lost by the project is kept to a minimum.
Manage by exception	Not only is it essential to use this principle and to ensure that it is implemented correctly but it is vital to see this as at the heart of empowering people to self-organize and stay in control with the appropriate level of governance when using PRINCE2 and agile together. Working in an agile way places a greater emphasis on allowing tolerance on what is delivered and restricting the tolerance on time and cost.	A project is established to create a **prototype** to be demonstrated at a trade show on a specific date. They give the project manager 25% tolerance on the amount of scope to be delivered, but zero tolerance for the delivery date.
Focus on products	Product descriptions, quality criteria and quality tolerances can be prioritized and decomposed in order to make flexing what is being delivered possible and therefore make it easier to stay in control and focus on the delivery of value.	A major conference wants people to pay using a credit or debit card. They prioritize the need for the payment as a 'must', and further prioritize the credit card option as a 'must' and the debit card option as a 'should'.
Tailor to suit the project environment	PRINCE2 Agile incorporates an agile assessment tool (the **Agilometer** – see Chapter 24), which enables further specific tailoring by assessing the risks associated with the agile way of working with respect to the project environment (e.g. How engaged is the customer? How easy is communication?).	A project is about to start and everyone is very excited about the months ahead. When assessing the project it transpires that a key customer representative is going to be on holiday for the next four weeks. The team decide to mitigate the risk of a reduction in customer involvement by using another person from another team during the missing weeks and creating a handover log to be updated throughout this period.

7.4 PRINCE2 AGILE BEHAVIOURS

When tailoring PRINCE2 to work in an agile context a PRINCE2 project manager and the project board will need to monitor specific behaviours from the project management team and the delivery teams. These behaviours need to function smoothly for agile to operate in the most effective way. As shown in Figure 7.1, they are:

● Transparency
● Collaboration
● Rich communication
● Self-organization
● Exploration.

7.4.1 Transparency

The more information that is out in the open, the better this is for the agile way of working. It enables speed, clarity and engagement, even if the news is not so good.

Essential to understanding this behaviour is to realize that there is more to transparency than just visibility. The most important elements of this principle come in the form of the common agile values of honesty, trust, integrity and respect. This openness is an essential ingredient for an agile way of working.

Take a situation, for example, where it is decided to show the progress of a three-month stage as a burn-down chart on the wall of the office. As each day passes the gap between the actual rate of progress and the planned rate keeps widening. The project team is aware of the situation and every day the team looks to close the gap by addressing the reasons for being behind (e.g. Is it extra work? Are the estimates too low?). Transparency means that everyone knows the situation and there are no surprises.

7.4.2 Collaboration

A motivated and respectful team is greater than the sum of its parts if people work together and provide cover for one another. More can be achieved this way than working in silos. Collaboration is not just internal to the team: it involves external collaboration with all stakeholders, especially the customer. Fully engaging with customers and working with them, rather than for them, will create shared understanding and ownership of goals and outputs.

An example of collaboration could be where a team is falling behind with work due to one person having difficulties with a technical problem. One person on the team is ahead of schedule on their own work, so they stop to help the colleague. The same thing happened in the previous sprint, although the roles on that occasion were reversed.

7.4.3 Rich communication

People should always use the most effective channel to communicate. Using face-to-face and/or visualization are many times faster and more effective than words on their own. A rich communication environment should be created where information passes freely in a culture of commitment and trust. There is still a need for documentation, but by using other more effective channels, it can be replaced or complemented and greatly reduced.

An example of rich communication is provided where an email thread has been circulating between three team members for over an hour about a possible design change. One of the team members decides to get the other two over to a whiteboard and discuss the point face-to-face. They agree a way forward in a matter of minutes.

7.4.4 Self-organization

The people closest to the work will usually know best how to get the job done. Therefore people should be trusted to do it. If they create a plan, then they own it and buy into it; it is far more likely to happen if they do. Self-organizing creates mutual respect. A project manager can leave a team manager to focus on product delivery where the team manager feels trusted. This principle extends far beyond the work. It includes the way the team works and the way team members behave towards one another. Although the project board is ultimately accountable for the direction of the project as a whole, the more a team is empowered at the delivery level, the more likely it is to perform well when working in an agile context and achieve the outcomes and goals of that direction.

A children's party can be a very good example of self-organization. At the end of a party it is likely that a house will be very untidy with toys and games everywhere. Let's say that the children have been promised a film, and that there is only a short time until the film starts. Instead of micro-managing the children, a parent lets the children know that they can all see the film if everything is put away tidily and in its right place. As a result, the house gets tidied and the children see the film.

7.4.5 Exploration

Projects are difficult, and in order to create 'the right thing' you need to be able to work out what 'the right thing' is! Frequent iteration and rapid feedback loops in any form provide an opportunity to learn. Learning helps to improve the products. However, feedback won't just happen; it needs to be sought out collaboratively – perhaps through **experiment**s and **spike**s, with people such as the customer, customer representatives, other team members or stakeholders.

Definition: Experiment

An investigation into something that is carried out in a series of specific steps (which may involve research) in order to prove or disprove a theory or idea. This can be used to validate an idea or to try and improve something such as the way a team is working.

Lots of small learnings about what the customer wants accumulate over time and make a big impact overall. By continually working in loops that deliver something and create feedback, the team can go forward. The shorter these feedback loops are, the quicker progress can be made and the smaller will be the impact of any mistakes. The sooner the team solves 'known unknowns' and uncovers 'unknown unknowns', the sooner they can arrive at the right destination.

Definition: Spike/spiking

A temporary piece of work used to understand more about a given situation. It may take the form of a prototype or some research and is often used to reduce uncertainty from a technical or customer viewpoint. Experiments are similar.

For example, as an experiment, a company decided to create a website to enable customers to print digital photographs. They were surprised to find that very few photos were printed but that many people joined the website to share photos with their friends.

7.4.6 How to ...

Table 7.2 Relevant agile guidance on PRINCE2 Agile behaviours

	Chapter and section references
Be transparent	Section 15.4.2, Appendix H
Collaborate	Chapter 10, in particular section 10.5.3
Communicate	Chapter 26
Self-organize	Sections 10.5.1 and 20.3.1; Appendix H
Explore	Sections 14.4.1, 20.4.2 and 25.6.1; Chapter 27

7.5 PRINCE2 PRINCIPLES SUMMARY

When using PRINCE2 in an agile context it is important to monitor these behaviours and ensure that they are happening as well as possible. Everyone involved in the project should be trying to behave this way as much as possible.

Ultimately, the project board or the project manager will need to monitor the situation, and one option is to use a simple traffic light dashboard to highlight any behaviours that are in need of attention or may be causing damage to the project (see Figure 7.2). The values will be subjective and may be for the project board or project manager only. A green light would mean that the situation is fine. Yellow/amber would indicate that there is cause for concern. Red would indicate that immediate action is needed.

Tip

Take two minutes just to look at your team. How are they acting? What are they doing? What are they saying? How are they adopting the principles and behaviours? The answer will be obvious, as long as you take time to look for it and not look away from it!

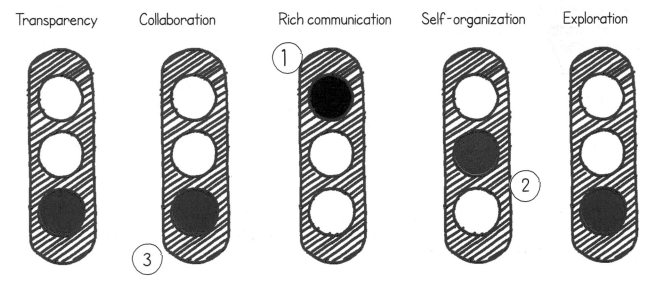

Notes:

1. This would usually trigger an exception
2. This would need attention as it will be causing some damage to the project
3. Although these are green they would still need to be monitored on a regular basis

Figure 7.2 How a behaviour dashboard may look if a project manager is reporting to a project board

8

Agile and the PRINCE2 themes

This chapter covers:

- The PRINCE2 themes
- The prominence of some themes over others

8 Agile and the PRINCE2 themes

8.1 THE PRINCE2 THEMES

PRINCE2 identifies seven integrated themes that are always present throughout a project.

The PRINCE2 themes are those aspects of project management that:

- Need to be addressed continually. They are not one-off activities. For example, risk management should be central to every decision: it is not a case of updating a register from time to time.
- Require specific treatment for the PRINCE2 processes to be integrated effectively. For example, the processes require a division of responsibilities between those people who direct (the project board), those who manage (the project manager) and those who deliver (the project [delivery] team) as defined in the Organization theme.

The themes provide guidance on how the process activities should be performed (and explain why). For example, numerous processes in PRINCE2 involve creating or approving plans: explanatory guidance can be found in the Plans theme, which is covered in Chapter 12 of this guide.

How PRINCE2 Agile is tailored for the PRINCE2 themes is described in Table 8.1.

8.2 SOME THEMES ARE MORE PROMINENT THAN OTHERS

Because most agile guidance is focused on product delivery, some of the themes are very prominent when combining agile with PRINCE2 (e.g. the Plans theme and the Progress theme), whereas others are less prominent (e.g. the Business Case theme and the Risk theme). However, all of the themes still need to be used, as they are equally important.

Image 8.1 Merging fixed with flexible ways of working

8.3 SUMMARY OF TAILORING GUIDANCE FOR THE PRINCE2 THEMES

PRINCE2 uses themes to describe aspects of project management that must be addressed continually. **It is essential to use all of the seven themes.** Table 8.1 provides a summary of guidance where particular areas of understanding may be required for each theme.

Table 8.1 Things to consider when tailoring the PRINCE2 themes to PRINCE2 Agile

Theme	Overview of the tailoring required and further considerations
Business Case	Although no changes are required to this theme, it may contain more information (and possibly emphasis) on the tolerances around benefits with respect to priorities, timescales and the amount of product being delivered. This business case could show the amount of product being delivered in the form of a best-case, a worst-case and an expected-case scenario in relation to the amount of the final product that may be delivered or flexed.
	It may be appropriate to explicitly define what would constitute a minimum viable product (MVP), as well as some indication of priorities within the overall scope and related quality criteria.
	When creating a business case, understanding is required of how the incremental delivery of a product and the value associated with it could impact project viability (positively or negatively) and also the ability to achieve the early delivery of some benefits.
	Where there is a high level of uncertainty the business case should be developed very quickly and the assumptions tested rapidly. This approach could be described as 'taking a leap of faith'.
Organization	Although no changes are required to this theme as defined in PRINCE2, additional delivery-level roles may need to be added, and the most common agile roles should be mapped appropriately to the roles of the project management team structure.
	Understanding is required of:
	● How a self-organizing delivery team operates and how this relates to the team manager role
	● The responsibilities of the most common agile roles such as product owner, Scrum master, agile coach, **business ambassador**
	● The potential limitations of the product owner role, where a wider view of the customer is needed – such as with multi-team projects
	● How the senior user role acts more as a 'super product owner' than a conventional product owner
	● Where more than one team is involved, how Scrum masters will liaise with the project manager.
	The full and uncompromised use of management by exception is essential to enable PRINCE2 and agile to be combined, in order to empower the project management team and enable it to self-organize within clearly defined boundaries.
Quality	It is important to understand the difference between scope and quality when defining customer quality expectations, acceptance criteria, product descriptions, quality criteria and quality tolerances. They need to be defined in such a way that flexing what is being delivered does not compromise the fitness for purpose of any product, or ultimately the final product. Further to this, carefully differentiating functional from non-functional requirements is important, as this can help with respect to prioritization.
	The use of agile concepts and techniques such as the **definition of 'done'** and the **definition of 'ready'** can be used to define quality criteria and acceptance criteria.
	The frequency of quality checking (in the form of reviews or tests) will have a significant impact on how a project is planned, as this will affect the iterative and incremental delivery of the project's products and how they are released.

Theme	Overview of the tailoring required and further considerations
Plans	Although no changes are required with this theme, many agile techniques and approaches exist in this area. They focus on the effort related to features (e.g. sprint planning) and often appear in an informal, low-tech, visible format such as a simple list or backlog.
	Planning is often done empirically.
	Agile typically looks at how much can be produced in a fixed timeframe such as a sprint or a release (or how much value can be delivered). This is often shown at the start in the form of a burn chart that can then be tracked.
	This is in contrast to creating milestones representing how long something will take and showing this on a **Gantt chart**, as this is of limited value. Gantt charts may be of value at the higher levels of plan but they should be synchronized to the agile way of working and should avoid the duplication of information that is being held in the form of backlogs.
Risk	The agile way of working addresses many risk areas such as avoiding too much detail at the start of a project (as it will not be fully understood at this point) but it comes with its own set of potential risks and these need to be proactively managed (e.g. ensuring that customer engagement is continual and that customer representatives are correctly empowered).
	Many agile techniques address risks, for example daily stand-up meetings, frequent delivery of products, frequent use reviews, customer interaction and empowered teams organizing themselves to deliver the right thing at the right time.
Change	Although no changes are needed to this theme, the agile way of working embraces change and responds to it. The PRINCE2 approach to change control needs to allow for this and helps to create a more accurate final product.
	The appropriate definition of product descriptions, quality criteria, quality tolerances and work packages is important. They can be defined in such a way as to allow for change, whilst at the same time creating a clearly defined baseline that can prevent a change to the very purpose of a product going undetected.
	A **change authority** may still be appropriate but is unlikely to function at the delivery level unless it carries out its duties informally, and the change authority needs to understand how detailed change is perceived and addressed in agile.
	A change budget is unlikely to exist, as the agile way of working uses the prioritization of what is being delivered as contingency.
	Configuration management will need to be set up in a way that also helps to embrace change, as it may happen frequently.
Progress	Similarly to the Plans theme, many agile techniques apply in this area where the emphasis is on tracking what is being delivered in the form of such things as **velocity**, **lead time**s or value. This is as opposed to tracking time and cost, which are not suitable as a measure of a project's progress. Tolerances would be set in accordance with this.
	Tracking progress will depend on the situation and what people need information on. If it is within a sprint then burn-up or burn-down charts may suffice (see section 15.4.1). If it is across releases, then showing the value accrued and how this relates to the business case may be more appropriate.
	The frequent delivery of products that meet the appropriate acceptance criteria/quality criteria is the primary source of information with respect to progress and provides the basis for forecasting future progress.

Tip

Planning poker is a technique used to estimate effort or the relative size of development goals. Each member of the development group selects one card from a set of numbered cards and places it face down on a table. The cards are revealed, and the estimates are then discussed.

Definition: Velocity

A description of the rate of progress a team is making. For example, if a team is completing 20 user stories per week, then this is their velocity and it can be used to empirically forecast their future rate of progress (assuming that the conditions remain the same).

Business Case theme

This chapter covers:

- PRINCE2 and agile approaches to the Business Case theme

- PRINCE2 Agile guidance for the Business Case theme

- Agile concepts and techniques

9 Business Case theme

9.1 THE PRINCE2 APPROACH TO THE BUSINESS CASE THEME

The purpose of the Business Case theme is to establish mechanisms to judge whether the project is (and remains) desirable, viable and achievable as a means to support decision-making in its (continued) investment.

It is a PRINCE2 principle that a project must have continued business justification.

In PRINCE2, the business case is developed at the beginning of the project and maintained throughout the life of the project, being formally verified by the project board at each key decision point, such as end stage assessments, and confirmed throughout the period that the benefits accrue (see Figure 9.1).

The business case should describe the reasons for the project based on estimated costs, risks and expected benefits. See section A.2 for the typical contents of a business case.

9.2 THE GENERAL VIEW OF AGILE WITH RESPECT TO THE BUSINESS CASE THEME

In a mature agile environment a business case would be created in some form. As part of the vision and product roadmap there would be sufficient information to ensure that the work is appropriately justified and that it is strategically aligned. This would need to take place before release planning takes place.

In some agile environments there may not be as much emphasis given to the concept of a formal business case, possibly for the following reasons:

- Teams talk in terms of the delivery of 'value' instead.
- The most common agile ways of working focus more on the value of delivering individual features rather than assessing the totality of the features as a whole in advance. Work is prioritized (in a product backlog) by a product owner, in an ongoing manner, based on value and maximizing that value. In effect this plays the role of a business case and is authorized by the product owner.

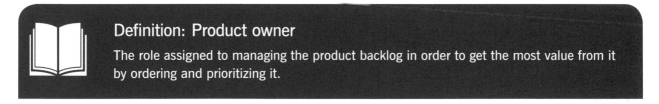

Definition: Product owner

The role assigned to managing the product backlog in order to get the most value from it by ordering and prioritizing it.

It is important to understand that in some agile environments this does not mean that a business case is not needed or is undesirable; it may just be assumed that one exists or that the rationale for the work being undertaken has already been justified.

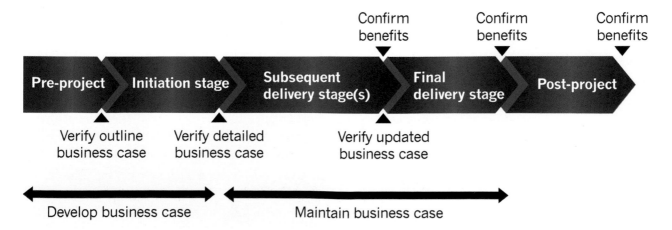

Figure 9.1 The development path of the business case

Scrum for example starts with a backlog of features – when Scrum is used in a project context it assumes that this backlog has already been created. In a BAU environment, a backlog will already exist and each entry on the backlog is prioritized on its relative merits in relation to the value it will deliver. In a project environment, upfront work is required (such as creating a backlog) and this would include the evolution of a business case, which would need to be authorized before delivery work could commence. A mature agile environment would cater for this although there isn't a commonly agreed standard for how to do this or what it would look like.

Definition: Visioning or project kick-off

An exercise or phase that aims to understand the overarching goal of something (e.g. a project). It would try to answer questions such as: Why is this work taking place? Who is it for? What might it look like?

One common approach that is used is to have a specific sprint at the beginning of a piece of work in order to address many upfront activities (e.g. forming a team, **visioning**, defining the architecture) and understanding and approving a business case would be part of this. This is commonly referred to as **sprint zero** (or iteration zero or (the) **discovery (phase)**) but the following points should be recognized:

● There isn't a formal standard for what sprint zero looks like.

● Sprint zero is perceived both positively and negatively by the agile community.

● The *Scrum Guide* (see Appendix H) does not support the concept.

Definition: Sprint zero

A specific sprint at the beginning of a piece of work in order to address many upfront activities (e.g. forming a team, visioning, defining the architecture): also referred to as iteration zero or (the) discovery (phase).

9.3 PRINCE2 AGILE GUIDANCE FOR THE BUSINESS CASE THEME

PRINCE2 Agile is based upon flexing what is delivered, and therefore the project board and the project manager should be aware that the business case is affected by the following:

● Flexing what is delivered may directly affect the expected benefits (e.g. fewer features than expected are delivered), so this needs to be appreciated when the business case is created and maintained as benefits are likely to be expressed in the form of a range, which relates to the amount delivered.

● After the project initiation documentation has been approved, time and cost tolerances, with respect to overruns, may be set to zero in order to focus solely on managing the quantity of what is delivered.

● The iterative and incremental delivery of products and sub-products aims to achieve the early delivery of benefit. The frequency of these incremental deliveries and the benefits they deliver can affect the business case both positively and negatively.

● How easy it is to deliver into the operational environment may also need to be taken into account.

● The business case should clearly state what the minimum viable product (MVP) is and may give an indication of when this will be delivered and whether it will be put into operational use. The appropriate tolerances would be created around this so that if the project is forecast to deliver the MVP late (or even not at all) then an exception condition occurs. More information on MVP can be found in section 20.4.2.

● The viability of the project is a different concept from an MVP. At all times during a project the project must remain viable and meet the needs of the business case.

PRINCE2 uses the business case and the Business Case theme throughout a project to provide a firm basis upon which agile concepts and techniques can be used effectively in the knowledge that the strategic alignment and business justification are in place. Mature agile organizations would already have these in place.

One way to present a business case is to describe best-case and worst-case scenarios that relate to the number of features that are planned to be delivered. The worst-case scenario (i.e. the lowest expectation of the amount delivered) would need to clearly show that the project is still viable. The best-case scenario could represent everything being delivered as planned. What would be useful to the project board assessing the business case, in an agile context, is to be given clear information on what is expected to be delivered, creating an expected case that is between the two extremes although this will not necessarily be the mid-point.

These scenarios can only be calculated when using high-level or (perhaps) intermediate-level requirements. It is unlikely that detailed requirements can be mapped directly to the business case.

When using agile, the business case (along with the project product description) will have much more emphasis on what features are being delivered and when partial deliveries or releases can be expected, and with them the benefits that will be achieved.

The business case is mandatory in PRINCE2 and needs to be created by someone who has the appropriate level of skill to create it correctly (e.g. it should be coherent, accurate and strategically aligned).

In situations of high uncertainty it may be appropriate that the creation of a business case takes very little time, so that tests can be carried out quickly in order to validate it (see section 20.4.2 on the Lean Startup method).

9.4 AGILE CONCEPTS AND TECHNIQUES

9.4.1 Defining value

Agile usually refers to 'value' whereas PRINCE2 usually refers to 'benefits'. Although not precisely the same thing the terms are often interchangeable (see section 9.4.2).

9.4.1.1 Agile and value

The very first principle of the Agile Manifesto refers to delivering value, but there is very little guidance in most agile sources on how to determine and define 'value'. The reason for this is because it is usually difficult to define and often involves subjectivity.

Another reason why this situation exists is because the most common agile frameworks are focused at the delivery level under the assumption that the work in general has already been justified. In some agile environments, this assessment of value takes place at the lowest levels of detail, which is probably the hardest place to do this.

9.4.1.2 Calculating value

Working out the value of carrying out a piece of work is easier at higher levels where some degree of aggregation has occurred. Forecasting the savings a particular project could make will normally be far easier than forecasting the savings that one particular requirement might achieve. This is why assigning relative values to a long list of detailed requirements or user stories will normally be quite subjective. A customer may find it easy to say that one **user story** is more important than another user story, but they may find it difficult to quantify what the value of each story actually is.

This may not always be the case, as there may be situations where the value measure being used can be derived quickly from historical data and can easily be validated by customer feedback. An example of this would be the desire to increase traffic to a website. In this scenario other websites could be analysed to see how beneficial certain features proved to be; then after implementing the feature, hard data would be available to measure the impact.

But even in the previous example measuring value may not be as straightforward as it looks. Should the customer be measuring the increase of visitors to a website or should they be measuring the increase in time spent on the website? Perhaps they shouldn't be measuring either and they should be focusing on how much revenue the website is generating.

Measures drive behaviours; therefore it is important to use the correct measure of value.

9.4.1.3 Measuring value

Measuring value can be quite difficult due to the fact there are so many things that may give value, such as increasing revenue, reducing costs, retaining customers, reducing risks, meeting regulatory targets, customer satisfaction, brand improvement and so on.

It is important to understand what kind of value is needed and to quantify it at the project level (i.e. in the business case). This will then help when assigning relative values at the delivery team level, because these people are working with the detail.

One thing that is more important than building the product right is to build the right product.

9.4.2 Defining benefits and value – an example

The following call centre scenario is intended to provide a guide to how benefits and value could be assessed at the beginning of a project and during it. The intention is to highlight how difficult this can be but at the same time illustrate its importance – and also demonstrate the way in which a project team working in an agile way can respond and adapt to the circumstances happening around them.

> *We need to close more customer incidents on the first call! We need a knowledge management (KM) system!*

Change in an organization can start from anywhere. There may be a problem to solve or an opportunity to take. Although the idea can come from anywhere it needs to be authorized at the right level and in the right way (e.g. at a strategic level).

Once a project begins to come into existence, it is essential to define the ultimate benefit and value that will be delivered. Asking for a KM system is asking for what PRINCE2 refers to as an output. Assuming that the KM system will result in more calls/incidents being closed on the first call, this is what PRINCE2 refers to as an outcome. However, more important than both of these are the benefit and value that are ultimately delivered. PRINCE2 refers primarily to benefit, whereas agile refers more frequently to value: although they are similar they are not the same and this is explored in the rest of this chapter. Value is sometimes referred to as 'net benefit' as it represents the benefits after the expenditure has been factored in.

Tip

AXELOS's *Management of Value* (MoV) says that value is subjective, with different people applying different criteria to assess whether they are getting good value. It is this subjectivity that makes it so essential to manage value deliberately, instead of leaving it as a by-product of any other management activity. Added value is provided by the delivery of enhanced, but useful, benefits and more effective use of resources. Not all perceived benefits are actually necessary. MoV provides a means of distinguishing between needs and wants. Likewise the supply of resources is often (indeed usually) limited. Effective expenditure is essential to make the most of what is available.

MoV recognizes that not all benefits are financial and that the differing priorities of key stakeholders need to be considered and reconciled. Expenditure must cover short- and long-term needs and recognize that resources are finite and must be conserved. Balancing and reconciling these conflicting demands, to maximize value, is one of the core principles of MoV.

9.4.2.1 Points to consider when starting a project

To correctly initiate a project, it is important to understand why it is taking place and what the best course of action is:

- Why is it assumed that a KM system will close more calls on the first call?
- What is the significance of closing an incident on the first call? Why is that different from closing an incident in two calls?

Spending time to work out exactly what the problem (or opportunity) is and how to solve it is essential to getting a project off to a good start.

The reasons for wanting a KM system could be that:

- If more information from around the company is made available, the information would be available to help close more calls on the first call.

The reason for wanting to close calls on the first call could be that:

- Existing measurements and metrics within the organization show that to re-visit an incident takes 25% more time in total because subsequent calls need to cover the same information again (e.g. customer details and security). This in turn is leading to the need to hire many temporary workers over and above the existing company headcount, and temporary personnel are relatively expensive.

9.4.2.2 Clarifying the output, outcome and benefit (or value)

Investigating the thinking behind the desire for a KM system can drive out the real reasoning behind it. Continually asking 'why?' can help to determine the answer, and may result in a well-defined statement such as:

> We want a KM system (output) so that we can close 80% of all incident calls on the first call (outcome) in order to reduce the workload in the call centre by 10% so that we will not need to hire as many temporary workers, and this will save us £200K per year (benefit).

Importantly, the outcome and benefits are now measurable. However, it is important to measure the current situation as well so that progress can be monitored (e.g. the percentage of calls closed on the first call is currently standing at 63%).

9.4.2.3 What if things change?

Assuming that the project has gone ahead, working in an agile way would focus on getting feedback as early as possible by the early delivery of features that should be of benefit and value.

If the new KM system was a 12-month project it may be appropriate to deliver certain important and useful features in the early months that are intended to help close calls on the first call. This then gives a chance to measure how effective they are.

After six months, if the percentage of closed calls on the first call has improved to 70% (from 63%) then this would probably be seen as a good sign. However, this is still an outcome. Has the expected benefit been achieved in saving the expense of the temporary workers? It may be the case that there is no reduction in the temporary personnel. A project that is benefit- or value-focused will react to this, whereas a project that is output-focused will continue to build the KM system (as this is what it has been asked to do).

As a surprise, what if the customer satisfaction ratings for the call centre have gone up recently by 4% due to the increase in calls closed on the first call? Perhaps the happier customers (due to calls being closed on the first call) are resulting in more calls to the sales teams, which in turn is resulting in more calls to the call centre! Which is why the number of temporary workers has not reduced.

Seeing that the KM system may be delivering benefit and value, but not quite in the way it was anticipated, can allow the project management team and the delivery teams to adjust how they work and what they work on.

It may be that certain premium customers are so impressed with the improved incident resolution time that they are buying other products and they do so in large volumes. Therefore, if the call centre focused more on closing premium customers' calls on the first call, this would deliver more benefits and value than with the original outcome, yet still deliver a KM system (the output).

Revising the earlier request may therefore be:

> *We want a KM system (output) so that we can close 90% of all incident calls from premium customers on the first call (outcome) in order to increase their customer satisfaction ratings by 3% so that we get an increase in sales of new products of £300K per year (benefit).*

9.4.2.4 The need to focus on benefits and value

To deliver as much benefit and value as possible it is important to be able to measure and track them. It is also important to be able to adjust the work taking place to maximize this. As feedback is received it will affect the priority of the requirements. This may generate new requirements that are essential (e.g. we need to know if a call is from a premium customer). This is why the business case needs to be flexible in that the benefits can be achieved by adjusting the originally defined outcomes and outputs, and therefore the setting of the appropriate tolerances (e.g. for scope, quality criteria and benefits) becomes important.

9.4.2.5 How collaboration helps

If the feedback being received by the early delivery of features is not quite what was expected, it is desirable if this is handled collaboratively by everyone on the project from the project board to the delivery teams – by the customer and the supplier. Agile teams respond to change. To react well to changes in circumstances means that anyone representing the customer needs to seize the opportunity to adjust the course of the project by working out what is happening and why, and then reprioritize accordingly. Equally, anyone from the supplier side needs to make clear what is possible (e.g. 'Have you thought of this?', 'We could do it that way.') More benefit and value are likely to be delivered if the team collaboratively focuses on benefits and value in preference to focusing on just the output. This is why the contractual side of the relationship needs to support this as much as possible.

9.5 BUSINESS CASE THEME SUMMARY

The popularity of PRINCE2 has had a significant impact on many organizations in terms of getting business cases created for most projects. Many agile frameworks do not have the concept of a business case, whereas in PRINCE2 it is mandatory. This provides an essential element to ensure that the project has been started correctly. Having a business case is one thing, but writing a good business case is another, and in PRINCE2 Agile it needs to be flexible and written on the assumption that what is being delivered will change in order to maximize the expected benefits of the project.

The Business Case theme supports the continued justification for the project and therefore helps to clarify the big picture. This in turn enables the decision-making that is being made at the more detailed levels to have a clearly defined position in this wider context and not just where requirements exist in isolation.

Tip

For any situation that arises on a project, a key question (for anyone) to ask is 'How does this affect the business case?' This represents the bigger picture or, to put it another way, the main thing is to keep the business case as the main focus.

As outlined in section 9.4.2, the skill of crafting a well-written project product description and business case will always be needed. Amongst other things this is essential to ensure a project's success but also to detect as quickly as possible if a project is no longer viable.

ACKNOWLEDGEMENTS AND FURTHER READING

Office of Government Commerce (2010). *Management of Value (MoV)*. TSO, London.

Eric Ries (2011). *The Lean Startup: How Constant Innovation Creates Radically Successful Businesses*. Portfolio Penguin.

Gabrielle Benefield. *The Mobius Loop*. http://www.gabriellebenefield.com/mobius/how-to-measure-value

Tom Gilb. *Quantifying Value: on-line resources*. http://gilb.com

10

Organization theme

This chapter covers:

- PRINCE2 and agile approaches to the Organization theme
- PRINCE2 Agile guidance for the Organization theme
- Differences between PRINCE2 and agile role concepts
- Agile concepts and techniques

10 Organization theme

10.1 THE PRINCE2 APPROACH TO THE ORGANIZATION THEME

The purpose of the Organization theme is to define and establish the project's structure of accountability and responsibilities (the who?).

10.1.1 Three project interests

The PRINCE2 principle of defined roles and responsibilities states that a PRINCE2 project will always have three primary categories of stakeholder, and the interests of all three must be satisfied if the project is to be successful. Figure 10.1 shows the three primary interests which make up the project board. PRINCE2 recommends that for completeness the project board should include representation from each of the business, user and supplier interests at all times.

● **Business** The products of the project should meet a business need which will justify the investment in the project. The project should also provide value for money.

● **User** PRINCE2 makes a distinction between the business interests and the requirements of those who will use the project's outputs. The user presence is needed to specify the desired outputs and ensure that the project delivers them. The senior user(s) will represent this stakeholder interest on the project board.

● **Supplier** The creation of the project's outputs will need resources with certain skills. The supplier viewpoint should represent those who will provide the necessary skills and produce the project product. The senior supplier(s) will represent this stakeholder interest on the project board.

10.1.2 The project management team

10.1.2.1 Project management team structure

A project management team is a temporary structure specifically designed to manage the project to its successful conclusion. The structure allows for channels of communication to decision-making forums and should be backed up by role descriptions that specify the responsibilities, goals, limits of authority, relationships, skills, knowledge and experience required for all roles in the project management team. Figure 10.2 illustrates the structure of the project management team and its reporting lines.

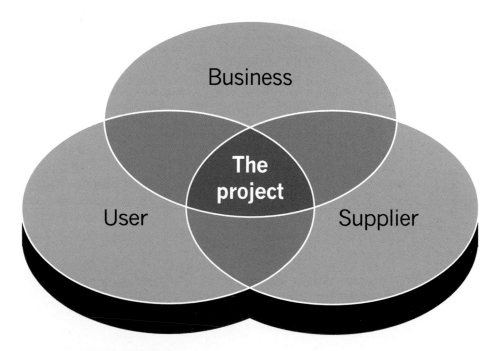

Figure 10.1 The three project interests

Corporate or programme management

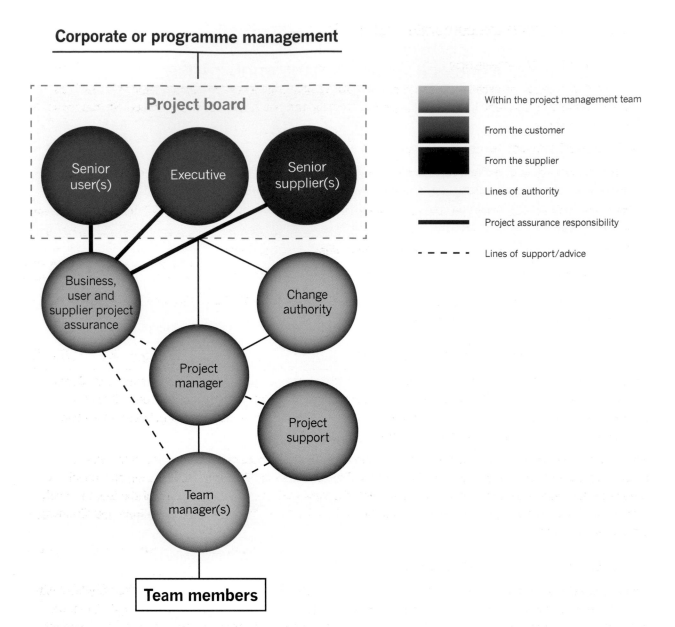

Figure 10.2 Project management team structure

10.1.2.2 Dealing with changes to the project management team

Ideally, the project manager and project board members should stay with the project throughout its life. In practice, however, this may not always be possible and the project management team may change during the project. A clearly defined team structure, together with comprehensive role descriptions outlining the responsibilities for each role, should help to alleviate disruption caused by project management team changes.

The use of management stages also allows a smooth transition for changes to the project management team. Project roles should be reviewed for the next stage during the Managing a Stage Boundary process. The use of end stage reports and stage plans can help to ensure that any handover procedure is thorough and well documented. Although ideally the project **executive** and project manager should stay with the project throughout its lifecycle, a stage boundary provides an opportunity to hand over the role during the project if this is necessary.

10.1.3 Working with the corporate organization

10.1.3.1 Centre of excellence

The concept of a centre of excellence is that of a central standards unit, which defines standards (such as processes, templates and tools), and provides skills, training and possibly independent assurance functions to a number of projects.

A centre of excellence can be useful where:

● Resource shortages, either in numbers or skills, make it difficult to supply people to perform project administration for each current project
● There are a number of small projects of a diverse nature that individually require only limited support from project support
● There is a large programme, requiring coordination of individual projects
● A large project requires several resources to handle project support roles.

Refer to AXELOS's *Portfolio, Programme and Project Offices* (OGC, 2008) for further information on the centre of excellence and its relationship to projects.

10.2 THE GENERAL VIEW OF AGILE WITH RESPECT TO THE ORGANIZATION THEME

There is a wide variety of structures and ways of organizing teams across the whole agile spectrum. Some agile approaches such as DSDM describe several roles with clearly defined levels of accountability and responsibility, whereas others such as Kanban define none. Scrum sits somewhere in between these two views as it has a few roles but these roles only apply to product delivery.

Agile puts a lot of emphasis on the way a team operates in that it should self-organize, be empowered, remain stable and have a large amount of autonomy. This creates a feeling of the team being collectively responsible for what it delivers, which contrasts with the view that the person in charge of the team is solely responsible. It also prefers the team members to be multi-skilled (i.e. they can offer more than one discipline) as much as possible.

10.2.1 Common viewpoints of agile and roles

Generally speaking the most well-known and well-defined agile roles operate at the product delivery level with relatively little reference made to roles which sit above this (e.g. sponsorship, technical strategy). A mature agile environment would have clearly defined roles that are responsible for such areas as vision and product roadmaps (e.g. a sponsor or a product manager). A summary of how agile views certain common roles is as follows:

● **The Scrum master** A common role in agile is that of the Scrum master, who is seen as a servant leader (see section 10.5.1). The Scrum master facilitates and coaches the Scrum process whilst removing impediments identified by the team working at the delivery level. It could be said that there is no equivalent role in PRINCE2. The team manager is the most obvious candidate, but in Scrum and in many agile belief systems the team does not need to be 'managed' per se – it needs to be 'led and coached'. When using agile in a PRINCE2 environment there will need to be a team manager or equivalent who is ultimately accountable for the delivery of a team's products, but this will need to be handled appropriately as described in section 10.4.1.
● **The product owner** Another common and perhaps pivotal role in agile is that of the product owner, and this role is often regarded as the key stakeholder. It is difficult to draw a simple parallel with a PRINCE2 role as it depends on the number of delivery teams involved on a project. Even making a general rule is difficult as there may be many teams with many product owners. The product owner role is discussed in detail in section 10.5.2. The business ambassador role in DSDM is similar to this.

- **The project manager (and team manager)** There is a significant body of opinion in the agile community that suggests there is no longer a need for the project manager role. This view is quite significant and has arisen primarily for two reasons:
  - There is a view that any work can be carried out and managed as if it were BAU by breaking the work down to a size and a level of certainty that allows it to be handled as routine work.
  - The term 'manager' is regarded as having negative connotations to many in the agile community as it infers a lack of trust in the people who make up the team – the belief being that they do not need a manager as they manage themselves collectively though self-organization.

  PRINCE2 and PRINCE2 Agile see the project manager role as essential for a project, although in an agile context the behaviours, relationships and responsibilities may be emphasized differently.

- **The requirements engineer/business analyst** The most common agile approaches give little prominence to a specific role for gathering the requirements for a project (e.g. a requirements engineer or business analyst). This role is usually undertaken by the product owner.

10.3 PRINCE2 AGILE GUIDANCE FOR THE ORGANIZATION THEME

Adding the project management team structure from PRINCE2 to the delivery-based roles of agile creates a very powerful combination. In simple terms the synchronization between these two is quite straightforward in that PRINCE2 provides very little specific guidance at the delivery/technical level, and similarly the most common agile frameworks provide very little specific guidance with respect to the roles of project management and project governance/direction. This is described at the beginning of Chapter 3 of this guide and illustrated in Figure 3.1.

The ease at which PRINCE2 and agile can be blended together depends upon the nature of the work involved. As soon as a piece of work involves more than just a few people and is difficult (i.e. it needs to be run as a project), there is a requirement to have clearly defined roles and responsibilities so that the correct communication and decisions can be taken at the right time and at the appropriate level (see Table 10.1).

Table 10.1 Combining PRINCE2 roles with agile roles

Type of work	Size/scale of work	Typical number of teams involved	Ease of synchronization
Routine	Small	One	Not applicable. Handled as BAU.
Difficult	Small	One	Probably straightforward. The project manager and team manager roles are combined. The most common agile roles should be aligned easily.
Difficult	Large	Many (at least more than one)	Probably requires a degree of care. The most commonly used agile roles need to be carefully aligned as there is more than one team and the alignment may not be obvious.

In a mature agile environment the contrasting concepts of the roles needed for a project context and how they integrate with the roles that commonly appear in agile will probably have been aligned. The concept that there is a need to represent a customer and a supplier (i.e. someone who wants the product and someone who builds the product) in some form – roles as opposed to job titles – is the same in PRINCE2 as it is in agile. However, there are concepts which are different.

10.4 DIFFERENT CONCEPTS REGARDING ROLES BETWEEN PRINCE2 AND AGILE

PRINCE2 operates in any environment and on a project of any size from something simple and straightforward to something more challenging. Some commonly used agile concepts and roles may therefore need to be adjusted and the following guidance applies:

- **Agile delivery teams prefer to be led and coached as opposed to managed.** Much of the agile way of working is founded on teams being self-organized and collectively responsible for what they deliver. The Scrum master is seen as a coach and a servant leader to the team and not a manager of the team. PRINCE2 defines the role of team manager, which has clear accountability at the team/delivery level; the mapping of this to any role in an agile team is not straightforward and needs to be handled appropriately (see section 10.4.1).

- **Common agile guidance refers to a single product owner.** If a project involves more than just a handful of people and needs to canvass the views of several stakeholders and perhaps conflicting views from the customer's side, PRINCE2 Agile recommends taking a more blended view of the customer rather than listening to one single voice. This would mean engaging with the customer at different levels of authority and ensuring that all areas of expertise were included in the decision-making and communication process (see sections 10.4.1 and 10.5.2).

- **Common agile guidance does not have a project manager role.** Unsurprisingly, PRINCE2 sees this role as mandatory on the basis that if a piece of work is difficult enough to be classed as a project then it requires someone to carry out the role of managing it.

10.4.1 Integrating the PRINCE2 team manager role into an agile delivery team

A PRINCE2 team manager has a clearly defined set of responsibilities which cover five areas as shown in the left-hand column of Table 10.2. The table also shows how these responsibilities correspond to the most common agile roles.

Table 10.2 Mapping the responsibilities of a PRINCE2 team manager to the common agile roles (in this case Scrum)

Team manager: areas of responsibility	Covered by the Scrum master?	Covered by the product owner?	Covered by the delivery team?
Planning	No, but may facilitate and support	Yes (prioritizing)	Yes (sprint planning)
Monitoring and managing progress	Yes (by way of coaching the team to self-organize)	Supports this through self-organization and by making the product backlog transparent	Supports this through self-organization and by making the sprint backlog transparent
Liaising with the project manager and other stakeholders	Most likely to but not necessarily (see guidance in this section)	No	No
Managing issues and risks	Yes	No, but will identify them	No, but will identify them
Final acceptance and handover of products	No	Yes	No (but the team is responsible for delivering them)

The team manager role in PRINCE2 needs to integrate with the delivery team as shown in Figure 10.3.

10.4.2 Relationship types linking the project manager and the delivery team

There are three options available when integrating an agile delivery team into a PRINCE2 project structure with respect to the team manager role. The key point is that the project manager needs to liaise with the team in the five areas of responsibility described earlier in Table 10.2 (see Appendix B for descriptions of roles).

PRINCE2 Agile does not have a preference for any one of the three options outlined in Table 10.3 as it will depend on the maturity of the delivery team and the relationship between the project manager and the delivery team. It may be that the project board, who are ultimately accountable for the project, express a preference or make a decision.

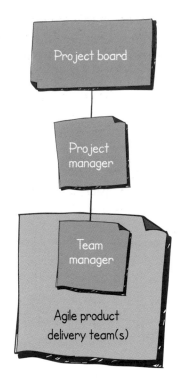

There aren't any direct mappings of the most commonly used agile roles to the PRINCE2 team manager role

This is the desired situation when using PRINCE2 in an agile context

Figure 10.3 Integrating the team manager role into an agile delivery team

Table 10.3 Integrating the project manager with the delivery team – options to consider

Option	Considerations
Leave the delivery team roles as they are	● Ensure that everyone is aware of who is responsible for each of the five areas. ● Role names remain the same (e.g. product owner, Scrum master). ● No-one is referred to as the team manager. ● The project manager will liaise with more than one person in the team.
Leave the delivery team roles as they are but identify a single point of contact for the project manager	● The single point of contact could be anyone from the team but is most likely to be the Scrum master and may be the product owner. ● Role names remain the same. ● The project manager will liaise with one person in the team, who will be able to provide the project manager with the information they need. ● The single point of contact may, or may not, be referred to as the team manager.
Create a team manager role in the delivery team	● This role would cover all of the areas of responsibility in Table 10.2. ● This is best achieved if the team manager is highly collaborative and facilitates the self-organization of the team – the team manager remains ultimately accountable for the outputs in these areas but not necessarily for creating the outputs. ● The project manager will liaise with the team manager.

These three options could be said to represent a range from 'very agile' (at the top) to 'less agile' (at the bottom) and could be a sign of how mature an organization is with respect to the agile ways of working. However, each project has its own set of unique circumstances and the choice should be made according to those circumstances.

The relationship between the project manager and the delivery team is one of the most important areas to get right when using PRINCE2 and agile together. This may need to be defined as part of a work package, and it should be defined in the project initiation documentation as this is where the project board (and perhaps the project manager) will need to agree on an appropriate interface between the project manager and the team manager/delivery team. Potentially, the relationship may be different from team to team.

How to integrate the responsibilities of the team manager into an agile delivery team is ultimately about balancing the needs of the project board and the project manager to enable them to direct and manage the project whilst at the same time creating an environment for the teams that motivates and empowers the people delivering the products.

10.4.3 The composition of a delivery team

There is no mention of the composition of the delivery team in PRINCE2. This is for two reasons. Firstly, PRINCE2 operates in a variety of situations and industry sectors; therefore defining delivery teams is difficult as there are a wide variety of disciplines to cover. Secondly, the technical delivery aspects of a project are separate from project management and project direction. All that is required by PRINCE2 is the clarification of the relationship between the project manager and the team manager.

Agile does define the roles in and around a delivery team, and they would usually represent some or all of the following:

- Someone to lead the team
- Someone from the customer (or at least someone to represent the customer)
- A team to create the product
- Someone to assure the quality of the product
- Someone to coach the team (which includes coaching them in agile).

How many of each role will vary according to the needs of the delivery team. One person could do more than one role (e.g. lead the team and coach it). Several people could carry out one role (e.g. create the product). Some roles may be peripheral to the delivery team (e.g. from customer areas that provide relatively minor input). A typical guide for the size of a team is seven, plus or minus two. It may be better for delivery teams that are larger than this to be divided into more than one team.

Many agile roles appear to assume an IT context: therefore role descriptions can look very much like IT roles, using terms such as 'developer' and 'business analyst'. There is usually very little mention of roles such as engineer, designer, editor etc. PRINCE2 Agile provides the following set of generic roles that can be used if desired (see Appendix B):

- Customer subject matter expert
- Customer representative (usually outside the delivery team)
- Supplier subject matter expert
- Supplier representative (usually outside the delivery team)
- Delivery team quality assurance (QA).

10.4.3.1 Multi-skilled people and roles

Many in the agile community promote the idea of teams made up of multi-skilled people, where any team member can do any other team member's job. Others agree with having more than one skill, but prefer some degree of specialization. There is very little appetite for single-function roles in an agile delivery team, as this makes self-organizing and the ability to respond to delays very difficult.

Organizations developing their agile capability and looking to broaden people's skill-sets need to allow enough time for this transition to take place. When using PRINCE2 with agile it is recommended to aim for delivery teams that are made up of 'generalizing specialists' (sometimes referred to as 'T-shaped' people as they have a lot of depth in one particular skill, and a breadth of knowledge, to a limited degree, in other skills). This creates a team where everyone has a core skill, but they also have the ability to help out other team members (to some degree) in other areas of expertise.

Further to this, the whole project management team needs to be set up in such a way that any stakeholder who needs to contribute is aware of their role (e.g. to provide information or to assure deliverables). Various techniques such as **RACI** (see box) exist for analysing stakeholder involvement – assessing the contribution, commitment and support levels of stakeholders in terms of whether or not their involvement is critical, desirable or non-essential. Such techniques can be used to ensure that the project management team is set up correctly and that the communication management strategy complements this. Ultimately, all of this will be approved by the project board.

It is essential that the delivery teams are clearly empowered, as they will be responsible for self-organizing and delivering products that are fit for purpose. Ensuring that the people in the delivery teams are appropriately trained in agile may also be needed. A lot of agile training is focused on specific delivery roles such as the product owner, the Scrum master and the agile coach, and corresponding qualifications also exist.

Definition: RACI

A widely used technique to define who is responsible, for what, on a project or with a process. RACI typically stands for (who is) Responsible, Accountable, Consulted and Informed with respect to certain deliverables or steps in a process. There are many variations of RACI that can be used.

In some senses, PRINCE2 has no interest in the inner workings of a delivery team. It uses the work package and the Managing Product Delivery process to ensure that the required product is delivered. However, to fully embrace agile, the PRINCE2 project team, and particularly the project manager, need to be aware of how people using agile work and behave – specifically at the delivery level. They must not meddle or interfere with the delivery teams as this is likely to be counter-productive, but the project manager needs to understand how agile is helping the project: this applies across the project as a whole and not just at the delivery level.

A PRINCE2 project manager using agile will be interested in how the delivery teams are working when liaising with their team managers. Therefore, they need to be aware of the delivery team roles and their typical behaviours.

10.4.4 Single-team project structure

If a project is small enough to be addressed by one team where the roles of project manager and team manager are combined, an expected configuration of the customer and supplier roles would look something like that shown in Figure 10.4.

Tip

An independent quality assurance (QA) role means that there is a separation of duties and people don't 'mark their own homework' (hence the need for the role).

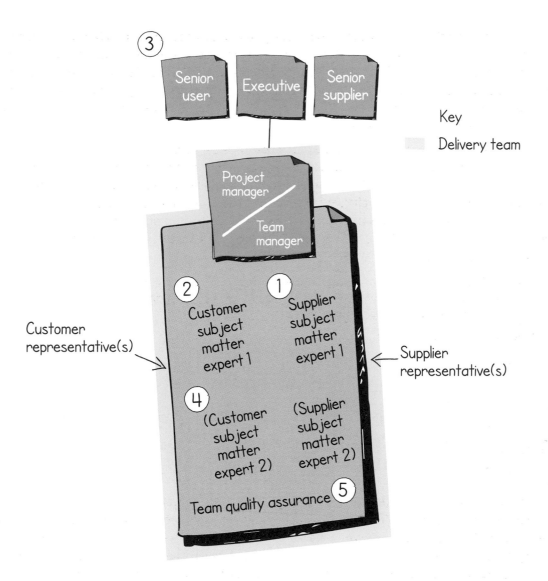

Notes:

1. Supplier subject matter experts (SSMEs) would typically be full-time.

2. Customer subject matter experts (CSMEs) may be full-time or part-time depending on their role within the organization as a whole (i.e. they may have a 'day job' as well as a role on a project).

3. On a single-team project the high-level view of the customer could be covered entirely by the senior user role, although other customer representatives at this level may be formally involved.

4. The detailed view could be covered by one CSME, although more than one CSME on a small project is quite normal when using PRINCE2 Agile. This will typically be similar to the product owner role, although in a basic agile context there is usually only one product owner.

5. Delivery team quality assurance may be the responsibility of just one person or it may be split into two roles (one to cover the customer side and one to cover the supplier side).

Figure 10.4 An example of an organizational set-up for a project with one team

10.4.5 Multiple-team project structure

If a project has more than one delivery team there will be one project manager and more than one team manager, and a typical configuration of the customer and supplier roles would look something like that shown in Figure 10.5.

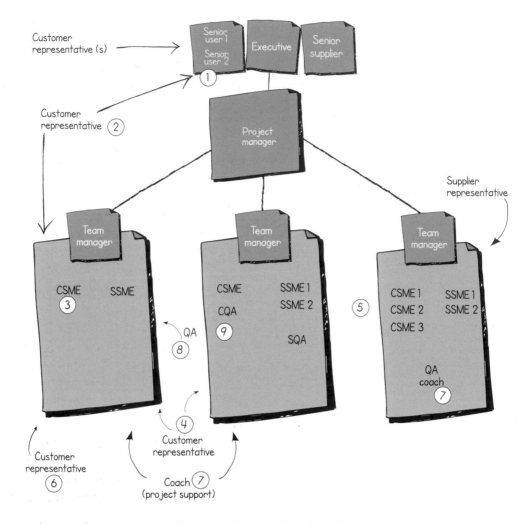

Notes:

1. There may be more than one person wishing to contribute to the high-level customer view as a senior user. In a mature agile environment, if there is one person ultimately responsible at this level, then this is sometimes referred to as a 'super product owner', 'senior product owner' or 'product manager'. The senior user role does not typically map to the role of product owner found in a delivery team.

2. A customer representative may wish to contribute to both the high-level and the detailed-level understanding of a project.

3. A customer subject matter expert (CSME) is the focal point for all information about the customer at the detailed level. They act as a conduit to the delivery team for all views that need to be taken into consideration from any customer representative who is impacted or who may wish to contribute. The high-level view is provided by the senior user.

4. A customer representative may contribute to more than one team at the detailed level.

5. A team may have more than one CSME. It may be appropriate to determine any reporting lines between CSMEs in the same team but usually this is not necessary.

6. Customer representatives need to have clearly assigned roles on a project, but their involvement is significantly less than that of a CSME. They usually contribute specific knowledge from certain areas.

7. A coach may exist as a person carrying out a specific role in a delivery team or the role could be covered by a person who is also carrying out another role for the team (e.g. team manager). Alternatively, a coach may work with several teams and be provided by project support.

8. QA may be split into customer QA (CQA) and supplier QA (SQA) and could be carried out by people from outside the delivery teams.

9. A CSME could also carry out CQA.

Figure 10.5 An example of an organizational set-up for a project with many teams

Tip

Customer QA and supplier QA are split into two so that it is possible to check that:

● The thing has been built right

and

● The right thing has been built.

10.4.6 Tailoring the PRINCE2 roles

Outside the delivery teams, PRINCE2 has agreed and identified roles and responsibilities. All of the roles apply when using agile and their responsibilities do not need to change. However, each role would need to be conversant with the fundamentals of working in an agile way. Additional guidance is provided in Table 10.4.

10.5 AGILE CONCEPTS AND TECHNIQUES

10.5.1 Servant leadership

This concept or philosophy is usually advocated as a best practice for the person 'leading' a team at the delivery level in an agile environment. The term 'servant leader' originates from books and essays written by Robert K. Greenleaf in the 1970s, although it could be said to date back to ancient history.

10.5.1.1 The basics

Although servant leadership can be used anywhere it is generally aimed at corporate or organizational leadership, or those who 'lead' as opposed to those who 'manage'. The term is referenced by the Scrum method (although the term is not explained); through the wide adoption of Scrum, servant leadership now has widespread adoption too as a concept, although how far it can be adopted is often affected by existing organizational constraints.

In simple terms the idea of servant leadership is that the best way to lead a team is to be a servant to the team. Therefore, as a leader of a team you would put team members' needs above yours. It would be your role to ensure that everyone is looked after, that they are okay and they have what they need. This in turn creates a happier, more effective and productive team, and performance improves accordingly.

When integrating agile with PRINCE2 this concept needs to be handled carefully, as it could be said that some of PRINCE2 would be in conflict with the philosophy of servant leadership. An example of this is where a team manager has clearly defined responsibilities such as planning and monitoring the team's work. Agile and servant leadership focus on everyone in the team as a whole being responsible for how they work and what they produce. Therefore, creating a role for this will automatically create a situation where the team may not feel that it is truly responsible. Even the title of the role itself can produce this effect. However, PRINCE2 does not have a preferred style of control and leadership, so it can support any style and this includes servant leadership.

10.5.1.2 Further information

The thing to focus on when using servant leadership with PRINCE2 is to create an environment for the team where they do feel truly empowered and responsible for the way they work and the products they produce, even if the team manager still remains ultimately responsible. This can be achieved by the team manager leading by example and working collaboratively with the team to achieve this.

When using PRINCE2 in an agile context, someone still needs to manage and lead the team, but by using the style of a servant leader their focus will primarily (but not solely) be on helping and supporting the team (i.e. serving). Therefore, leadership of the team is a secondary focus and comes from how well the primary focus is achieved.

Table 10.4 Guidance on the PRINCE2 roles and possible agile mappings

Role	Overview of the tailoring required and further considerations
Project board	Needs to be fully conversant with the agile way of working and needs to understand: ● The fact that everything might not get delivered. ● The implications of the degree of agility being used – the project board needs to authorize the intended level of use of agile and ensure that it does not create unnecessary levels of risk. Risks can be created by using too much agile, or not enough agile, in relation to the project environment. The mixture of PRINCE2 and agile is a coherent blend and they do not exist in parallel. ● The different emphasis on self-organizing and communications techniques will necessitate that the appropriate boundaries are correctly set up to enable management by exception, giving the project board the appropriate level of control and the project manager and the delivery teams the necessary empowerment and trust. ● The general level of agile knowledge within the organization and how this will impact the project (e.g. agile knowledge of the people representing the customer on a project).
Executive	Needs to be familiar with the term 'value' as this will be frequently used by the project management team and the delivery teams. The term is often used interchangeably with the word 'benefits' and although they are similar in how they can be used, they are not identical. Knowledge of how PRINCE2 integrates with Management of Value (MoV) would be beneficial. This role broadly maps to agile environments that refer to a role of 'sponsor'.
Senior user(s)	This role is unlikely to map to the common agile role of product owner, although it may function as a 'super product owner' under some circumstances. It is an important role in PRINCE2 Agile, in that it is the role that is ultimately responsible for the prioritization of the work being delivered in order to maximize value and realization of the customer's goals.
Senior supplier(s)	No further guidance is required to that already mentioned for the project board above and the role description in Appendix B.
Project manager	Needs to be fully conversant with the agile way of working and how to manage a project using agile. Further to this the project manager is responsible for ensuring that the use of agile is happening in the right way and that the project management team is receiving the appropriate coaching and support. The project manager needs to be seen as a friend of the delivery teams and not a figure of authority. This role does not naturally correspond to the Scrum master.
Team manager	This is an important role when using PRINCE2 in an agile context and represents the main interface between project management and product delivery. See section 10.4.1 for a detailed explanation of the tailoring required.
Change authority	Will need to be aware of the agile way of working (e.g. the focus of tolerances set for the project will be in the form of flexing what is being delivered, and the delivery teams will be empowered and self-organizing).
Project assurance	This has an important role to play in ensuring that management by exception is operating correctly to support the agile way of working. They need to assure that the project manager is being agile and applying agile in the appropriate way. They also need to assure that the delivery teams are using agile appropriately, and this would include the team manager. They may wish to put particular emphasis on the interface between the project manager and the team manager role as this may have been set up with a particularly agile emphasis or a more formal emphasis. Either way, it needs to be functioning in the most effective way possible for each team (see section 10.4.2).
Project support	May be responsible for the provision of agile coaching to the project management team or at the delivery team level unless the delivery team already has someone in that role.
Corporate and programme management	Will need to be aware of the agile way of working (e.g. the use of empowering the project management team and frequent releases of products to enable and provide benefits). They may also be looking at the organization as a whole and how the agile way of working can be applied or improved.

In some cases different terminology is used to achieve the servant-leadership philosophy (e.g. 'facilitative' leadership or 'collaborative' leadership).

A lot of the thinking behind servant leadership is that people feel more valued when they work as equals and share responsibility. This is in contrast to autocratic, dictatorial or authoritarian leadership where those in charge enjoy the feeling of power and the kudos that comes with it.

Servant leadership will fit into any PRINCE2 Agile role where leadership skills are needed (e.g. project board, project manager and team manager) although certain areas of responsibility may need to be defined. An example of this would be to clarify the difference between leadership and management. Leadership normally refers to such things as vision, direction and the ability to inspire. Management focuses more on the work to be done and the people doing the work. There is an overlap between these two, as leaders sometimes need to manage people, and managers always need to lead in some form.

Some of the agile behaviours focus on collaboration, respect and honesty, which is very much in keeping with the servant-leader philosophy; these behaviours would be typical of an agile team manager managing a team with a servant-leader style.

It is possible for a team to naturally select its own leader/Scrum master, and this may be anyone from the team – not necessarily the most senior or most experienced.

10.5.1.3 Hints that may prove useful

A team manager running a team in a servant-leader style would create an environment to help grow and develop team members. The team manager would be a team player, always coaching the team and building consensus along the way. The same applies to a project manager in the wider context of a project management team. Creating a culture where people are comfortable to ask for help, and when they do it is welcomed, is a significant part of creating the right environment.

To help further understand the typical attributes a servant leader would need, the following lists may be of use.

From *Servant Leadership: A Journey into the Nature of Legitimate Power and Greatness* by Robert K. Greenleaf (2002):

● Listening
● Empathy
● Building community
● Healing
● Awareness
● Commitment to the growth of people
● Foresight
● Persuasion
● Stewardship
● Conceptualization.

Ann McGee-Cooper and Duane Trammell summarized servant leadership as:

● Listen without judgement
● Be authentic
● Build community
● Share power
● Develop people
● Co-create shared vision.

These attributes are ideal for any team, as this way of working builds on the behaviours that personify agile, by creating empowered and creative teams working in an iterative style and responding to change. Involving the team in decision-making and organizing work would be seen as a normal agile practice by the project manager or team manager even though they are ultimately accountable in a PRINCE2 environment.

10.5.1.4 Context is important

Servant leadership is a very powerful concept, and how far to utilize this depends on many factors. One such factor affecting how effective this can be would depend on the context in which it was being used. How open is a team, department or organization to this style of working? A mature agile organization would use servant leadership and self-organization a lot. Another factor that could limit servant leadership is that a project team is temporary and therefore needs time to grow and bond, whereas an existing BAU team that is stable and has been together over a long period may have evolved its own way of working.

Ultimately, PRINCE2 can support as much or as little of this style of working as is desired because it has no preferred style. There is nothing in PRINCE2 that limits this.

10.5.2 How to incorporate the wider customer view and the product owner role

In agile, the customer view is often represented by a role called the product owner. It is one of the three Scrum roles and is hugely significant in agile terms: executing this role correctly is critical to the successful use of agile because this role is so commonly used. This may require an individual to be trained in how to be a product owner, or they may need the support of a proxy who has the appropriate skills.

However, there is a paradox with this role in that it is simple to define it and assign someone to it, but this simplicity needs to be tailored when used in a project context – even when working in a mature agile environment. The reason for this is that the product owner role is commonly associated with a scenario where there is one team, one product, and work is ongoing such as in a BAU environment. When using the product owner role in more challenging situations adjustments will probably need to be made.

10.5.2.1 The basics

In simple terms the product owner is the 'voice of the customer' and this role covers the following responsibilities as described in the *Scrum Guide* (see Appendix H):

- Clearly expressing product **backlog item**s
- Ordering the items in the product backlog to best achieve goals and missions
- Optimizing the value of the work the development team performs
- Ensuring that the product backlog is visible, transparent and clear to all, and shows what the Scrum team will work on next
- Ensuring the development team understands items in the product backlog to the level needed.

Other definitions of the product owner responsibilities in more mature agile environments include the product vision, creating product roadmaps and business case justification.

In terms of their attributes and style of working, a product owner should be:

- Very knowledgeable of the customer domain
- An effective communicator
- Able to canvass the opinions of key stakeholders
- Empowered
- Clear on the vision for the product
- Able to define requirements and user stories
- Able to define what a successful outcome would look like
- Available at all times to the delivery team.

Ultimately, the product owner has the final say on everything to do with the final product. They own it, and they are solely accountable for it. This means that the product owner has the authority to decide what goes into the product, and they are not accountable to anyone else with respect to having to justify it.

10.5.2.2 The simplicity of the product owner role

Crucial to this role, as commonly expressed in agile frameworks, is that there is only one person doing this. This creates the simplicity which many people (e.g. from the technical delivery side) find attractive as it creates a very clear single point of contact and a single version of the truth.

The simplicity of the product owner role can work well in a straightforward BAU context, but there are limitations when working on a project.

10.5.2.3 Limitations due to project size

Project teams (small or large) would typically require a wider and more representative view of a customer's interests than are perhaps required in a BAU situation.

It may not be appropriate to have one person from the customer side responsible for the many views and angles that exist on a project. There may be high-level views held by certain stakeholders that need to be taken into account (e.g. strategic), along with other more detailed views from a different set of stakeholders (e.g. to do with how the product looks).

10.5.2.4 Limitations due to size of the role in a project context

It is one thing to assign several responsibilities and attributes to a role, but it is something different altogether to find an individual who can carry out that role effectively. The product owner role contains some responsibilities that even in isolation may require advanced levels of skill and may form a discipline (or role) in its own right, in the context of a project.

Gathering requirements, defining them, facilitating communication with the wider customer community of project stakeholders (which would include many contrasting perspectives) and creating buy-in to the way forward is a significant undertaking for even the most experienced individual.

This can be too much for one person as it involves a lot of work, and some of this work involves a high degree of technical skill (e.g. requirements engineering).

A project requires many customer roles in order to correctly reflect the customer's view. A single product owner may not be the best way to achieve this.

10.5.2.5 Representing the customer view on a project

A one-team, one-product BAU situation can operate very effectively with one product owner. More challenging work needs to be structured as Figures 10.4 and 10.5 show. Most of the common agile frameworks do not have the structures to accommodate this naturally, although DSDM is an exception to this general rule and mature agile organizations will have created their own.

The PRINCE2 Agile role of customer subject matter expert (CSME) is similar to product owner if it is inside a delivery team, and it can still be referred to as 'product owner' if the team already uses and understands this term and what the role entails. However, in a PRINCE2 Agile context this role would take the general function of providing the customer's voice at the detailed level. The senior user would be responsible for the wider and higher-level customer view and also be ultimately accountable for what goes into the final product. The executive would be responsible for the business case.

10.5.2.6 Specialist role to support capturing the customer view

Another option is to have a role that can help to define the project's products (often referred to as requirements) by acting as a catalyst between the customer view and the supplier view. Roles such as a requirements engineer or business analyst would be examples of this. The role could work inside the delivery teams, the project management team or both. This role would be responsible for some or all of the following:

● Acting as a translator, as both the customer and supplier will have their own terminology, and then ensuring that both parties understand the requirements

● Gathering and correctly writing and defining requirements/user stories along with quality criteria and acceptance criteria

● Helping where appropriate by providing support with testing from the customer perspective

● Ensuring that requirements prioritization is appropriate (this includes being prepared to challenge decisions where necessary)

● Creating and evolving models and supporting documentation

● Facilitating discussions and running workshops with the wider stakeholder community

● Contributing to information held in the business case

● Using techniques to ensure that requirements align with strategic and/or project objectives

● Liaising with the senior user, customer SMEs and other customer stakeholders.

10.5.2.7 Getting a blended view

It is very important to represent the customer view appropriately on a PRINCE2 project. The product owner is a very powerful concept but it needs to be adjusted to work in a project context. To create a fully representative view of the customer at all levels and in all areas affected by a project, it is important to build a blended and comprehensive view of the customer needs and perhaps involve specialists to help with this, such as a requirements engineer or a business analyst. It is essential to do this as well as possible as the customer will be impacted by the final product, and they are ultimately justifying the investment.

On a PRINCE2 project the senior user is ultimately responsible for the appropriateness of the delivered product, and the executive is responsible for the justification of the project itself. The product owner role as commonly defined in agile (e.g. in Scrum) operates in the best way from inside the delivery teams.

10.5.3 Working agreements and team ground rules

Many concepts in agile relate to multi-skilled teams that are empowered and self-organize. Creating working agreements is a concept that is used to evolve the effectiveness of a team that is self-organizing. This is achieved by collectively developing a set of team guidelines, or rules, to bring some structure to how the team works and behaves.

Tip

Working agreements and team rules include or are similar to policies, team norms or team charters.

10.5.3.1 The basics

These agreements can operate at many levels. Some of them may relate to concepts such as values (e.g. 'we should be honest', 'we should be open') whilst others may relate to simple rules about how long a stand-up meeting lasts (e.g. 10 or 15 minutes), or agreeing the core working hours for the team. They are created and reviewed by the team members themselves (typically during a retrospective) and their purpose is to improve the effectiveness of the team by reducing mistakes and promoting successful behaviours and practices.

Typically they are made visible (perhaps displayed on the wall) and the team develops them over time. The team manager should make sure that everyone is involved, that improvements to the rules are facilitated and that everyone can contribute freely as the features evolve.

10.5.3.2 Further information

All teams are different, and most of the way a team works and acts should develop naturally and not need to be defined. Therefore any rules that are defined should help strengthen the way the team works and provide a focus. Having too many rules could have the opposite effect.

10.5.3.3 Hints that may prove useful

Team ground rules can help with the internal workings of the team. They could be included as part of a work package as long as everyone is in agreement – i.e. the team, the project manager and the team manager.

Agreements and rules are potentially destructive if they are not built carefully by consensus and involve all of those impacted. Some teams prefer to make their commitment to the rules visible by signing them for all to see. Other teams prefer a more cautious approach based on trust and may even avoid using the word 'rule', as they perceive this word to have negative connotations because it looks like an order or a command.

A balance between when to guide and when to force is needed. An example of this would be the definition of 'ready', which is more of a guide to people, whereas the definition of 'done' is something that should be complied with. However, both should be defined collaboratively in order to get commitment to both.

10.5.3.4 The Pastor of Fun

Many in the agile community who have experience of mature agile environments put a lot of emphasis on and effort into creating a collaborative culture in the teams and fostering motivated and happy people. An example of this is where a team creates a role for a person called the Pastor of Fun, and this role is responsible for ensuring that the team develops a close bond by organizing social activities (perhaps inside and outside of work) and coming up with ideas to make certain work activities or events more fun and enjoyable. This typically results in bringing out the more human side of everyone, and in turn this creates behaviours such as loyalty and openness.

Tip

The Pastor of Fun is not an official PRINCE2 role.

10.5.3.5 Assessing the needs of the team

Collectively creating agreements on how the team works can be productive, but it needs to suit the requirements of the team. They should decide at what level or levels these agreements need to operate and on what scale they add value. For example, a working agreement could include the following parameters:

- Everyone's views should be listened to and respected.
- The team is greater than the sum of its parts.
- There is no such thing as a silly question.
- Don't be afraid to say 'I was wrong', 'I need help' or 'I don't know'.
- Stand-ups start at exactly 9:30am.
- If we can't solve it ourselves we escalate it quickly.
- Ask don't tell.
- It's OK to challenge someone's view.
- It's OK to have fun!

10.6 ORGANIZATION THEME SUMMARY

How a PRINCE2 project is organized when in an agile context is very important. Many considerations have to be taken into account in order to arrive at the best blend. One area of consideration is the specific responsibilities involved with each role and how they can be mapped and tailored. However, it is also important to understand and allow for the language involved, as this can have a significant effect in an agile context. The exact wording or title of a role can give off a negative impression in some situations, as can responsibilities that use terms such as 'reporting to' and 'assigned to'. It is important to ensure that PRINCE2 operates as effectively as possible and is not compromised by terminology, but sometimes care is needed to create a positive effect.

Tip

Assess carefully the people representing the customer side of the project. Are they empowered? Are they respected? One useful 'rule' is to engage with people who the customer 'won't let you have access to' (people who are seen as indispensable and the customer cannot afford to lose them to project work for any length of time).

ACKNOWLEDGEMENTS AND FURTHER READING

Bill George (2007). *True North: Discover Your Authentic Leadership*. John Wiley & Sons.

Robert K. Greenleaf (2002). *Servant Leadership: A Journey into the Nature of Legitimate Power and Greatness*. Paulist Press.

Patrick M. Lencioni (2002). *The Five Dysfunctions of a Team: A Leadership Fable*. John Wiley & Sons.

Duane Trammell, Ann McGee-Cooper and Jack Lowe (2012). *Being the Change: Profiles from Our Servant Leadership Learning Community*. Ann McGee-Cooper and Associates.

Bruce W. Tuckman (1965). Developmental sequence in small groups. *Psychological Bulletin* 63, 384–399.

Geoff Watts (2013). *Scrum Mastery: From Good to Great Servant Leadership*. Inspect & Adapt, Cheltenham, UK.

Belbin team roles: http://www.belbin.com

Insights discovery: https://www.insights.com

Myers-Briggs Type Indicator: http://www.myersbriggs.org

11

Quality theme

This chapter covers:

- PRINCE2 and agile approaches to the Quality theme

- PRINCE2 Agile guidance for the Quality theme

- Agile concepts and techniques

11 Quality theme

11.1 THE PRINCE2 APPROACH TO THE QUALITY THEME

The purpose of the Quality theme is to define and implement the means by which the project will verify products that are fit for purpose.

The Quality theme defines the PRINCE2 approach to ensuring that the project's products:

● Meet business expectations
● Enable the desired benefits to be achieved subsequently.

The 'product focus' principle is central to PRINCE2's approach to quality.

The specific treatment for quality in PRINCE2 is the focus on products from the outset, requiring systematic activities to:

● Identify all the project's products (i.e. to the level at which the project intends to exert control)
● Define them in product descriptions – including the quality criteria by which they will be assessed; the quality methods to be used in designing, developing and accepting them; and the quality responsibilities of those involved
● Implement and track the quality methods employed throughout the project.

The PRINCE2 approach to quality can be summarized simply by the quality audit trail depicted in Figure 11.1.

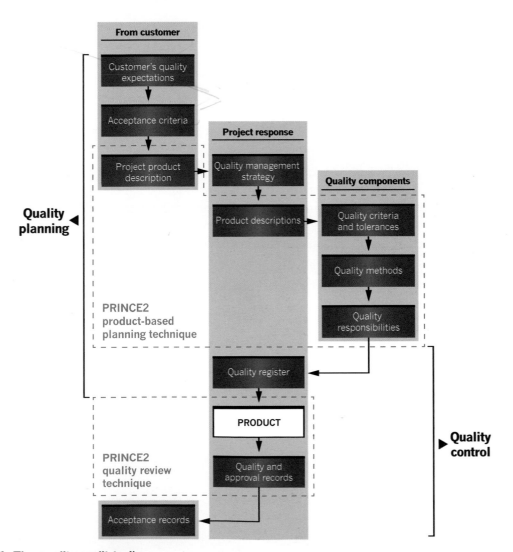

Figure 11.1 The quality audit trail

11.2 THE GENERAL VIEW OF AGILE WITH RESPECT TO THE QUALITY THEME

There is a lot of emphasis put on quality throughout the whole agile movement, and some of the most prominent agile techniques address this area (e.g. the definition of 'done' in Scrum and the general use of acceptance criteria). However, perhaps surprisingly, the Agile Manifesto does not contain the word 'quality', although it does refer to working software.

Tip

Acceptance criteria are commonly used in agile to define how to know if a user story has been completed. See the glossary for definitions of 'acceptance criteria' and 'quality criteria'.

Certain concepts that have evolved in most agile approaches are very different from traditional views about how to ensure quality. A Waterfall approach would typically see activities such as quality checking and testing take place after a product has been built. Agile takes a much more dynamic view and uses such concepts as integrating the testing and quality checking 'as you go', or even doing this before you start ('test first'). This contrasts greatly with performing this afterwards or at the end.

In some agile environments there may not be a lot of emphasis given to quality planning and quality management during the start of a project, whereas there will usually be a lot of focus on quality control during product development. One approach commonly used in agile is to evolve the definition of quality gradually over time. This is achieved by refining and honing the definition of 'done' as work progresses. Another approach is to ensure that all of the quality-checking approaches and tests are written and defined before work commences on building the product.

11.3 PRINCE2 AGILE GUIDANCE FOR THE QUALITY THEME

11.3.1 How to use the PRINCE2 product description

Although product descriptions are mandatory in PRINCE2, they are very flexible and can be written in the form of epics or user stories as long as they meet the requirements of the product description outline (as defined in Appendix A). These represent what are commonly referred to as the project's 'requirements' (see Figure 25.1 for an example of decomposition).

Product descriptions can be formal or informal, and they can evolve during the project to allow for change as long as it is clear what the baseline is and what level of plan they have been baselined to (e.g. they could be baselined at the stage plan level). The project management team may decide that the higher-level product descriptions need to be more formally defined (e.g. they are to be baselined in a configuration management system) and the lower-level product descriptions can be informal (e.g. captured as user stories on index cards).

When using agile with PRINCE2, full advantage should be taken of the flexibility built into the product description outline as shown in Table 11.1.

11.3.2 Creating the project product description

This can be crafted in a similar way to the product description in that the customer's quality expectations, acceptance criteria and project-level quality tolerances are defined with a level of formality and detail that embraces the agile way of working.

Further to this, when using agile the preferred way to define the purpose of the project product description is to use a clearly defined outcome (or outcomes) – see section 9.4.2 for more information on outcomes. This can also help if the contractual side of the project is to be based on a more agile style of working (see Chapter 28).

Table 11.1 How to use some of the product description components to provide flexibility

Product description component	Guidance
Quality criteria	This usually equates to acceptance criteria (e.g. for a user story), although sometimes the definition of 'done' in Scrum is used for the same purpose. It should avoid too much unnecessary detail that will restrict positive change but does need to be of sufficient clarity so that it can be quality checked.
Quality tolerances	Use a range of values (perhaps prioritized) to allow for change.
Quality method	Select the appropriate technique for the agile environment – sometimes some form of automated '**test-driven**' approach may be desirable/required (e.g. when writing software) whereas at other times a more conventional quality review may be the more appropriate (e.g. when producing a brochure).
	Using the quality method to define the approach to quality would be specific to a particular product. A more general view across all products would be contained in the quality management strategy.

11.3.3 Quality management and quality planning

The tools and approaches that are to be used should be defined as part of the quality management strategy: working in an agile way needs the appropriate choice of tooling and techniques as teams may be distributed and the testing may be 'test-driven' (see section 11.3.4).

Definition: Test-driven

The concept of writing tests or quality checks before building the product or sub-product as opposed to after.

The role of the customer should be well defined as the customer is an essential ingredient when working in an agile way. Apart from their continual involvement and commitment, their responsibilities should be understood by all with respect to such things as:

● Customer acceptance

● Customer documentation

● Canvassing a wider customer view

● Attendance at product demos.

It is the upfront quality planning that enables PRINCE2 to develop a strategy for how testing and quality checking will be carried out in advance of the work taking place. If several frequent releases are planned, then this enables the resources needed (human or otherwise) to be assessed and costed so that they can be factored in to the business case.

Quality control considerations that look at what quality methods to use (e.g. the frequent use of demos and sprint reviews) are a natural evolution from this planning.

Ultimately the learnings from many projects contribute to the evolution of the wider quality management system for an organization, and part of this will involve development of the use of agile.

PRINCE2 takes a holistic view of the whole area of quality, which exists throughout a project and operates at all levels.

11.3.4 How to test: test-first, test-driven and test-as-you go concepts

When using PRINCE2 with agile, a decision has to be made early on, as part of the quality management strategy, as to how much of the testing and quality checking can be carried out in the preferred agile manner of 'test/check first' or at least 'test/check as you go'. This is the one area where transferring agile concepts and techniques from the software development domain needs to be handled carefully. Software can be built iteratively and tested frequently using automated testing. The frequency can be as short as days, hours or minutes in terms of these iterative builds. This approach can still be used for a product such as a marketing campaign but it may not be as easy to build it so quickly or through the use of lots of automation.

The challenge here when using PRINCE2 and agile together is to apply this concept as much as possible. The more it can be applied then the more agile the project will be. In an agile software context one approach is to use test-driven development (TDD) in the creation of software. Although this is a software-specific approach, the fundamental thinking behind it has led to similar techniques that can be used at a higher level and not necessarily in an IT context. One such example is behaviour-driven development (BDD); see Table 11.2. BDD can be applied to both 'building the right thing' and 'building the thing right' – sometimes referred to by two separate processes called 'validation and verification' (or V&V).

The idea of continually writing tests or quality-checking processes before building a product or sub-product may seem counterintuitive to many but this is one of the concepts of the agile way of working, and when this works in partnership with developing the product iteratively and refactoring the product (see Table 11.2), this helps to build the appropriate level of quality into the final product.

This can be quite challenging but it is agile best practice and is one of the reasons why the agile way of working has become popular (because it ensures that quality is built into a product).

Table 11.2 Common agile terms that relate to quality

Term	Description
Definition of 'done'	See Appendix H: The definitive guide to Scrum. See section 11.4 for an example.
Definition of 'ready'	A similar concept to the definition of 'done' except that this is a list of criteria to determine if work can be started on something such as a user story or a sprint. See section 25.6.1 for an example.
Test-driven development (TDD)	This is a software development process that uses a very short development cycle whereby: ● A developer writes an (initially failing) automated test for a new function. ● The developer then produces the minimum amount of code to pass that test. ● Finally, the new code is refactored to meet the appropriate coding standards. TDD is related to the test-first programming concepts of eXtreme Programming (XP) from the late nineties: it requires automation and usually takes place at the 'unit-testing' level (i.e. the smallest testable part of a system).
Behaviour-driven development (BDD)	This is a software development process based on TDD. BDD is usually more collaborative and uses the general techniques and principles of TDD in a wider behavioural context (e.g. what the customer may want to achieve). It uses a style of language that is easy for the customer to understand (hence the use of words such as 'behaviour' in preference to 'test').
Refactoring	In a software context, this is defined by Martin Fowler as '…the process of changing a software system in such a way that it does not alter the external behavior of the code yet improves its internal structure' (*Refactoring: Improving the Design of Existing Code* by Martin Fowler). The same concept can be applied to any product irrespective of whether or not it contains software.
Technical debt	Another term mostly used in the software domain, which is a metaphor referring to the eventual consequences of poor system design, software architecture or the software development itself. The debt can be thought of as work that needs to be done before a particular job can be considered complete. If the debt is not repaid, then it will keep on accumulating interest, making it hard to implement changes later on. Unaddressed technical debt increases the level of disorder in the software and therefore its overall level of quality. In a PRINCE2 context tolerances may be applied to this, and if the debt is forecast to become too significant it will cause an exception.

11.4 AGILE CONCEPTS AND TECHNIQUES

Examples of the 'definition of 'done' and behaviour-driven development (taken from Table 11.2) are given below.

Definition of 'done':

- The user documentation is up to date.
- The customer has seen the product demonstrated and is happy that it has met their acceptance criteria.
- The product has been peer-reviewed.
- The support team has been notified of when it will be released.
- The product meets the organization's accessibility standards.

The 'given, when, then' format used in BDD:

- **Given** Some initial context (the givens)
  - *Given* the account is in sufficient credit
  - *And* the card is valid
  - *And* the dispenser contains cash
- **When** An event occurs
  - *When* the customer requests cash
- **Then** Ensure some outcomes
  - *Then* ensure the account is debited
  - *And* ensure cash is dispensed
  - *And* ensure the card is returned.

11.4.1 How to ...

Table 11.3 Relevant agile guidance for the Quality theme

	Chapter and section references
Create a definition of 'done'	Appendix H
Create a definition of 'ready'	Section 25.6.1
Write acceptance criteria and user stories	Section 25.6.1
Identify outputs, outcomes and benefits	Section 9.4.2
Tailor any of the PRINCE2 management products	Chapter 23

11.5 QUALITY THEME SUMMARY

It is important when using agile to distinguish between the quality of a product (defined by quality criteria) and the scope (defined by the products themselves). Some project management philosophies see a reduction in scope as a reduction in quality. PRINCE2 does not see it this way. From the beginning of a project the customer's quality expectations (and associated acceptance criteria) are set, and this level of quality needs to be maintained. At the end of a project if 10% of the scope is not delivered but the remaining 90% that has been delivered has achieved the desired quality level, then this is seen by PRINCE2 as a reduction in scope, not a reduction in the quality level.

Tip

If you don't know how to test a requirement, then assume you haven't understood the requirement yet.

Furthermore, and as part of the thinking behind flexing what is being delivered, it is the de-scoping that enables the quality level to be protected and therefore avoids incurring ownership costs (e.g. due to maintenance) throughout the life of the final product.

ACKNOWLEDGEMENTS AND FURTHER READING

Chris Matts: https://theitriskmanager.wordpress.com

Dan North: http://dannorth.net/introducing-bdd

12

Plans theme

This chapter covers:

- PRINCE2 and agile approaches to the Plans theme

- PRINCE2 Agile guidance for the Plans theme

- Agile concepts and techniques

12 Plans theme

12.1 THE PRINCE2 APPROACH TO THE PLANS THEME

The purpose of the Plans theme is to facilitate communication and control by defining the means of delivering the products (the where and how, by whom, and estimating the when and how much).

PRINCE2 recommends three levels of plan to reflect the needs of the different levels of management involved in the project, stage and team.

PRINCE2's planning levels are illustrated in Figure 12.1.

12.2 THE GENERAL VIEW OF AGILE WITH RESPECT TO THE PLANS THEME

Agile puts a lot of emphasis on planning, and there are several concepts and techniques (e.g. planning and estimating with story points) that could be said to be common to the agile way of working. However, not only are there significant differences between agile and conventional approaches to planning, there are also differences between the various agile frameworks. This means that there are choices to be made when planning, and care is needed to use the most appropriate approach to suit the situation.

12.2.1 Empiricism

A fundamental principle upon which most agile methods are based is the concept of empiricism. This involves making decisions based on experience – i.e. what is happening or has already happened. A simple example of this would be to start a piece of work and then calculate how much work is left to complete by comparing it with how much work is getting done. This then allows the team to forecast or create an end date.

Starting work and seeing how much is getting done is sometimes called 'calibration' (in a similar way to manually setting weighing scales to zero), or calculating 'velocity' (i.e. the rate of progress). Another expression used to encapsulate this is 'using yesterday's weather' as it can often be the best indicator of what is to follow. Future estimates are then based on this.

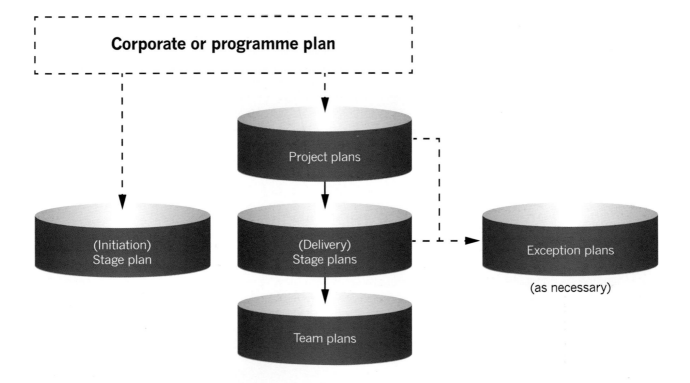

Figure 12.1 PRINCE2's planning levels

The opposite of this is called 'rationalism' whereby reasoning or logic is used to make predictions and plan what should happen.

In a BAU context **empirical** planning is a common agile technique and works well in an environment where work is ongoing. This means that when planning a two-week sprint, the primary information to use would be that of the previous sprint and the sprints prior to that.

12.2.2 Planning style

Agile plans are often created in a particular style which involves:

● Basing planning around requirements and features
● Making planning a team-based exercise
● Planning at the last responsible moment (also known as JIT or just-in-time planning).

The first point means that the focus of any agile plan is on what features are being delivered as opposed to focusing on technical phases such as design, build and test (see section 2.1).

The second point is a vital component of the agile mind-set that creates ownership of plans and underpins the ability of a team to self-organize. In some agile environments this may only happen at the delivery level. A project would be seen as more agile if the same ethos applied to plans created at the project management and project direction levels.

The third point enables a team to adapt easily to changing circumstances by planning as near as possible to the point where a product is being created. However, care is needed to avoid taking unnecessary risks by leaving decisions too late or procrastinating.

Agile planning can be very effective even though it is sometimes quite simple and low-tech, such as a simple list which is referred to as a backlog. The aim is to do the right amount of planning at the right time.

12.2.3 Using points to plan

As agile has evolved over the years many people have moved from controlling their work with a timeboxing approach (e.g. Scrum) to using flow-based systems through the use of Kanban (see Figure 12.2). This has created choice for agile teams whereby teams can use a point-scoring system to negotiate and plan (e.g. effort points per story), or they can choose to forecast according to such things as lead times (i.e. how long it takes a piece of work of this type to complete). There are advantages and disadvantages when using points in their many forms, so care should be taken to use them appropriately as described in the guidance later in section 12.4.1.

It is important to note that the use of 'points' for estimation is seen by some as fundamental to working in an agile way. Although they are still popular and still useful, they should be seen as 'a way' and not 'the way' (see section 12.4.1). A middle ground is often used whereby a simple form of estimation is used where work is classified as either large, medium or small, or high, medium and low, and this can be used with either a timeboxed or flow-based approach.

12.3 PRINCE2 AGILE GUIDANCE FOR THE PLANS THEME

PRINCE2 supports any type of planning style from a conventional Gantt chart to a simple backlog list. Both styles are in keeping with the product description for a plan (see Appendix A.16). It may be the case that more than one planning style is used on a single project. There may be a tendency to use more conventional planning techniques for the higher levels of planning (e.g. where departmental and organizational dependencies may exist) but this may not be necessary. When using PRINCE2 in an agile environment a Gantt chart can be of limited value as it is not geared to monitor and control the amount of products delivered and their quality.

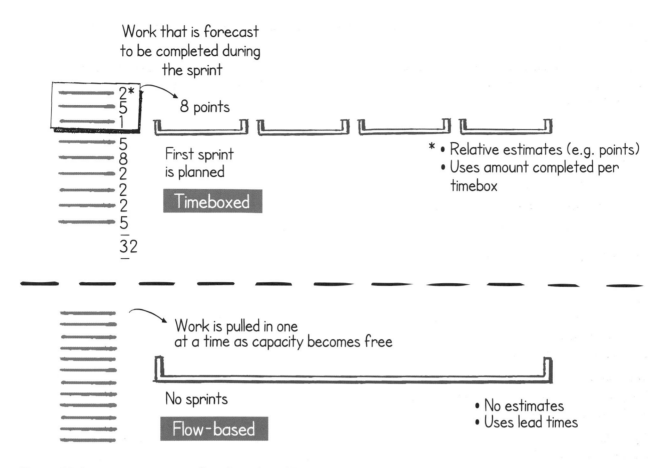

Figure 12.2 Timeboxed versus flow-based working

12.3.1 Collaborative planning

Agile planning Is collaborative, for all types of plan and at all levels, and this is desirable in order to create an environment where the people involved in a project can respond to changing circumstances. If a group of people are working to a plan that was created by someone else (e.g. the project manager) there is likely to be less commitment and responsiveness.

This does not mean that the role of the project manager or team manager is any less important, but it does mean that they need to facilitate this style of planning.

12.3.2 Using empiricism to plan

Empiricism has many advantages, and to use PRINCE2 in an agile environment this needs to be fully understood and embraced as far as is practicable. A potential drawback with some of the agile planning techniques is that in a project context (where a project is finite), we need to estimate and plan *before* we start and not *after*.

PRINCE2 needs a **project plan** with an end date for the following reasons:

● It will enable the project to be justified and therefore authorized.

● It will provide a baseline against which progress can be measured and stages defined.

● Projects are finite pieces of work that are 'bounded'; therefore without an end date PRINCE2 and PRINCE2 Agile would not see the work as a project.

● From a supplier perspective it enables them to give the customer a price and a delivery date.

● It will show if a minimum viable product (MVP) can be created in time.

Stage plans and team plans are similarly affected, albeit at a lower level.

12.3.3 Planning horizons

Having an end date is one thing, but how accurate and realistic it is can be something quite different.

Both agile and PRINCE2 accept the premise that the further you look into the future the more uncertainty there is. This means that longer-term estimation will need an increasing margin of error compared with shorter-term estimation. This leads to the use of the term 'planning horizon' whereby a plan for the next two weeks would be quite detailed and have a relatively low margin of error, whereas a plan for the next 12 months would be much less detailed and have a relatively high margin of error (see Figure 12.3).

Long-term planning addresses the uncertainties and unknowns (sometimes referred to as the 'cone of uncertainty') by providing a level of confidence or a range with each estimate in the form of agreed tolerances (see section 25.4).

Estimation and planning are seen as evolutionary when using agile and not a one-off activity. They are carried out throughout the project and for every level of plan (see Table 12.1).

Empirical and **emergent** planning is more likely to occur in the lower levels of plan such as with product delivery within the Managing Product Delivery process (i.e. where agile is predominantly used) because the timescales (and therefore the planning horizons) will be short, perhaps in the order of two to four weeks. The tasks at this level of plan will be so small (e.g. a matter of days or hours) that feedback in the form of metrics will be frequent and planning will have a relatively low margin of error. 'Just-in-time' (or JIT) planning at these low levels of plan is sometimes referred to as 'rolling-wave planning' or 'progressive elaboration'.

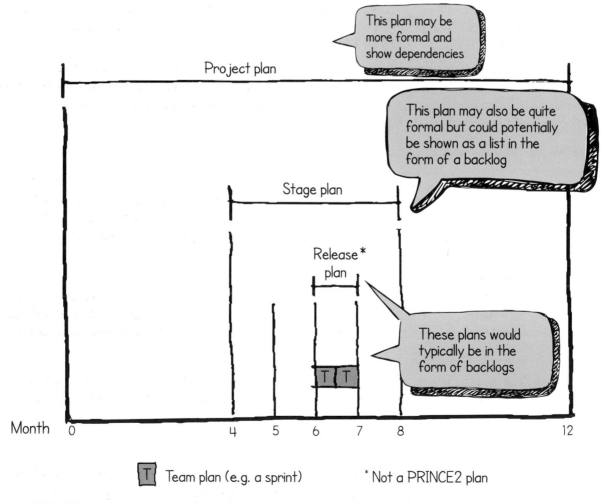

Figure 12.3 Different planning levels, horizons and formats

Table 12.1 Estimation approaches that may be used at each PRINCE2 plan level

PRINCE2 plan level	Possible agile equivalent	Typical estimation approaches and/or techniques
(Corporate or programme)	Product roadmap	
Project	Project	By analogy with other projects or by using more predictive or 'rational' means or expert knowledge
Stage	Release (one or more)	Effort per feature in the form of points and expected value or by using existing lead times if available
Team	Sprint (one or more)	Effort per backlog item in the form of points or by using existing lead times if available

Definition: Emergent

A concept in agile that refers to creating solutions and making decisions in a way that gradually converges on an accurate solution and doesn't involve a lot of upfront work. The opposite would be to spend time and try to predict how things will happen. An example would be 'emergent architecture' whereby work could be started on the product and then the best architecture would emerge as the product develops. The alternative would involve doing a lot of work in advance to decide how the product would be built.

A more predictive style of the planning would typically be applied for higher-level plans (e.g. project plans and possibly stage plans) as these have a relatively higher margin of error. However, empiricism can still be used at these levels, and it would be a good sign of an organization's maturity if measures and metrics from previous projects and stages were used to estimate without a lot of ceremony.

Either way, over-planning should be avoided as it is not possible to cover and plan for every eventuality. Therefore the attitude should be to do 'enough' planning and no more, otherwise the extra work will outweigh the potential benefits as with the law of diminishing returns. The Agile Manifesto puts emphasis on responding to change rather than following a plan.

12.3.4 Align product-based planning to features

One of the most powerful techniques in PRINCE2 is that of **product-based planning**, and this can be applied very easily in agile situations. When creating a product breakdown structure or product description the focus will typically be similar to the content of a requirement or user story. It would not be appropriate to use technical phases during this exercise in an agile context (e.g. analysis, design, build and test) as this is not the focus of the agile way of working.

When using PRINCE2 in an agile context it is important to plan around features and groups of features. Due to the primary focus of agile being based on flexing what is being delivered (see Chapter 6) features expressed in the form of requirements or user stories represent the contingency on a project when combining PRINCE2 with agile. Conversely, time and cost are not used as contingency and are therefore likely to remain stable.

Clearly illustrating what constitutes the MVP is recommended.

Product-based planning can be used for any level of plan in PRINCE2. Perhaps at the lowest level a team may prefer to use its own form of activity planning but the option to use product-based planning should at least be considered.

12.3.5 A possible limitation with sprint planning by priority only

When working at the delivery level with agile, planning centres around the immediate future and this often relates to a timebox of two to four weeks. Although flow-based approaches do not typically use a timebox, both flow-based and iterative timeboxing approaches focus predominately upon prioritization. That is to say the focus is on doing the highest-priority work as soon as possible.

This is typified by sprint planning in Scrum (see Appendix H) whereby the highest-priority items in the product backlog are broken down into tasks by the team that will be developing them. An indication of a well-maintained product backlog is that each entry in the product backlog is independent of any other entry, thus increasing the likelihood that work can be carried out by any member of the team with the appropriate skills, without impacting on any of the others. However, there will typically be limitations due to people having certain types of skill and experience, and which people are available; therefore a balance will always need to be struck.

Projects by their very nature are challenging, and therefore when planning at the levels above the product delivery level it is usually too simplistic to create a prioritized to-do list and start working from the top. Longer-term planning needs to consider many factors such as dependencies (internal and external to the project) and the grouping together of similar work items.

12.4 AGILE CONCEPTS AND TECHNIQUES

12.4.1 Agile estimation

One of the most popular techniques used in agile environments is to estimate the work to be done using a points system. This technique can be used for any type of plan in PRINCE2 (see 'sprint planning' in Appendix H). Although the technique is reasonably straightforward and commonly used, many of its advantages are not that obvious and sometimes overlooked.

12.4.1.1 The basics

The principal thinking behind this technique is to start estimating by using 'relative' estimates (not 'actual' estimates) and to do this by harnessing the knowledge of the whole team in a way that everyone can contribute without being prejudiced by other team members.

The most common form of relative estimation is achieved by giving requirements or user stories a points value that means something relative to another requirement or user story. If painting a wall was given a value of one point and painting a ceiling was given a value of two points, this would mean that painting the ceiling would require twice the effort compared with painting the wall. Importantly, this does not give any indication of how long either task will take, but it does mean that if painting the wall turns out to take five days then painting the ceiling should take something in the region of 10 days – assuming that we have made a correct relative estimate.

Creating these relative estimates is carried out as a team, where each team member simultaneously gives their opinion by using pre-numbered playing cards or pieces of paper showing their chosen points value. The reason for using playing cards or similar is to avoid people having their estimates affected or prejudiced by other people's views. One area that can affect people's judgement is the tendency for people to put too much emphasis on the first estimate suggested. This is known as 'anchoring'.

When everyone reveals their points estimates it is important that any differences, small and large, are discussed and the reasoning behind the differences is understood. Then another round of voting takes place, which leads to the team estimates converging towards a collectively agreed point value.

Ultimately, a team can work out how many points they can do in a timebox and can forecast future work throughput, although this does need a degree of stability in the working environment so that like is being compared with like.

12.4.1.2 Further information

There are many variations of numbering systems used and most are based on the Fibonacci sequence of 1, 1, 2, 3, 5, 8, 13, 21, 34 etc. Pre-printed playing cards are commonly used with a sequence of 1, 2, 3, 5, 8, 13, 20, 40 and 100 or similar, possibly with extra cards too.

Therefore, using this points system a requirement estimated at eight points would involve four times the effort compared with a requirement classified as being worth two points.

Table 12.2 Using ratios along with T-shirt sizes

Size	Ratio
S	1
M	2
L	4
XL	8
XXL	16

Another very popular technique is called 'T-shirt sizing'. This involves classifying each requirement or user story as being either small (S), medium (M), large (L) or extra-large (XL) and so on. Even a simple rating of 'high, medium or low' as a guide to effort can still be effective. These systems are deliberately abstract in that they can be carried out without any relative values or ratios. In effect they just say that a medium task is bigger than a small and not as big as a large.

Ratios (or values) can be used with these approaches if desired as shown in Table 12.2. The reason why the numbers increase exponentially, and not in a linear manner, is because there is more uncertainty as the size of a task increases.

12.4.1.3 Hints that may prove useful

When starting the estimation exercise, see if the team can agree on a single base story that represents a value of one (or another number if preferred) so that every other story has something relative to refer to from the start.

If a story is estimated at a very large number (e.g. 40 or 100) then it would normally indicate that there is not enough known about the story to provide a realistic estimate. Further investigative work is likely to be required to understand more about the story.

Avoid using actual times instead of the points when using this technique. It can cause teams to work less hard or too hard if the estimate is inaccurate, and estimates would need to be based on some form of standard day, which may be difficult to calculate. Points are arbitrary and therefore reduce the likelihood of this problem and the potential for conflict.

Do not compare your relative estimates with the relative estimates of other teams. Each team has its own individual way of doing this, and the approach may not be the same across teams (e.g. the degree to which they factor in their own risk appetite might vary).

When using playing cards or paper to estimate, do not at any time average out the point scores. It is the debate and interaction between the team members that will result in a greater understanding of the task and therefore produce a more accurate estimate.

When considering the relative effort involved it is best not to think of the actual effort required, as this defeats the purpose of the technique. Ultimately these relative estimates can be converted into actual estimates of time and cost if desired but this may not take place (e.g. a delivery team might try and do as much work as possible (measured in points) in the allotted time period). However, in a project context deadlines will need to be forecast so it may be necessary to go some way in converting the relative estimates into times. Please note that when using the more common agile frameworks in the BAU domain, teams are quite happy dealing with relative estimates in the style of points (or similar) and do not convert them to an actual effort figure such as hours or days.

The concept of team-based estimation is often referred to as 'the wisdom of crowds', and focuses on bringing different areas of knowledge and experience together in order to get the best estimate possible. Unusual estimates from certain team members may contain great insight. One of the benefits of this technique is the amount of communication and understanding that the team generates during this exercise.

Painting

In terms of complexity

The window is a high complexity task:
• Avoid painting the glass
• Dismantle the handles
• Leave open to dry

The wall is a low complexity task.

In terms of effort, the window and the wall are about the same.

Figure 12.4 Painting a wall – comparing effort with complexity

The points values are usually referred to as story points as they typically relate to a user story and the amount of effort involved to complete it. Another similar term used for this is 'complexity points' where estimates are based on complexity. This is not the same as effort, which already factors in the level of complexity and is illustrated in Figure 12.4.

12.5 PLANS THEME SUMMARY

Planning in PRINCE2 operates at several levels and throughout a project. PRINCE2 Agile planning is very comprehensive (e.g. the plans include the requirements/user stories) and when this is carried out in a very collaborative and feature-focused planning style, it creates a lot of knowledge transfer about the plan and the ownership of it.

Tip

An estimate should always have at least two parts: the estimate itself and a level of confidence for that estimate.

ACKNOWLEDGEMENTS AND FURTHER READING

Mike Cohn (2005). *Agile Estimating and Planning*. Prentice Hall.

James Grenning: http://www.renaissancesoftware.net/blog

13

Risk theme

This chapter covers:

- PRINCE2 and agile approaches to the Risk theme

- PRINCE2 Agile guidance for the Risk theme

- Agile concepts and techniques

13 Risk theme

13.1 THE PRINCE2 APPROACH TO THE RISK THEME

The purpose of the Risk theme is to identify, assess and control uncertainty and, as a result, improve the ability of the project to succeed.

13.1.1 What is a risk?

A risk is an uncertain event or set of events that, should it occur, will have an effect on the achievement of objectives. It consists of a combination of the probability of a perceived threat or opportunity occurring, and the magnitude of its impact on objectives, where:

- Threat is used to describe an uncertain event that could have a negative impact on objectives
- Opportunity is used to describe an uncertain event that could have a favourable impact on objectives.

13.1.2 Risk management procedure

PRINCE2 recommends a risk management procedure comprising the following five steps:

- Identify (context and risks)
- Assess (i.e. estimate and evaluate)
- Plan
- Implement
- Communicate.

The first four steps are sequential, with the 'communicate' step running in parallel because the findings of any of the other steps may need to be communicated prior to the completion of the overall process. All of the steps are iterative in nature in that when additional information becomes available, it is often necessary to re-visit earlier steps and carry them out again to achieve the most effective result.

Figure 13.1 shows the elements of the risk management procedure.

13.1.2.1 Identify

Identify context

The primary goal of the 'identify context' step is to obtain information about the project in order to understand the specific objectives that are at risk and to formulate the **risk management strategy** for the project. The risk management strategy describes how risks will be managed during the project. The project's risk management strategy should be based on the corporate risk management policy or on the programme's risk management strategy.

13.1.2.2 Assess

Estimate

The primary goal of the 'estimate' step is to assess the threats and opportunities to the project in terms of their probability and impact.

Evaluate

The primary goal of the 'evaluate' step is to assess the net effect of all the identified threats and opportunities on a project when aggregated together.

13.1.2.3 Plan

The primary goal of the 'plan' step is to prepare specific management responses to the threats and

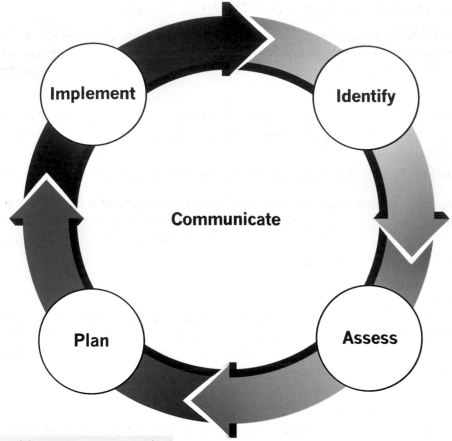

Figure 13.1 The risk management procedure

opportunities identified, ideally to remove or reduce the threats and to maximize the opportunities. Attention to the plan step ensures as far as possible that the project is not taken by surprise if a risk materializes.

13.1.2.4 Implement

The primary goal of the 'implement' step is to ensure that the planned risk responses are actioned, their effectiveness monitored, and corrective action taken where responses do not match expectations.

13.1.2.5 Communicate

Communication is a step that is carried out continually. The 'communicate' step should ensure that information related to the threats and opportunities faced by the project is communicated both within the project and externally to stakeholders.

13.2 THE GENERAL VIEW OF AGILE WITH RESPECT TO THE RISK THEME

In general terms there is relatively less prominence given to the area of risk in agile when compared with other areas such as planning and progress. Issues (often referred to as blockers or impediments) are explicitly addressed (e.g. during a stand-up meeting) but risks and the management of them are handled more implicitly.

Agile, by the very nature of some of its concepts, mitigates many risks associated with other approaches (e.g. Waterfall) by preferring the detail to emerge later rather than sooner, and thereby reducing the impact of changes.

It could be said that risk management happens due to the responsive and proactive nature of the agile way of working, where the delivery teams are working to short delivery cycles and continually reacting to feedback and looking out for anything that will hinder progress. Further to this, the team approach to being aware of risks means that there is not usually a role accountable for managing it. In a mature agile environment this will exist and it will be clear who manages risk at the project level and at the delivery level.

13.3 PRINCE2 AGILE GUIDANCE FOR THE RISK THEME

The Risk theme in PRINCE2 brings a level of formality to the management of risk, which can be very effective in any agile environment. In many situations it may be possible to manage risk in a real-time way but PRINCE2 puts a lot of emphasis on planned risk management, clearly defining who is accountable for this.

In PRINCE2:

● It is the responsibility of the role that is managing the *team* (i.e. the team manager) to manage risk at the delivery level, and the responsibility of the role managing the *project* (i.e. the project manager) to manage risk at the project level.

● Risk management is formalized and planned, but at a level that is appropriate for the situation.

That does not mean to say that the team-based approach to risk management is no longer needed. The opposite is the case in that when using PRINCE2 with agile the whole team should look out for risks and take ownership of risks when appropriate, but ultimately the accountability for managing them lies with the person managing the team and/or managing the project.

13.3.1 Level of formality

Formalizing risk management does not mean creating processes or documents that are bureaucratic. The level of formality should be appropriate to the needs of a project. On some projects, a risk register of a few columns manually updated on a team board may suffice (see Figure 13.2) whereas other projects may require a dozen columns electronically held and accessible remotely.

13.3.2 Addressing risk during stand-up meetings

Due to the implicit nature of risk management in some forms of agile, it is good practice to ensure that the delivery teams understand the difference between something that 'has happened' or 'is happening' (referred to as an 'issue' in PRINCE2) versus something that '*may* happen' (referred to as a 'risk' in PRINCE2).

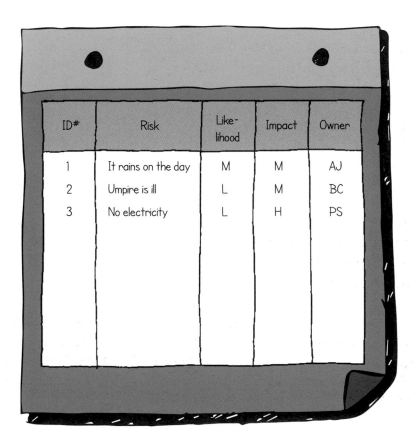

ID#	Risk	Like-lihood	Impact	Owner
1	It rains on the day	M	M	AJ
2	Umpire is ill	L	M	BC
3	No electricity	L	H	PS

Figure 13.2 An informal risk register may be appropriate in certain situations

This is particularly relevant in stand-up meetings (or daily Scrums – see Appendix H). When asking team members if anything is blocking their progress (sometimes called an 'impediment'), it is good practice to also ask if they are aware of anything that 'may potentially' block their progress. This does not necessarily need to be a separate question but the distinction is important, as the two questions require different responses.

When dealing with projects and difficult situations it is essential to actively manage risk. PRINCE2 sees this as essential in all situations. It is not optional.

13.3.3 Agile risks

Much of the agile way of working has been created to address the many risks associated with Waterfall projects – for example, avoiding detailed specifications at the early stages because the details may change, or delivering early and often to highlight misunderstandings. Although the agile way of working may reduce many common risks (which is one of the reasons for its growth in popularity) it does have risk areas of its own, such as:

● Agile relies on customer involvement, so what happens if the customer lacks commitment or is not empowered to make decisions?

● Agile relies on people interacting quickly and effectively, so what happens if a team is split over more than one site and in different time zones?

● Agile benefits from iterative and incremental delivery of products, so what happens if this is difficult to do due to the limitations of the existing infrastructure or legislation?

Another risk that should not be overlooked when working in an agile way is that value is delivered before it has been planned. Although this may be a positive situation and will not happen as a surprise (due to frequent customer involvement), it is still a risk and needs to be managed accordingly (e.g. end-users need training earlier or benefits that are delivered earlier can be applied to other projects).

A PRINCE2 project using agile will face many risks faced by any project but it is vulnerable to specific agile risks and these need to be managed. PRINCE2 Agile contains an agile risk assessment tool called the Agilometer and this is described in Chapter 24.

13.4 AGILE CONCEPTS AND TECHNIQUES

Some of the concepts and techniques relevant to managing risk are described in Table 13.1.

13.5 RISK THEME SUMMARY

PRINCE2 places focus on the Risk theme, and with its alignment to Management of Risk (M_o_R) it brings a wide body of knowledge to this area offering many benefits to the agile way of working, such as with planning a risk strategy and managing risks throughout the project.

When using PRINCE2 Agile it is important to ensure that the behaviours, concepts, frameworks and techniques of agile are correctly in place as many elements of the agile way of working manage and mitigate risk by their very nature – for example, concepts such as working iteratively and incrementally, and techniques that help to prioritize the work.

The most important areas that help with managing risk in an agile context are the five behaviours in PRINCE2 Agile of transparency, collaboration, rich communication, self-organization and exploration (see section 7.4). If these are then complemented by appropriate planning and ongoing risk management (see section 13.1), it greatly increases the chances of completing a successful project.

Table 13.1 Agile concepts and techniques relevant to risk management

Approaches and techniques associated with risk	Description
M_o_R (*Management of Risk*)	AXELOS's M_o_R offers an effective framework for taking informed decisions about the risks that affect performance objectives. The framework allows organizations to assess risk accurately (selecting the correct responses to threats and opportunities created by uncertainty) and thereby improve service delivery.
Risk burn-down charts	Originally introduced by John Brothers and then elaborated on by Mike Cohn, this technique multiplies the probability of a risk occurring by the impact it will have in days lost. This then creates a value for the days that may be lost from a timebox. When this is accumulated for all risks associated with a timebox, a total exposure (in potential days lost) can be calculated. This is shown graphically in the form of a burn-down chart that can be addressed (i.e. burnt down) by mitigating or addressing the identified risks. On a PRINCE2 risk register entry, 'expected value' can be used to record this, although it will usually be measured in days or hours.
Spiking, prototyping, proof of concepts, experiments	Techniques that can be used to explore and learn about areas of a project that are uncertain and need to have the level of uncertainty reduced to help with such things as planning and risk mitigation.

Tips

A good project manager prefers to be good at managing risk and not good at fighting fires.

Quick check: Are risks getting identified during daily stand-up meetings?

14

Change theme

This chapter covers:

- PRINCE2 and agile approaches to the Change theme

- PRINCE2 Agile guidance for the Change theme

- Agile concepts and techniques

14 Change theme

14.1 THE PRINCE2 APPROACH TO THE CHANGE THEME

The purpose of the Change theme is to identify, assess and control any potential and approved changes to the baseline.

Change is inevitable during the life of a project and every project needs a systemic approach to the identification, assessment and control of issues that may result in change.

Issue and change control is a continual activity, performed throughout the life of the project. Without an ongoing and effective issue and change control procedure, a project will either become unresponsive to its stakeholders or drift out of control.

14.2 THE GENERAL VIEW OF AGILE WITH RESPECT TO THE CHANGE THEME

Agile embraces change. One of the four values of the Agile Manifesto is about 'responding to change' and one of its principles is 'welcoming changing requirements, even late in development'.

Agile sees change as inevitable and a normal situation. The understanding of a project will change as the project proceeds: 'unknowns' will surface and unexpected events will happen. Responding positively to change when it happens results in a more accurate product being delivered, and because agile puts a lot of emphasis on flexing what is being delivered, this is where most of the change is managed and is the focus of PRINCE2 Agile.

14.2.1 Changes to what is being delivered

Changes to the detailed understanding of the product being created would typically be viewed in a positive light, as this greater understanding improves what is being produced. However, if the changes mean that the baseline upon which the work was justified is being compromised, then this may not be seen in a positive light, as it may be a symptom of significant misunderstandings from earlier on in the project.

One caveat to the idea of baseline change perhaps being unwelcome is that in a wider context it may be positive news – in the sense that it results in the fast failure of the project that would ultimately have delivered an unsuccessful outcome. This could represent good news in general, but perhaps not good news for that particular project.

In simple terms these different types of change to what is being delivered can be described as detail or baseline changes (see Figure 14.1).

14.2.2 Other types of change

Agile usually refers to change as something that affects a project's products. PRINCE2 sees anything that affects the agreed baseline as change and handles it accordingly. If a team member becomes ill and will be unavailable for two weeks, then this would be handled as a change in the form of an issue as it will impact planning. A typical agile response to this (assuming the team was of sufficient size) would be for the delivery team to re-organize and aim to deliver less due to the reduced capacity, although this would depend on the level of collaboration with the customer.

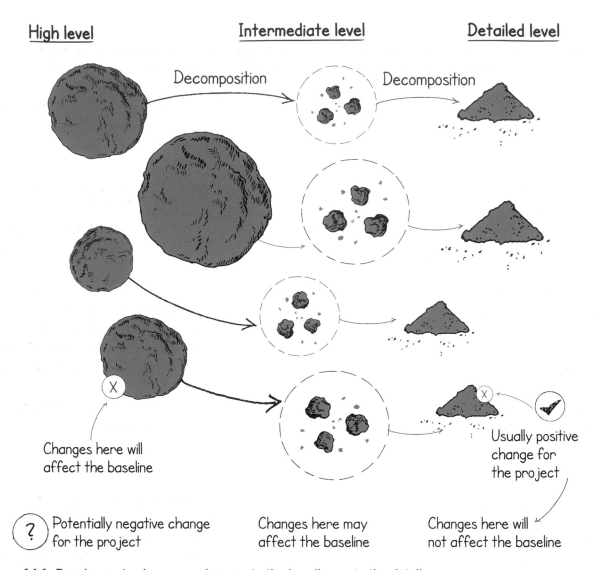

Figure 14.1 Requirements change can happen to the baseline or to the detail

14.3 PRINCE2 AGILE GUIDANCE FOR THE CHANGE THEME

Both PRINCE2 and agile see change as inevitable but there is a contrast between the two in that agile embraces change and could be described as 'change friendly', whereas PRINCE2 is somewhat more cautious and could be said to 'control it'. These views are not contradictory, and when combining PRINCE2 with agile it creates a blend of controlling significant change, whilst giving freedom to allow for responsive change at the detail level.

This means allowing change at the product delivery level in order to harness the benefits of positive change, whilst at the same time putting in place the appropriate governance to handle change, which may affect the agreed baseline upon which the project was justified. Techniques for handling change are described in section 14.4.

One particular area of note when handling change is to assess if the change has any impact on the ability to deliver a minimum viable product (MVP) at the right time, as this will immediately raise an exception.

14.3.1 Allowing for change

During pre-project and the initiation stage, PRINCE2 creates plans and product descriptions that form baseline definitions of what is to be delivered. To enable a more agile way of working, these baseline definitions should allow enough room for manoeuvre by being defined at the right level, to cater for the inevitability of change whilst at the same time providing enough clarity to ensure that the justification for the project is still sound.

When setting this baseline, using the correct level of detail is important in an agile context, as per the following examples:

● **When a high degree of accuracy is needed** When making a mirror or a lens for a telescope used in space, a deviation by a single micrometre may have a seriously damaging effect on its effectiveness.

● **When a lesser degree of accuracy is needed** The operating temperature for radio equipment used by a soldier may be best specified by a range which can be prioritized ('must' work at $-10°C$, 'should' work at $-20°C$, 'could' work at $-30°C$).

The examples illustrate that sometimes requirements definition is like a binary condition in that it is either exactly right or it is not, whereas at other times it is more of a spectrum in that there is a varying degree of correctness. When defining requirements, it is important to avoid defining those requirements that have varying degrees of correctness in a binary form. Doing so reduces the options available if adjustments to the scope, or a product's quality criteria, become necessary later in the project thus reducing the ability to work in an agile way.

Further refinement of these products happens during Managing a Stage Boundary and Managing Product Delivery, but this should not affect the baseline described in the project initiation documentation.

14.3.2 Relationships between the Change theme, the Risk theme and configuration management

In order to be more proactive about change in an agile setting, as well as controlled and consistent after responding to change, it should be noted that in PRINCE2 there is a close relationship between the Change theme, the Risk theme and the activity of configuration management. In this way a good risk management strategy and good risk management can lessen the impact of change by formally allowing for it and planning for it. A good **configuration management strategy** and good configuration management will then ensure that changes have been applied correctly and consistently. Whether or not this only happens at the higher levels of the project structure depends on where the baseline has been set and whether or not it impacts the teams working at the delivery level.

14.3.3 Delegation of decision-making

It is very important to deal with change at the appropriate level of management. PRINCE2 establishes many controls that can be used but they should be used at the right level and at the right time. The most prominent of these controls are the tolerances in the product descriptions and the work packages.

Generally speaking, an empowered self-organizing team working at the delivery level should be free to handle change quite dynamically as long as that change is at the detailed level and is within defined tolerances. This is where specifying the quality criteria for a product description as a range or spectrum can prove beneficial. Any significant change that may impact baselines set at the stage or project level may need to be escalated to the project board or to a change authority if one has been set up.

In either situation it is useful to track the type of change – for example, is it an off-specification that the supplier needs to rectify or is it a request for change that the customer has raised? This can be useful for learning lessons from the project in terms of where these changes originated; they may also be relevant in contractual terms depending on how the contract was created (see Chapter 28 for a description of an agile style of contract).

It is important when establishing controls to handle change that they create an environment which enables quick and accurate change when the change has a positive effect on the project, whilst at the same time protecting the project from change that may have a more unwelcome impact.

PRINCE2 has a clearly defined issue and change control procedure; for a baseline change this needs to be carried out as quickly as possible, although it may take several days. For a detail change the same process is used but it may take seconds: a quick discussion, a decision on what to de-scope or which priorities to change, and the procedure is complete. This is how an empowered delivery team should work.

14.4 AGILE CONCEPTS AND TECHNIQUES

14.4.1 The feedback loop

A fundamental concept in agile is to gather feedback from a customer as quickly as possible. This is in keeping with the PRINCE2 Agile behaviour of exploration. This takes the form of a cycle where something is delivered, gets used, creates feedback (which can be in many forms) and then drives further decisions and deliveries (see Figure 14.2).

Lean Startup puts particular focus on this and aims to make this cycle as short as possible in order to become more responsive. It refers to this as 'accelerating the feedback loop'. How short a timescale this feedback loop will be varies considerably between different organizations in different sectors, but the aim is to move from months to weeks, weeks to days and even days to hours. Sprint reviews and release reviews are examples of where this feedback can be collected.

Ideally, this feedback should be as 'true' as possible and involve the end customer. Having said that, any feedback about the project process or the product being created is going to have value. The ultimate goal is to have real customer feedback in as short a time as possible: this may require continual customer involvement.

The feedback loop is of great importance to being truly agile. A lot of emphasis on effort should be channelled into making this as short and effective as possible.

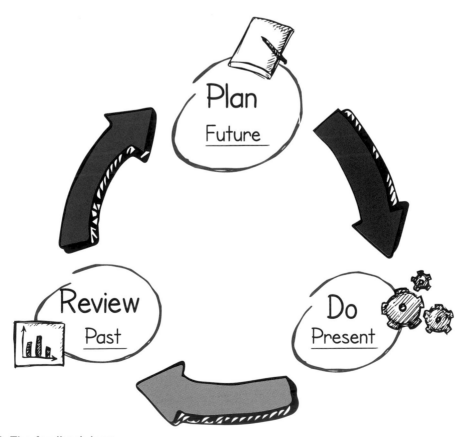

Figure 14.2 The feedback loop

Other forms of feedback loop exist such as:

- OODA (Observe, Orient(ate), Decide, Act)
- PDCA (Plan, Do, Check, Act)
- PDSA (Plan, Do, Study, Act)
- Build, measure, learn (Lean Startup).

14.5 CHANGE THEME SUMMARY

Change will happen, and the combination of PRINCE2 and agile in this area typifies the marriage of these two. A project increases its chances of success if it can be responsive at the detail level (e.g. by flexing or trading detailed requirements) and remain in control at the higher levels (e.g. by ensuring that the business case is still viable at the end of a stage).

The processes for Starting up a Project and Initiating a Project also help to create an environment where change can happen, and be responded to, at the correct level and at the correct point in a project. Many projects are poorly started and this results in change happening due to the incorrect level of detail being defined. If there are too many detailed requirements during the pre-project stage, they are unlikely to have been understood correctly. Equally, a project could be in the initiation stage with only a few high-level requirements defined and important decisions being made that are not based on enough information.

Successful projects need to handle change easily, and with PRINCE2 ensuring that the wider project context is under control, many of the agile behaviours, concepts, frameworks and techniques such as prioritization, timeboxing, exploration and collaboration can play their part in embracing change and delivering the best possible solution for the customer.

Tips

The devil is in the detail – so expect it, allow for it and respond to it.

The customer will ask for changes, so don't let this come as a surprise.

15

Progress theme

This chapter covers:

- PRINCE2 and agile approaches to the Progress theme

- PRINCE2 Agile guidance for the Progress theme

- Agile concepts and techniques

15 Progress theme

15.1 THE PRINCE2 APPROACH TO THE PROGRESS THEME

The purpose of the Progress theme is to establish mechanisms to monitor and compare actual achievements against those planned; provide a forecast for the project objectives and the project's continued viability; and control any unacceptable deviations.

Two of the principles of PRINCE2 are managing by stages and continued business justification. The Progress theme provides the mechanisms for monitoring and control, enabling the critical assessment of ongoing viability.

The Progress theme provides such mechanisms for all management levels (delivering, managing, directing) within the project management team, and for corporate or programme management outside the project.

15.1.1 What is progress?

Progress is the measure of the achievement of the objectives of a plan. It can be monitored at work package, stage and project level.

15.1.2 What are progress controls?

Progress controls ensure that for each level of the project management team the next level of management can:

● Monitor progress
● Compare level of achievement with plan
● Review plans and options against future situations
● Detect problems and identify risks
● Initiate corrective action
● Authorize further work.

15.1.3 Exceptions and tolerances

An exception is a situation where it can be forecast that there will be a deviation beyond the agreed tolerance levels.

Tolerances are the permissible deviation above and below a plan's target for time and cost without escalating the deviation to the next level of management. There may also be tolerance levels for quality, scope, benefit and risk.

Progress control involves measuring actual progress against the performance targets of time, cost, quality, scope, benefits and risk, and then using this information to make decisions (such as whether to approve a stage or work package, whether to escalate deviations, whether to prematurely close the project etc.) and to take actions as required.

15.2 THE GENERAL VIEW OF AGILE WITH RESPECT TO THE PROGRESS THEME

In a similar way to the Plans theme, agile sees the Progress theme as of particular importance and many agile concepts and techniques exist to address the need to track progress. Although most of this is focused at the delivery level, more mature agile environments use these techniques in a wider context where there is a need to see how a piece of work relates to other teams or other projects and what value is being delivered as a whole.

Agile typically tracks the progress of the amount of work being completed and the amount of value being delivered. Ideally this value is provided to real customers in an operational environment.

It is important to understand that agile monitors and controls the work being carried out as much through some of its fundamental values and not just the use of specific techniques. Burn charts and work-in-progress boards are very common techniques used in agile, and although they are very effective in their own right, they actually form part of a bigger picture in that they help enshrine some of the key agile values such as transparency, simplicity and empiricism. People new to agile often see these displays first, and not only do they look appealing, they are also very effective.

Fundamental to the agile way of working is the desire to respond quickly to learnings and new information. By working iteratively there is a great sense of immediacy to this responsiveness and agile aims to create the conditions where progress is monitored 'real time'.

15.3 PRINCE2 AGILE GUIDANCE FOR THE PROGRESS THEME

Both PRINCE2 and agile provide an abundance of guidance on tracking progress. There is nothing contradictory between the two. However, there are different areas of emphasis and when combining PRINCE2 with agile it is important to draw on the strengths of both to create a strong blend that provides comprehensive coverage in all areas and at all levels of a project.

When using PRINCE2 with agile, flexibility in what is delivered is the primary aspect of performance that is of most interest to the whole project management team; therefore displaying this in the form of a burn chart is quite natural irrespective of the project level.

It is also quite natural for a project manager to know that they will need to react quickly to how things are progressing as it may take several sprints or releases to understand how much work is going to be delivered by tracking overall velocity.

15.3.1 Control

Whenever an organization invests time and money into a project it is essential that this investment is monitored and controlled appropriately. Although common phraseology, such as the use of the terms 'progress' (in PRINCE2) and 'velocity' (in agile), gives a positive feel when helping to answer the question 'How are things going?', it should not be overlooked that behind all of the techniques and concepts lies the necessity to be in control at all times. The word 'control' does not resonate well with many in the agile community as they see it as inferring 'command and control'. This is certainly not the case as PRINCE2 is more focused on creating guiding boundaries that empower people to carry out their work by self-organizing. PRINCE2 creates these boundaries by using such things as tolerances (as well as stage boundaries and the role of project assurance), and if these are forecast to be exceeded, it will trigger an exception. This then acts as a safety net to catch a situation that has gone outside what was reasonable to expect.

15.3.2 Progress at different levels

PRINCE2 tracks progress at different levels (see Figure 12.3) and many techniques can be used at any level. Using only agile techniques for delivery and only traditional techniques for direction and management would be limiting, as many of the agile concepts and techniques can prove effective at all levels for tracking progress. Care may need to be taken as the audience for any technique will need to be comfortable with the information it is conveying (e.g. to use a burn-down chart for the project board may prove counter-productive if the project board members are not familiar with this format). However, many of the PRINCE2 products can be created by using agile artefacts. For example:

● **An agile technique used at the direction level** On a PRINCE2 project where scope and quality criteria are variable, it is often good practice to communicate progress to the project board by way of a graphical burn chart showing how much has been successfully completed against what had been forecast. Adding the tolerance levels for the scope may enhance the graphic further.

● **A PRINCE2 theme at the delivery level** On a project using timeboxing, it is recommended to first define the stage boundaries, and then to build in the appropriate number of releases and/or sprints (of suitable length) inside each stage.

In either example progress is typically tracked by completed products (as opposed to days or hours).

15.4 AGILE CONCEPTS AND TECHNIQUES

15.4.1 Burn charts

One of the most popular techniques used in agile environments is to display progress using lines plotted on a graph. These graphs are known as burn charts and they come in two forms: burn-down charts and burn-up charts (see Figure 15.1).

15.4.1.1 The basics

Burn-down charts are the most well known and they are used to show how much work remains whereas burn-up charts are slightly more complex and they are used to show how much work has been done. Both types of chart aim to provide two important pieces of information:

● What is the situation regarding progress – i.e. what is the current situation and what should it be?

● At the current rate of progress what will be the situation at the end of this time period (which could be a sprint, release, stage, project or any other period of time)?

Typically the vertical axis shows the amount of work to do in terms of effort and the horizontal axis shows time in some form such as days or dates.

15.4.1.2 How a burn-down chart works

In its most simple form the burn-down chart has two lines (see Figure 15.1). A straight line that shows where the 'ideal' rate of progress should be (in black on the figure) and a line that is updated on a regular basis (usually daily) that shows the amount of work done (in purple on the figure). The work remaining is shown by the end of the purple line. When the purple line is above the black line this means that work is behind schedule. If the purple line is below the black line this means that work is ahead of schedule.

The current rate of progress can be determined by the trend of the line (i.e. its gradient) showing effort remaining. This is commonly referred to as 'velocity' by the agile community. Assuming that there is stability and constancy in the team, this can then be used to project forward and forecast when the work will be complete and importantly determine if the deadline is likely to be met.

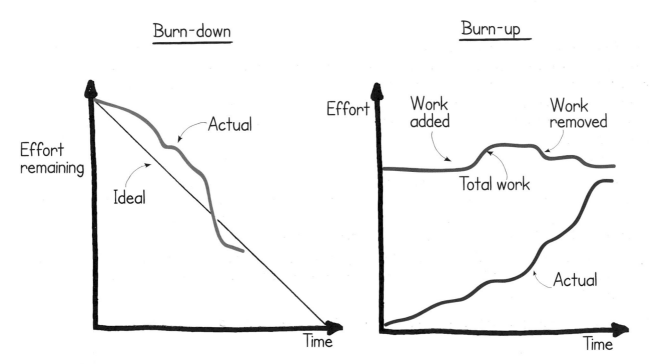

Figure 15.1 Burn-down and burn-up charts

15.4.1.3 How a burn-up chart works

One limitation with burn-down charts is that they assume the amount of work doesn't change. This is not a significant limitation in most situations (e.g. where a two-week sprint has been agreed and locked-in/baselined) but if the amount of work is likely to change, or does change, then this will not be picked up by a burn-down chart easily, and therefore a burn-up chart should be used (see Figure 15.1). The purple line shows work completed, which can now be used in tandem with the red line showing the total amount of work. The work remaining is therefore the difference between the red and purple lines. Any work that has been added or removed during the time period can now be seen by the red line.

15.4.1.4 Further information

The reason why burn charts are so prevalent in agile environments is because agile is based on what is (or is not) being delivered and where time and the team size are fixed. Therefore to monitor progress, an agile delivery team (or team manager or project manager) will focus on what, of the planned work for a specific time period, has been completed. Depending on the level at which this work is taking place this could refer to such things as requirements, user stories or tasks.

The recommended way to display a burn chart is for it to be physically mounted on a wall or board and updated manually. This intentionally creates a simple and tactile way of showing and interacting with the information regarding progress. It is not always possible to do this, such as when teams are distributed. However, the temptation to move to capturing and displaying the information electronically should be taken carefully as the benefits of the technology may not outweigh those of the physical engagement created by the tactile experience.

15.4.1.5 Hints that may prove useful

When updating a burn chart, only record information according to completed work. If a two-day task is 50% complete do not mark anything as completed on the burn chart. The same applies even if it is 95% complete.

Burn charts are less accurate if the size of the tasks being reported on are relatively large for the given time period (e.g. a five-day task in a two-week sprint). When working in an agile way it may be appropriate for teams working in sprints (which should last no more than four weeks) to break down tasks to a size that needs only a few days of effort or less. Primarily this is needed in order to help make it easier for a team to organize its work. A desirable side-effect of this is to make burn charts more sensitive (to issues/impediments) and accurate. However, there is an overhead with this as time needs to be spent breaking down work into smaller work items.

Either type of burn chart can be used in a wide variety of situations throughout a project. They can be applied to anything that involves time lasting from a few hours, to many months or years.

Make sure the axes reflect the correct units being used. The left-hand axis will typically show effort in the form of points such as story points. However, this needs to reflect the units used when the work was estimated.

15.4.2 Information radiators

When entering a room where an agile team is working you would expect to see lots of information displayed on the walls or boards and you would also expect to see this information conveyed in a 'low-tech' style with the abundant use of sticky notes, large sheets of paper, colour, symbols, pictures and graphics.

15.4.2.1 The basics

One of the best ways to convey most information is visually, and if this can be accessed quickly then this is even better. If a room contains large sheets of paper or large whiteboards and the information on them can be seen clearly from a distance, then this creates a 'push' of information that can be accessed immediately. If information is held on someone's desk or computer it is not immediately accessible and also needs to be 'pulled'.

Further to this, and of similar importance, the creation and maintenance of this information is best carried out manually – i.e. physically writing on charts and moving sticky notes. This can happen very quickly and in any format or style that is felt to be appropriate. For example spontaneous annotations and informal codes and symbols such as ticks, crosses, red dots, green stars etc. can be used. Although this can be achieved electronically, and perhaps it can be printed off, this takes longer and can be seen as being sterile and not as engaging as the 'low-tech' option.

Tip

Information radiators include or are similar to information displays, big visible charts (BVCs), team boards, Kanban boards.

Image 15.1 An example of a team board

15.4.2.2 Further information

Transparency (or visibility) is one of the key behaviours that is at the heart of most agile approaches. It is a hugely significant part of agile and the use of visible information, handcrafted, simple to understand and instantly available to digest, contributes significantly in this area. The idea is to make information visible to all and understood by all. However there is a risk that comes with this. In order to be fully, or truly, transparent all information about a project needs to be visible and that includes displaying information that may at times be negative as well as positive. This is where another key behaviour which is also at the heart of most agile approaches (and perhaps at the heart of manage by exception) can be enhanced: that value being trust. The opposite of this is when the information is massaged which is sometimes referred to as 'gaming'.

15.4.2.3 Hints that may prove useful

A good guide to help with deciding on the correct size, format and layout of anything being displayed is to see if the information can be digested by someone walking past. Put another way, does someone need to leave their desk and walk over to the information in order to be able to read it? This is why words like 'big' and 'large' are used to describe these figures and charts. Many people use the abbreviation BVC which stands for 'big visible chart'.

A wide variety of information can be displayed using this approach. The most commonly displayed information relates to work and how it is progressing (e.g. a burn-down chart or a WIP (work-in-progress) board). Other information commonly displayed would cover quality and defects, risks and issues, vision statements (or similar) and working practices (see Figure 15.2).

Information displayed this way needs to be regularly updated and it won't update itself! Holding a daily stand-up meeting by these displays, and moving the information across immediately, is one way to achieve this.

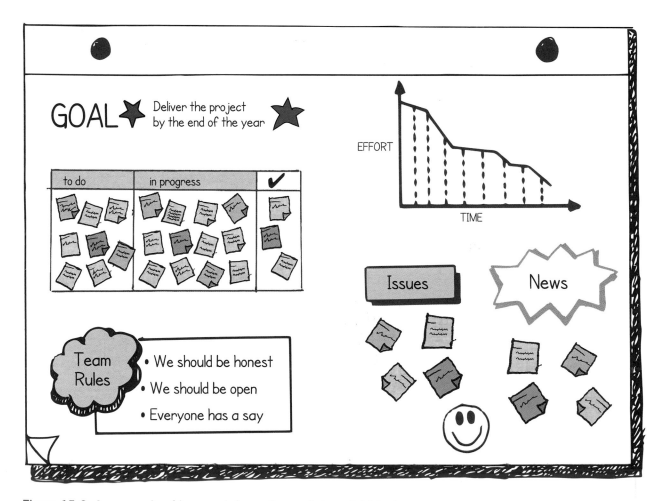

Figure 15.2 An example of how an information radiator might look

If a project management team is not co-located this is hard to recreate, but technology, webcams, digital photography and virtual systems can go part of the way to achieving some of the benefits that this brings to how the team communicates.

Don't underestimate the positive impression these graphs and charts give off simply by their attractive appearance!

15.5 PROGRESS THEME SUMMARY

Progress on a project can be assessed in several ways and at several levels. PRINCE2 Agile monitors many areas of the project such as whether or not the business case will be met, or how many features have been delivered so far in a particular sprint.

When combining PRINCE2 and agile, the different levels of planning a project need to show progress in a form that is suitable for the audience looking at the information or looking to monitor and control the situation.

The most effective use of PRINCE2 and agile is achieved when progress is managed within an appropriate set of responsive and flexible tolerances that cover the six aspects of the PRINCE2 Agile hexagon (see Figure 6.1).

Tip

If progress is visible and transparent it goes a long way to making life easier. You get all the news (good or bad) quickly.

One of the principles of PRINCE2 is to manage by exception; therefore, to have transparency of how a project is progressing is an essential ingredient to help stay in control.

ACKNOWLEDGEMENTS AND FURTHER READING

Alistair Cockburn (2001). *Agile Software Development*. Addison Wesley.

Kent Beck: http://www.threeriversinstitute.org/blog

Martin Fowler: http://martinfowler.com/intro.html

16

Agile and the PRINCE2 processes

This chapter covers:

- The PRINCE2 processes
- Tailoring guidance for the PRINCE2 processes

16 Agile and the PRINCE2 processes

PRINCE2 is a process-based approach to project management and has seven processes (containing activities) which apply to all levels of a project. All seven processes are required, and agile needs to be incorporated into all of them in some form. The amount of agile that is relevant to each process varies significantly, and therefore the amount of tailoring required varies accordingly.

16.1 THE PRINCE2 PROCESSES

PRINCE2 is a process-based approach for project management. A process is a structured set of activities designed to accomplish a specific objective. It takes one or more defined inputs and turns them into defined outputs.

There are seven processes in PRINCE2, which provide the set of activities required to direct, manage and deliver a project successfully.

Figure 16.1 shows how each process is used throughout a project's life.

PRINCE2 can be used on projects irrespective of project scale, complexity, geography, culture etc. PRINCE2 can also be used whether the project is part of a programme or is being managed as a stand-alone initiative. This reflects the principle that PRINCE2 must be tailored to suit the particular project context; PRINCE2 Agile is an example of such tailoring to suit an agile context.

A mature agile environment may have many processes in existence that address the areas of project direction and stages (or an equivalent concept to stages), as well as processes to ensure that a project is started and ended in a controlled way.

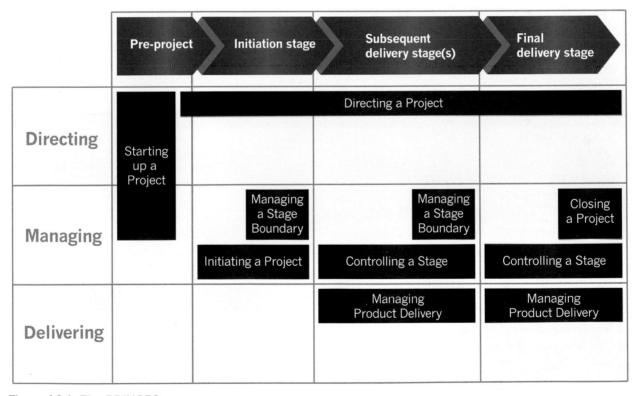

Figure 16.1 The PRINCE2 processes

16.2 TAILORING GUIDANCE FOR THE PRINCE2 PROCESSES

Figure 16.2 shows the seven PRINCE2 processes and the PRINCE2 management products (see Table 16.1 for a key to the abbreviations). More detail of how sprints and flow-based timeboxes are incorporated are shown in the inset, which has been expanded in Figure 16.3.

The numbers in Figures 16.2 and 16.3 refer to the PRINCE2 management products as identified in the PRINCE2 manual and shown in Table 16.2 (see Chapter 23 and Appendix A for further information about the products).

Figure 16.3 shows how releases and low-level timeboxes (i.e. as sprints or flow-based) may appear inside a PRINCE2 management stage. The figure assumes a common agile situation where a product backlog is used to create a series of releases, and each release in turn creates a series of sprints (e.g. when using Scrum) or is run as one timebox using a flow-based approach (e.g. when using Kanban).

Table 16.1 Key to abbreviations in Figures 16.2 to 16.4

Abbreviation	PRINCE2 process	Key agile artefacts and events that may exist within the process
DP	Directing a Project	
SU	Starting up a Project	Vision, product roadmap
IP	Initiating a Project	Product backlog
CS	Controlling a Stage	Release(s), release backlog, release retrospective
MP	Managing Product Delivery	Sprint(s), sprint backlog, sprint review and retrospective
SB	Managing a Stage Boundary	As for CS
XSB	Managing a Stage Boundary (when an exception has occurred)	As for CS
CP	Closing a Project	Project retrospective

Table 16.2 Key to the PRINCE2 management products

Baseline management products, shown in red	Records, shown in black	Reports, shown in blue
1 Benefits review plan	5 Configuration item records	3 Checkpoint report
2 Business case	7 Daily log	8 End project report
4 Communication management strategy	12 Issue register	9 End stage report
6 Configuration management strategy	14 Lessons log	10 Exception report
16 Plan (covers project, stage and, optionally, team plans)	23 Quality register	11 Highlight report
17 Product description	25 Risk register	13 Issue report
19 Project brief		15 **Lessons report**
20 Project initiation documentation		18 Product status account
21 Project product description		
22 Quality management strategy		
24 Risk management strategy		
26 Work package		

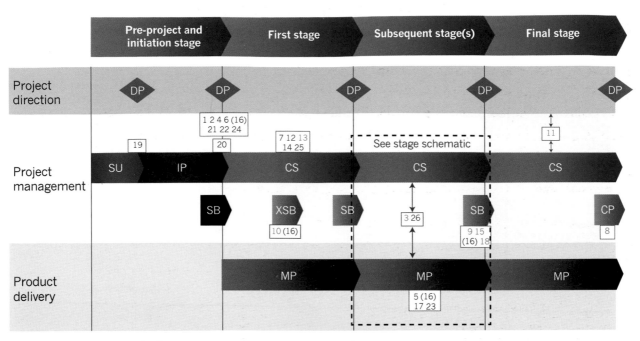

Figure 16.2 The PRINCE2 processes and management products

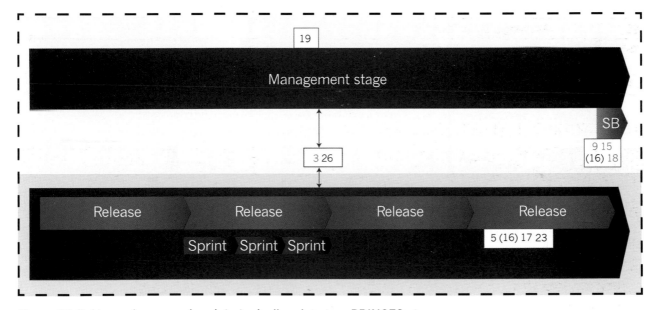

Figure 16.3 How releases and sprints typically relate to a PRINCE2 stage

Although this represents a common approach there are many other equally valid situations (see Figure 16.4). Examples of such situations might be:

● Releases and release backlogs are not used because sprints and sprint backlogs are all that are required. In this case a sprint may result in a release of features into operational use, or a release of features into a staging area or an interim deliverable which is of use to the project.

● Releases happen so frequently that they are not treated as a type of timebox or in need of a release backlog. In this case a release may happen at the end of each timebox or on more than one occasion during the timebox.

● A management stage could relate to just one release.

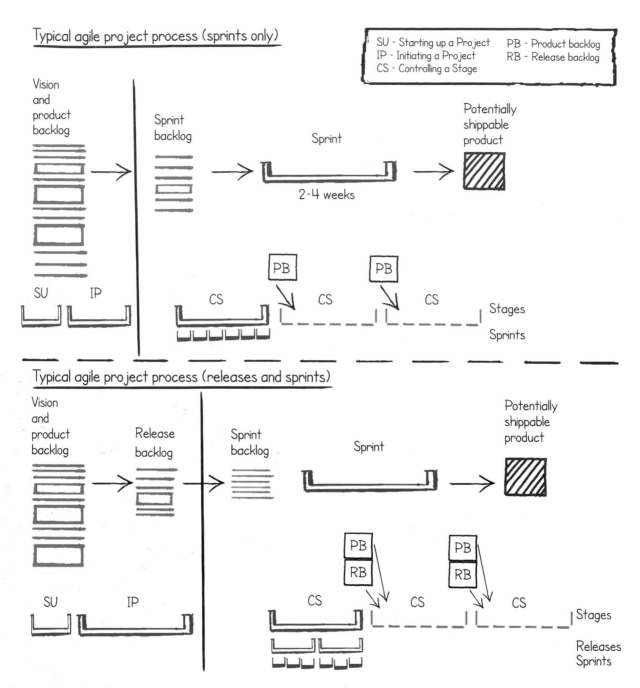

Figure 16.4 How typical agile processes would relate to the PRINCE2 process model

17

Starting up a Project;
Initiating a Project

This chapter covers:

- PRINCE2 guidance on Starting up a Project and Initiating a Project

- Agile ways of working that may already exist

- PRINCE2 Agile guidance on Starting up a Project and Initiating a Project

- Agile concepts and techniques

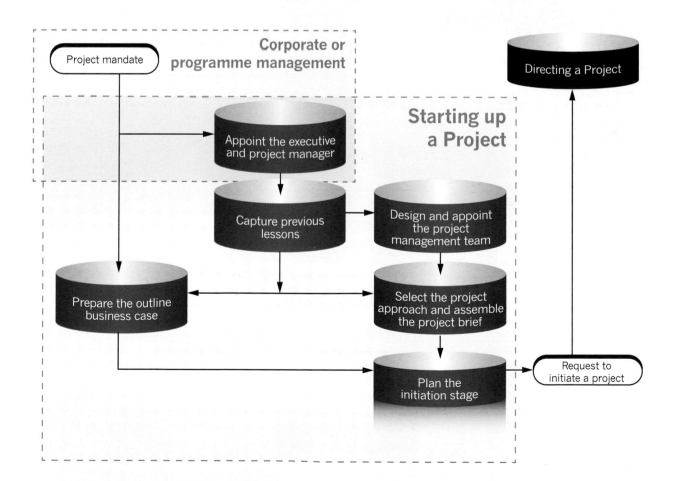

17 Starting up a Project; Initiating a Project

17.1 PRINCE2 GUIDANCE ON STARTING UP A PROJECT AND INITIATING A PROJECT

17.1.1 Starting up a Project

The purpose of the Starting up a Project process is to ensure that the prerequisites for Initiating a Project are in place by answering the question 'Do we have a viable and worthwhile project?'

It is as much about preventing poorly conceived projects from being initiated as it is about approving the initiation of viable projects. As such, the Starting up a Project process is a lighter task compared to the more detailed and thorough Initiating a Project process. The aim is to do the minimum necessary in order to decide whether it is worthwhile to even initiate the project (see Figure 17.1 for an overview).

17.1.2 Initiating a Project

The purpose of the Initiating a Project process is to establish solid foundations for the project, enabling the organization to understand the work that needs to be done to deliver the project's products before committing to a significant spend.

Initiating a Project is aimed at laying down the foundations in order to achieve a successful project. Specifically, all parties must be clear on what the project is intended to achieve, why it is needed, how the outcome is to be achieved and what their responsibilities are, so that there can be genuine commitment to it.

The Initiating a Project process allows the project board, via Directing a Project, to decide whether or not the project is sufficiently aligned with corporate or programme objectives to authorize its continuation.

Figure 17.1 Overview of Starting up a Project

If, instead, the organization proceeds directly from Starting up a Project to Controlling a Stage, then it may be forced to commit significant financial resources to a project without fully understanding how its objectives will be achieved. Without a firm definition, the project board will be taking a leap of faith.

All activities within the Initiating a Project process need further consideration if the relationship between the customer and the supplier is a commercial one (for example, the reasons for undertaking the project as defined in the supplier's business case may be different from those defined in the customer's business case).

During the Initiating a Project process the project manager will be creating the suite of management products required for the level of control specified by the project board. The project manager should have agreed (as part of the initiation stage plan) the means by which the project board will review and approve the management products – the two extremes are one at a time or all at once (see Figure 17.2 for an overview).

Please note that Starting up a Project and Initiating a Project are separate processes in PRINCE2, but they have been combined into the same chapter in this manual as the guidance when using PRINCE2 with agile is the same for both processes because they both relate to getting a project off to a good start. It is important to note that this does not mean that they are combined into one step when using PRINCE2 Agile. They should be used as two distinct processes as with PRINCE2.

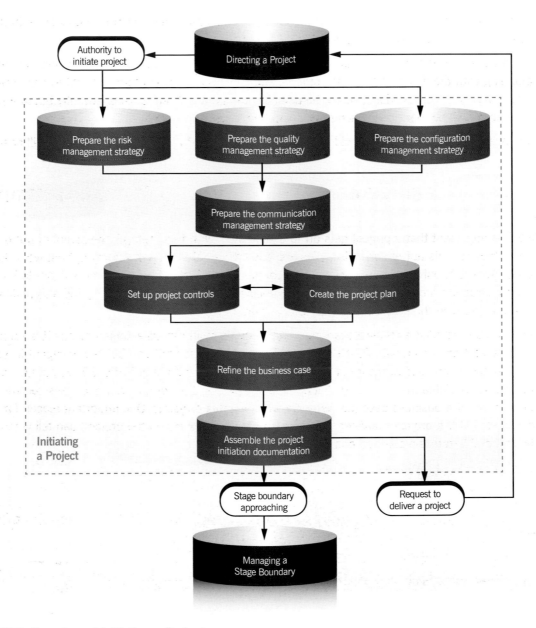

Figure 17.2 Overview of Initiating a Project

17.2 AGILE WAYS OF WORKING THAT MAY ALREADY EXIST

The most common agile approaches focus on product delivery and therefore they do not have processes beforehand to formally define any upfront work. Some agile approaches such as DSDM, DAD and FDD (see Table 2.1) do acknowledge the need to do this work; however, there is little standardization in this area across the agile community.

In simple terms this is usually for one of two reasons. Either the agile approach assumes that the upfront work would have already taken place, or it does not need it to be done.

Mature agile organizations using agile build their own processes for upfront work when they use agile in a project context.

Two concepts that occur quite frequently in agile are:

● Project chartering or visioning
● Sprint zero (iteration zero or (the) discovery (phase)) – see section 9.2.

Project chartering or visioning in agile is typically used to gain a basic understanding of the project and is seen as a short process where information is captured and recorded in a very simple form often using bullet points and visualization.

Sprint zero is a similar idea widely used by Scrum and agile teams but the concept is controversial in that it is seen by some as unnecessary and is not part of the *Scrum Guide*.

The amount of upfront work that takes place in an agile context is often a question of balancing the need to do some planning with the desire to let things emerge and use empiricism in order to adapt to changing circumstances. In a BAU context doing very little planning can be a very effective philosophy but in a project context where work will be more challenging this could be too risky.

A lot of guidance in agile starts with a backlog of features to build but in a project context this will need to be created.

17.3 PRINCE2 AGILE GUIDANCE ON STARTING UP A PROJECT AND INITIATING A PROJECT

In PRINCE2 it is important that a project gets off to a good start with the appropriate amount of upfront work. Not only that but this upfront work is typically broken down into two parts. Most upfront work done in some agile environments only concerns getting ready for delivery. PRINCE2 provides more rigour to this work by putting more structure around what 'being ready' means (during Initiating a Project), and also making sure it is worth getting ready in the first place (during Starting up a Project).

Upfront work can be regarded as unnecessary to a degree by some in the agile community as it is seen as being 'predictive' and not 'emergent'. PRINCE2 is predictive to a degree but can be very emergent if required (e.g. by reducing the length and formality of the initiation stage). However, any PRINCE2 project needs to be justified and has to be viable from the start. Fundamentally, part of this upfront work must answer the 'why?' question in the form of a business case (i.e. Why are we doing this project?). One important reason for knowing this is so that the project manager (and perhaps anyone involved on the project) can tell when it needs to be stopped before the planned end date.

Definition: Disruptive

A widely used term that has more than one definition but in general terms refers to situations where there are high degrees of uncertainty (e.g. with product innovation) and the product being developed will significantly disrupt (intentionally or accidentally) the existing environment or marketplace (e.g. 3D printing).

Lean Startup is often cited as demonstrating how agile can work when faced with high levels of uncertainty, and there are parallels between growing a small company (often using '**disruptive**' technologies) and running a challenging project in that even dynamic ground-breaking start-ups need to justify coming into existence to investors and need to be held to account at funding reviews from time to time.

Collecting enough information means that a lot of areas need to be looked at because they can all impact the business case in one form or another (e.g. risks, organizational structure, quality planning, communication planning and how the project is tailored).

How this information is presented depends on the needs of the project and the project board. Typically this may be in a document but it could be delivered along with a face-to-face presentation. Alternatively, most, if not all, of this information could be visible on the walls of a team room using lots of visualization.

As part of these two processes (Starting up a Project and Initiating a Project), the suitability of using agile needs to be assessed. The use of agile will bring many advantages but it will also bring with it a set of risks if agile is used inappropriately. This is assessed using the Agilometer (see Chapter 24).

17.3.1 Further guidance that may also be appropriate

The project product description (and the business case) should be defined with more focus on how the output can be described so that the outcomes and benefits can be adjusted during the project. If the project product description just focuses on the intended solution then the supplier is more likely to focus on this than the value it intends to deliver. This in turn may impact contractual arrangements made before delivery commences (e.g. how much the style will reflect the agile way of working).

The high-level and intermediate-level requirements are likely to be held as a list which may take the form of a spreadsheet or a low-tech list on a wall and may be referred to as a backlog.

An early definition of 'done' is likely to be part of the quality management strategy or an existing one that has been used from a previous project.

The mapping of existing agile roles to the PRINCE2 roles will be defined and understood (e.g. how the team manager role will be fulfilled).

Understanding is required of agile terminology such as project chartering, discovery phase, visioning, sprint zero and product roadmaps.

Agile suitability needs to be assessed by looking at what agile ways of working exist or need to exist, and what are their respective advantages and disadvantages (e.g. is co-locating the team a good idea or will it be too expensive and undermine the business case?)

Workshops are likely to be used to collaboratively create and understand deliverables.

Levels of uncertainty need to be explicitly stated as these may affect the choice of agile techniques such as the use of prototyping, spikes or experiments and the choice of how long to make timeboxes. Sometimes a project may be taking place in a very volatile context or where there are vague requirements. At other times the context could be more stable and there is less need for prototypes, spikes and experiments.

The level of formality will be decided with respect to such things as control, communication and planning (e.g. how will progress be tracked – on a wall or using a tool?).

If there are high levels of uncertainty then this phase is likely to be very short.

The impact of frequent releases should be assessed with respect to areas such as how quality will be managed and how the frequent delivery of products (or products in differing states) will take place (e.g. whether they will always go directly into operational use).

Table 17.1 shows PRINCE2 activities for start up and initiation and how they relate to agile artefacts and events (all product description references for PRINCE2 products are located in Appendix A).

Table 17.1 PRINCE2 Agile activities for start up and initiation

PRINCE2 activities and products	Applicable agile artefacts and events
● Appoint the executive and the project manager: 　● Create daily log, A.7	● Event(s): 　● **Project kick-off**
● Capture previous lessons: 　● Create lessons log, A.14	● Event(s): 　● (Previous) project/release retrospectives
● Design and appoint the project management team: 　● Update the daily log, A.7 　● Create project management team role descriptions 　● Create project management team structure	● Event(s): 　● Project kick-off
● Prepare the outline business case: 　● Create the outline business case, A.2 　● Create the project product description, A.21 　● Update the daily log, A.7	● Artefacts: 　● Vision ● Event(s): 　● Project kick-off
● Select the project approach and assemble the project brief: 　● Create/select the project approach 　● Create additional role descriptions 　● Assemble project brief, A.19 　● Update the daily log, A.7	● Artefacts: 　● Vision 　● Product backlog ● Event(s): 　● Project kick-off
● Plan the initiation stage: 　● Create the stage plan, A.16 　● Update the daily log, A.7	● No common equivalent
● Prepare the risk management strategy: 　● Create the risk management strategy, A.24 　● Create and populate the risk register, A.25	● Event(s): 　● Project kick-off
● Prepare the configuration management strategy: 　● Create the configuration management strategy, A.6 　● Create the initial configuration item records, A.5 　● Create and populate the issue register, A.12	● Event(s): 　● Project kick-off
● Prepare the quality management strategy: 　● Create the quality management strategy, A.22 　● Create the quality register, A.23	● Artefacts: 　● Vision 　● Definition of 'done' ● Event(s): 　● Project kick-off
● Prepare the communication management strategy: 　● Create the communication management strategy, A.4	● Event(s): 　● Project kick-off
● Set up project controls 　● Create project controls 　● Update role descriptions 　● Update project management team structure	● Artefact(s): 　● Information radiators ● Event(s): 　● Project kick-off 　● Release planning

Table continues

Table 17.1 continued

PRINCE2 activities and products	Applicable agile artefacts and events

● Create the project plan:
   ● Create the project plan, A.16
   ● Create product descriptions, A.17
   ● Create and update the configuration item records, A.5
   ● Update the project management team structure
   ● Update role descriptions
	● Artefacts:
	   ● Vision
	   ● Product backlog
	● Event(s):
	   ● Project kick-off
	   ● Release planning

● Refine the business case:
   ● Create the benefits review plan, A.1
   ● Create the detailed business case, A.2
	● Artefacts:
	   ● Vision
	   ● Product backlog
	   ● Release backlog
	● Event(s):
	   ● Project kick-off
	   ● Release planning

● Assemble the project initiation documentation:
   ● Assemble the project initiation documentation, A.20
	● Event(s):
	   ● Project kick-off

17.3.2 How to …

There are many behaviours, concepts, frameworks and techniques that are used in agile and referenced throughout this manual. Table 17.2 provides cross-references to some of the most relevant for use during Starting up a Project and Initiating a Project.

Table 17.2 Relevant agile guidance for Starting up a Project and Initiating a Project

	Chapter and section references
Define outcomes	Section 9.4
Use concepts from Lean Startup	Section 20.4.2
Identifying risks to the agile way of working with the Agilometer	Chapter 24
Use the project product description	Section 23.1, A.21
Define a business case in an agile context	Chapter 9
Know what is covered by sprint zero (iteration zero or (the) discovery (phase))	Section 9.2
Run workshops to kick off a project	Section 26.4.1
Assess different levels of uncertainty with Cynefin	Section 17.4.1
Use more informal communication channels	Chapter 26
Plan the frequency of releases	Chapter 27
Create and manage a product backlog	Sections 2.2, 25.6, Appendix H
Write a definition of 'done'	Section 11.4, Appendix H
Map agile roles to PRINCE2 roles and describe the considerations to take into account	Section 10.4
Communicate on a project using agile	Chapter 26
Plan and control a PRINCE2 project using agile	Chapters 12, 15
Tailor any of the PRINCE2 management products	Chapter 23

17.4 AGILE CONCEPTS AND TECHNIQUES

17.4.1 The Cynefin framework

The Cynefin framework (pronounced kuh-nev-in) was created by David Snowden. It is a decision-making framework that has been designed to help with understanding and determining what level of complexity exists in a given situation or environment.

In the context of PRINCE2 Agile this can be used to help understand the level of complexity facing a project or potential project.

17.4.1.1 The five domains

The Cynefin framework identifies five domains which describe the relationship between 'cause' and 'effect' of events and interactions, and therefore determines how complex an environment is. In simple terms, if *x* happens and results in *y*, what is the relationship between *x* and *y*? Is it to be expected and always happens, or could it be completely unexpected and in fact random?

The five relationships are identified as:

- **Obvious** Where the relationship is obvious and is usually addressed by 'best practice'
- **Complicated** Where some form of analysis or expertise is required to understand the relationship, which is usually addressed by 'good practice' where there may be several different options available
- **Complex** Where the relationship can only be understood in retrospect and is addressed by 'emergent practice' which may evolve to a new way of working
- **Chaotic** Where there is no apparent relationship, and any way of working is described as novel
- **Disorder** Where the relationship is unknown.

The Cynefin framework is shown in Figure 17.3. The central area of the figure represents the fifth domain of 'disorder'. The boundary between 'obvious' and 'chaotic' is, in fact, a 'cliff'. To transition between these two domains is regarded as potentially catastrophic, whereas transitioning across any of the other boundaries is not.

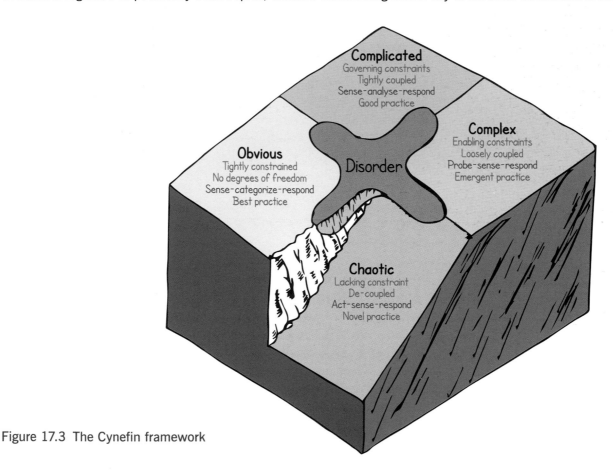

Figure 17.3 The Cynefin framework

17.4.1.2 When to use Cynefin and what to use it for

During Starting up a Project and Initiating a Project this framework can be used to understand (or attempt to understand), the complexity of a project. The framework can be used to analyse two areas:

- The level of complexity of the final product in terms of the output, outcome and benefits (e.g. whether it is highly innovative and there is little knowledge of how well it will sell)
- The level of complexity of the project environment in terms of such things as the levels of co-location, collaboration and experience (e.g. there are many teams involved from all around the world).

17.4.1.3 Assessing the level of complexity

Correctly assessing the level of complexity of the product and the project environment can help to determine the appropriate use of PRINCE2 and agile. It can be the case that certain areas of a project have different levels of complexity (e.g. the user interface of a control panel may be highly volatile and difficult to design, whereas the internal mechanics may be reasonably straightforward).

17.4.1.4 An example of a complex or chaotic situation

If the output from a project is a highly innovative children's toy that is very different from anything currently in the marketplace then approaches such as Lean Startup (where strong emphasis is placed on learning quickly) and techniques such as spiking and prototyping are likely to be appropriate at the delivery level.

Making the PRINCE2 processes as short as possible and using many stages may also be appropriate and the project could feel very much like an experiment, or a series of experiments.

17.4.1.5 An example of a complicated situation

As an alternative to the previous example, if the same organization was creating a new board game for adults and it had done this many times before, it may use four-weekly timeboxes to execute the delivery and may have very few stage boundaries.

In the second example it may even be the case that the level of complexity does not warrant the use of PRINCE2 and the work should be carried out as BAU.

The Cynefin framework should not be used as a categorization tool, as one of the principles behind it is that people have a natural tendency to categorize complexity according to their own experiences and preferences. A person who is used to working in the complicated domain may well have a tendency to approach a problem by analysing it, whereas a different person who is used to working in the complex domain may approach the same problem by running an experiment.

If the level of complexity is assessed collaboratively there is more likelihood that it will be correctly determined and PRINCE2 will be configured appropriately.

When a project is in progress it is possible that the level of complexity of the project, or the product, may change and migrate across the domain boundaries. PRINCE2 and the agile approaches being used may then need to be tuned (e.g. timebox durations may need to be shortened or lengthened; more customer demos may be required).

17.4.1.6 Evolving PRINCE2 in an agile context with Cynefin

The Cynefin framework can also be used to apply the learnings from a project to other projects and evolve the use of PRINCE2 and agile as a whole throughout an organization. A project framework may typically exist in the complicated domain ('good practice') but that is a matter of choice for an organization as it may be more beneficial to see it in the complex domain ('emergent practice'). One approach would be to assign different areas of the project framework to their most appropriate domain (e.g. some innovative agile techniques that may be unproven may be used when in the chaotic domain).

One specific area the Cynefin framework focuses on is the area of complacency which exists between the obvious and the chaotic domains (referred to earlier as the cliff). An example of this would be where the use of PRINCE2 Agile becomes robotic and routine through it being applied inappropriately and not being adapted to suit the environment or the level of uncertainty. Perhaps it has become stale as it only exists in the obvious domain and therefore does not change or evolve and is regarded as a simple thing to do. This can lead to what Cynefin describes as a crisis or catastrophe, where a sudden realization occurs that an approach is no longer fit for purpose (e.g. a major project disaster occurs because the underlying process is no longer appropriate).

17.4.1.7 Appropriateness

The Cynefin framework can help with how PRINCE2 is configured for projects of varying degrees of uncertainty. In a similar way to driving a car, there is a need to understand the prevailing conditions (e.g. it is snowing, it is dark – then drive in the most appropriate way by using the controls that are available).

17.5 SUMMARY

A distinguishing feature of PRINCE2 is that a project needs to be set up and started in a controlled and appropriate manner in order to increase the chance of project success.

Ideally when using PRINCE2 in an agile context the processes of Starting up a Project and Initiating a Project would involve lots of interaction between the relevant stakeholders. The use of workshops and the visual capture of key information to identify the benefits, outcomes and outputs for the project would be prevalent.

The use of agile would be appropriate to the environment and the level of uncertainty. Prioritized requirements would be clearly defined in measurable terms, not in too much detail and understood by all. Along with this a strategy for how the level of quality will be achieved and a plan for how the project will be executed will be created and agreed before delivery commences.

This will create the right conditions for a project so that it can be run as effectively as possible by starting at the right time when just enough information has been collected in order to appropriately authorize delivery to commence.

ACKNOWLEDGEMENTS AND FURTHER READING

Dave Snowden: http://cognitive-edge.com

18

Directing a Project

This chapter covers:

- PRINCE2 guidance on Directing a Project
- Agile ways of working that may already exist
- PRINCE2 Agile guidance on Directing a Project

155

18 Directing a Project

18.1 PRINCE2 GUIDANCE ON DIRECTING A PROJECT

The purpose of the Directing a Project process is to enable the project board to be accountable for the project's success by making key decisions and exercising overall control while delegating day-to-day management of the project to the project manager.

The objective of the Directing a Project process is to ensure that:

- There is authority to initiate the project
- There is authority to deliver the project's products
- Management direction and control are provided throughout the project's life, and that the project remains viable
- Corporate or programme management has an interface to the project
- There is authority to close the project
- Plans for realizing the post-project benefits are managed and reviewed.

The Directing a Project process starts on completion of the Starting up a Project process and is triggered by the request to initiate a project.

The Directing a Project process does not cover the day-to-day activities of the project manager, but the activities of those at the level of management above the project manager: that is, the project board. The project board manages by exception. It monitors via reports and controls through a small number of decision points. There should be no need for other 'progress meetings' for the project board. The project manager will inform the board of any exception situation. It is also important that levels of authority and decision-making processes are clearly identified.

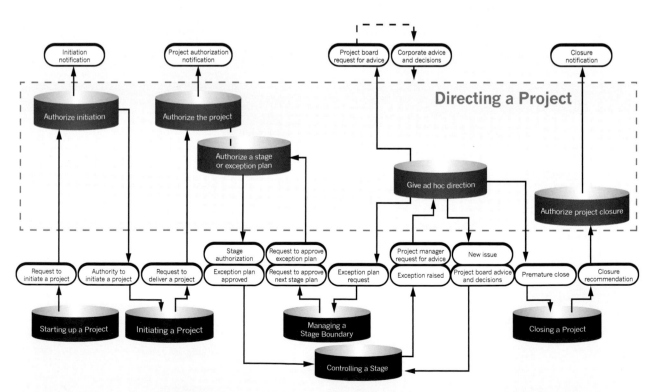

Figure 18.1 Overview of Directing a Project

There needs to be a two-way flow of information between the project board and corporate or programme management during the project. It is a key role of the project board to engage with corporate or programme management and to act as a communication channel. This need, and how it is to be satisfied, should be documented in the communication management strategy. .

The project board should provide unified direction and guidance to the project manager. If the project board is unable to provide a single view or if independent, possibly contradictory, advice is given, then the risk of project failure significantly increases. In such cases, the project manager should defer to the executive.

The project board is responsible for assuring that there is continued business justification. The Directing a Project process provides a mechanism for the project board to achieve such assurance without being overburdened by project activity.

One of the functions of the project board is to provide informal advice and guidance to the project manager as well as formal direction. The project manager should seek advice whenever necessary during the course of the project.

18.2 AGILE WAYS OF WORKING THAT MAY ALREADY EXIST

Agile usually sees steering and direction as the role of a product owner, although this depends on the number of teams involved and whether or not there is an 'overall' product owner. Alternatively this role could be carried out by the role of sponsor.

18.3 PRINCE2 AGILE GUIDANCE ON DIRECTING A PROJECT

Although it is essential to use this process it is vital to ensure that management by exception is operating effectively for the whole project management team as this creates an environment conducive to the agile way of working where people are empowered and self-organize.

In terms of progress reporting the project board should expect there to be more emphasis placed on the amount being delivered, and the information flows may be regular, rich and informal. The project board may even attend reviews.

Decision-making could be further enhanced by attending key demos.

Decision-making may be based more on information pulled from the project as opposed to formally reported.

Some, or most, of the benefits are likely to be enabled or delivered during the project.

Corporate and programme management should understand the rationale behind agile and how it delivers products and benefits.

18.3.1 How to ...

There are many behaviours, concepts, frameworks and techniques that are used in agile and referenced throughout this manual. Table 18.1 provides cross-references to some of the most relevant for use during Directing a Project.

Table 18.1 Relevant agile guidance for Directing a Project

	Chapter and section references
Use information radiators and pull information	Section 15.4.2
Be facilitative and collaborate	Sections 10.5.1, 26.4.1, 7.1
Empower the project manager and the teams	Section 7.2
Use tolerances when working in an agile way	Chapter 6
Communicate effectively	Chapter 26
Identify risks to the agile way of working with the Agilometer	Chapter 24
Assess value in relation to outputs and outcomes in an agile context	Section 9.4.1
Tailor any of the PRINCE2 management products	Chapter 23

18.4 SUMMARY

In PRINCE2 the project board is ultimately accountable for the ongoing viability of a project. It needs to provide direction and authorization as required.

In an agile context this needs to happen quickly and should take the form of empowering the project manager and the delivery teams so that information can be pulled; the use of transparency and collaborative interaction helps to ensure that the project remains viable and on target, and that any deviations to this can be detected quickly and responded to immediately.

19

Controlling a Stage

This chapter covers:

- PRINCE2 guidance on Controlling a Stage
- Agile ways of working that may already exist
- PRINCE2 Agile guidance on Controlling a Stage
- Agile concepts and techniques

19 Controlling a Stage

19.1 PRINCE2 GUIDANCE ON CONTROLLING A STAGE

The purpose of the Controlling a Stage process is to assign work to be done, monitor such work, deal with issues, report progress to the project board, and take corrective actions to ensure that the stage remains within tolerance.

The objective of the Controlling a Stage process is to ensure that:

- Attention is focused on delivery of the stage's products. Any movement away from the direction and products agreed at the start of the stage is monitored to avoid uncontrolled change ('scope creep') and loss of focus.
- Risks and issues are kept under control.
- The business case is kept under review.
- The agreed products for the stage are delivered to stated quality standards, within cost, effort and time agreed, and ultimately in support of the achievement of the defined benefits.
- The project management team is focused on delivery within the tolerances laid down.

The Controlling a Stage process describes the work of the project manager in handling the day-to-day management of the stage. This process will be used for each delivery stage of a project. Towards the end of each stage, except the final one, the activities within the Managing a Stage Boundary process will occur.

The Controlling a Stage process is normally first used after the project board authorizes the project, but it may optionally be used during the initiation stage for large or complex projects with a lengthy initiation.

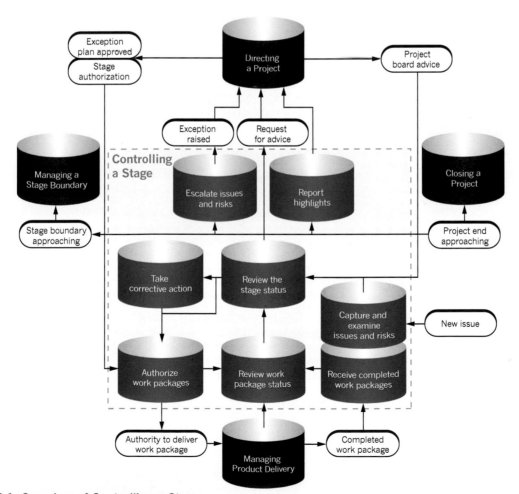

Figure 19.1 Overview of Controlling a Stage

Work packages are used to define and control the work to be done, and also to set tolerances for the team manager(s). In the case where the project manager is fulfilling the team manager role, work packages should still be used to define and control the work of the individual team members being assigned work. Where this is the case, references to team manager throughout the Controlling a Stage process should be regarded as references to the individual team member being assigned work.

Central to the ultimate success of the project is the day-to-day control of the work that is being conducted. Throughout a stage, this will consist of a cycle of:

● Authorizing work to be done
● Monitoring progress information about that work, including signing off completed work packages
● Reviewing the situation (including that for product quality) and triggering new work packages
● Reporting highlights
● Watching for, assessing and dealing with issues and risks
● Taking any necessary corrective action.

Towards the end of the last stage, the Closing a Project process will be invoked.

19.2 AGILE WAYS OF WORKING THAT MAY ALREADY EXIST

The nearest equivalent to a stage within agile would be a higher-level timebox that acts as a container for a set of lower-level timeboxes. This may be referred to using terms such as release, iteration or increment. These could involve more than one team and they would be typically managed by a project manager or product manager (the latter being at a higher level than a product owner).

It should be noted that a management stage is slightly different from such concepts as a release, iteration or increment in that it focuses on the commitment of resources and grants the project manager the authority to spend within the context of ongoing project viability. This is in contrast to a timebox such as a sprint or a release, which delivers a distinct set of features.

A concept known as a 'Scrum of Scrums' is sometimes used in agile when there are multiple teams and this provides a mechanism to move information between the teams. It provides an opportunity for Scrum masters to raise project-level issues and discuss inter-team dependencies. This does not conflict with the role of the PRINCE2 project manager as it is not a mechanism for control. It is more focused on ensuring transparency and collaboration across the related teams. However, a Scrum of Scrums meeting would not typically involve the project manager.

Scrum of Scrums is not part of the *Scrum Guide* and therefore the use of this technique and its role should be agreed collectively. Ultimately the project manager is responsible for the successful completion of the stage and should use this technique as appropriate in order to help with areas such as communication and coordination. The project manager has three alternatives with respect to Scrum of Scrums meetings:

● Doesn't use them
● Attends and facilitates the meetings
● Uses them but may or may not attend the meetings (and uses other sources of information to help with the management of the stage – for example, the use of information radiators and liaising with the delivery teams by other means such as informal discussions).

19.3 PRINCE2 AGILE GUIDANCE ON CONTROLLING A STAGE

19.3.1 The structure of a stage

● Stages are likely to be made up of timeboxes (e.g. one or more releases, containing one or more sprints), with the focus being on delivering sets of features ideally into operational use and therefore enabling their respective benefits.

19.3.2 Work assignment

- Planning, scheduling and estimating are likely to be carried out as a collaborative team-based exercise.

- At the delivery level team members typically select the next piece of work to be done based on the order decided by the customer SME (such as a product owner) who is in the delivery team. As a result, work is typically not assigned to specific team members.

- Work packages provide the flexibility (e.g. through tolerances) needed to enable teams to self-organize, and their sign-off may be informal. Reviews and demos at the end of a sprint or a release provide rich and regular feedback to the customer as a means to validate that the acceptance criteria for the agreed work package have been met.

- A work package may contain several timeboxes (e.g. in the form of sprints) and although each one will deliver something, they may not necessarily deliver something into operational use.

19.3.3 Monitoring progress and reporting

- Within agile environments, teams report progress to one another during the daily stand-up. The project manager or team managers may be invited to attend/assist stand-up meetings if appropriate, and/or facilitate stand-up meetings.

- Reporting of progress during a sprint within a release to which it belongs is typically done via information radiators.

- Reporting of progress at the end of a sprint or a release is done via the sprint or release review and the optional product demo, which provides the opportunity to discuss planned features which were not delivered or those that were but were not originally planned for the release.

- Monitoring and forecasting in general is more likely to be in an empirical style (based on evidence).

- Progress is more likely to be shown as a burn chart rather than a Gantt chart.

- Although PRINCE2 identifies six aspects of control the project manager will focus on flexing the scope and the quality criteria of the defined products. The details of these products may be held in the form of backlogs for the project as a whole, the stage, a release inside a stage or a sprint.

19.3.4 Risks and issues

- The daily stand-up provides the delivery team with the opportunity to identify issues. Issues may be referred to as blockers, impediments or smells by the delivery team. This approach ensures that issues are uncovered and escalated quickly to ensure that sprint and release goals are not compromised.

- Sprint and release retrospectives also provide an opportunity for risks and/or issues that may have been missed in the daily stand-ups or review sessions to be highlighted by the team.

- Risks and issues identified by the agile assessment need to be monitored regularly.

- During retrospective sessions teams are encouraged to select only those corrective actions that they can reasonably expect to be able to implement in the next sprint or release. This makes it more likely for the corrective action to be successful and to have the greatest positive effect for the team.

Table 19.1 shows PRINCE2 activities for Controlling a Stage and how they relate to agile artefacts and events (all product description references for PRINCE2 products are located in Appendix A).

Table 19.1 PRINCE2 Agile activities for Controlling a Stage

PRINCE2 activities and products	Applicable agile artefacts and events
● Authorize a work package: ● Create a work package, A.26 ● Create/update the configuration item record(s), A.5 ● Update the quality register, A.23 ● Update the risk register, A.25 ● Update the issue register, A.12 ● Review team plan, A.16 ● Update the stage plan, A.16	● Artefacts: ● Product backlog ● Release backlog ● Sprint backlog ● Event(s): ● Release planning ● Sprint planning
● Review work package status: (NB: A work package can contain one or more releases and one or more sprints) ● Review checkpoint report, A.3 ● Review team plan, A.16 ● Update stage plan, A.16 ● Update configuration item record(s), A.5 ● Update the risk register, A.25 ● Update the issue register, A.12	● Artefacts: ● Burn charts ● Sprint backlog (done/not done) ● Information radiators ● Event(s): ● Daily stand-ups ● Sprint reviews ● Release reviews
● Receive completed work packages: ● Confirm configuration item record(s), A.5 ● Update stage plan, A.16	● Artefacts: ● Potentially shippable product ● User story acceptance criteria ● Event(s): ● User acceptance (during a sprint demo or release demo) ● Sprint review ● Sprint demo ● Release review ● Release demo
● Review the stage status: ● Update the risk register, A.25 ● Update the issue register, A.12 ● Update the stage plan, A.16 ● Update the lessons log, A.14 ● Create/update the issue report, A.13	● Artefacts: ● Burn charts ● Sprint backlog (done/not done) ● Information radiators ● Event(s): ● Daily stand-ups ● Sprint reviews ● Release reviews
● Report highlights: ● Create highlight report, A.11	● Artefacts: ● Burn charts ● Information radiators ● Event(s): ● Sprint demos ● Sprint reviews ● Release demos ● Release reviews

PRINCE2 activities and products	Applicable agile artefacts and events
● Capture and examine issues and risks: 　◦ Update the daily log, A.7 　◦ Create issue report, A.13 　◦ Update issue register, A.12 　◦ Update risk register, A.25	● Artefacts: 　◦ Impediments from daily stand-ups 　◦ Information radiators ● Event(s): 　◦ Daily stand-ups 　◦ Sprint planning 　◦ Sprint reviews 　◦ Sprint retrospectives 　◦ Release planning 　◦ Release reviews 　◦ Release retrospectives
● Escalate issues and risks: 　◦ Create exception report, A.10 　◦ Update issue register, A.12 　◦ Update risk register, A.25 　◦ Update issue report, A.13	● Artefacts: 　◦ Impediments from daily stand-ups 　◦ Outputs or decisions from a retrospective, sprint review or release review
● Take corrective action: 　◦ Update issue register, A.12 　◦ Update risk register, A.25 　◦ Update issue report, A.13 　◦ Update stage plan, A.16 　◦ Update configuration item records, A.5 　◦ Update daily log, A.7	● Artefacts: 　◦ Daily impediments 　◦ Sprint backlog 　◦ Release backlog

19.3.5 How to …

There are many behaviours, concepts, frameworks and techniques that are used in agile and referenced throughout this manual. Table 19.2 provides cross-references to some of the most relevant for use during Controlling a Stage.

Table 19.2 Relevant agile guidance for Controlling a Stage

	Chapter and section references
Plan stages, release and sprints	Chapters 12, 27, Appendix H
Understand the benefits of transparency, collaboration and self-organization	Section 7.4
Estimate	Section 12.4.1
Create a work package	Section 20.3.1
Use tolerances	Chapter 6
Carry out stand-ups, Scrum meetings and sprint reviews	Appendix H
Use information radiators	Section 15.4.2
Use burn charts	Section 15.4.1
Carry out retrospectives	Section 19.4.1
Tailor any of the PRINCE2 management products	Chapter 23

19.4 AGILE CONCEPTS AND TECHNIQUES

19.4.1 Retrospectives

The retrospective is a very common technique and is used regularly when working in an agile way. It involves looking back and reflecting on how things went in terms of how a team worked, in order to make improvements to how they work going forward. A retrospective is a type of review that specifically looks at the way of working as opposed to looking at what was produced (e.g. sprint review).

> **Tip**
>
> Retrospectives include or are similar to continual improvement, Kaizen, inspect and adapt.

19.4.1.1 The basics

The role of retrospectives is extremely important. It could be said that this is as significant as any concept, technique or behaviour in agile. It is central to learning lessons and can be part of any continual improvement process. Therefore, not only do retrospectives need to be carried out, but they need to be carried out well.

The most important point to understand about retrospectives, and running them well, is that they must be planned, structured and facilitated. If they are run as an unstructured meeting, they can become ineffective and they may also become a chore. How to run a retrospective is decided by the team, so it may become quite informal; however this does not imply any lack of structure.

> **Tip**
>
> PRINCE2 uses the term 'review' for a specific purpose (i.e. when using the quality review technique) whereas it is used frequently in many forms when using agile.

Not only do retrospectives need to be planned, but they also need to be adapted to keep the participants stimulated. Retrospectives are only as good as the contributions made by the people who take part.

19.4.1.2 Further information

The first step in all PRINCE2 processes is to take the learnings from previous projects or stages. A retrospective can last any length of time but it is usually proportionate to the duration of activity that is being reviewed. A retrospective for a two-week sprint may take two hours, whereas a retrospective of a six-month project may take a whole day. In effect a retrospective is a mini-workshop. Section 26.4.1 describes how powerful workshops can be; all of the tools, techniques and considerations involved in workshops can also be used by retrospectives. Examples would be the choice of tool or technique, how to manage conflict, laying out the room etc.

A lot of guidance exists on how to run a retrospective and it closely aligns with how to run or facilitate a workshop. Section 26.4.1 refers to the five preparation steps needed to run a successful workshop and the same steps apply to a retrospective. There are many suggested formats and many tools and techniques available. A retrospective would have a similar structure to the following:

● **Objective** This could be very specific to a certain area or more broadly based
● **Attendees** Usually this would just be the team and all of them should be present
● **Agenda** Needs to be adjusted to suit the situation (see section 19.4.1.3)
● **Logistics** The same as for any workshop (e.g. layout, materials, refreshments)
● **Pre-reading** Distributing key information and results in advance can result in a faster start to the retrospective and therefore it takes less time.

19.4.1.3 Agenda

Many techniques exist to capture lessons (or 'learnings') but typically a retrospective will involve an agenda with the following steps in some form:

● Agreeing the objective, agenda and any house rules
● Reflecting on what has happened in terms of actual results and measures (e.g. 42 story points were delivered, 7 defects were found)
● Generating views on what went well and what didn't go so well
● Actions on what to do next time, who is responsible for each one and when they are due to be completed
● Close.

19.4.1.4 Hints that may prove useful

Including someone from project support in a retrospective could be useful to capture the lessons in order to transfer the learnings across projects and the organization as a whole. The team would need to be comfortable with this, as they may prefer to pass on their findings after the retrospective.

Occasionally, key documents and artefacts could be specifically reviewed (e.g. the definition of 'done' or working agreements).

It is often a good idea to ensure that only a few changes to the process are suggested at each retrospective, as opposed to working on too many improvements at the same time. In other words it is better to produce two actions from a retrospective that are actioned, because the work involved is easy for the team to take on, as opposed to ten actions which can psychologically seem like too much extra work for a team, and therefore

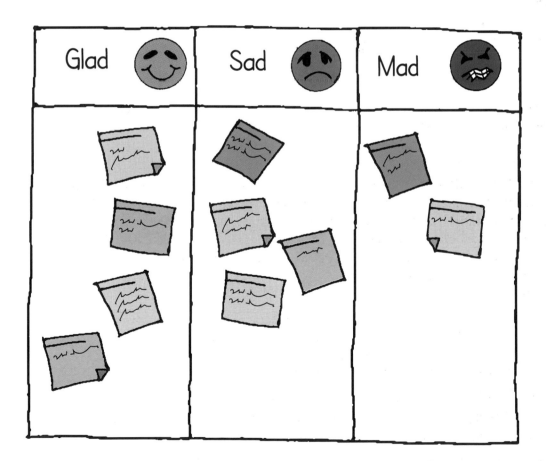

Figure 19.2 A Glad! Sad! Mad! board

Definition: Glad! Sad! Mad!

This is a feedback technique that can be used by a team in a retrospective. Each team member writes one or more sticky notes and puts them into the appropriate column. This lets everyone else know what made them 'glad' during the last timebox, what made them 'sad' and what even made them 'mad' (see Figure 19.2)!

not worth starting. Feedback can be prioritized using a simple classification system of 'high, medium and low' or by plotting the feedback on an impact/effort grid (which contains two axes that show the effect of the change and the amount of work involved in it).

A final step in a retrospective could be to reflect on how well the retrospective process worked. Put another way it would be a retrospective retrospective!

Even if a team has become very good at doing retrospectives in a certain way, it can be worth introducing new techniques to keep people's creativity fresh.

Introducing an independent facilitator can be very effective. If the group does not choose this option then the person leading the retrospective should still be facilitative.

To introduce some variety to retrospectives it may be worth using some of them to look for improvements on specific areas of the process, whereas other retrospectives may have no specific area of focus.

Involving the people who use the process in improving the process ensures that there is buy-in to any changes, and that any change is permanent.

Kanban would refer to retrospectives as service delivery reviews at a team level, and operations reviews at a higher level, but they can be run in the same style or similar.

During a retrospective, feedback usually comes in two forms: facts and feelings. Sometimes it is beneficial to separate feedback when it covers both of these (e.g. having separate steps in the agenda). Facts are usually objective and measurable, such as 'the customer was not available during week two'. Feelings are usually subjective and harder to quantify, such as 'I felt let down by the release team as they promised me they would be ready'. It is the latter that is more likely to cause emotional responses and possibly conflict during a retrospective.

19.4.1.5 Learn gradually

Identifying lessons and learning from them are two different matters. This is why a retrospective needs to carefully draw out the learnings from a group, analyse them and then distil them into decisions and actions that ensure the continual improvement of the process and the way the team works. This can then be recorded in the lessons log.

The best way to improve how a team works is little by little, and little and often. This applies to a sprint, a release, a stage or the whole project.

19.5 SUMMARY

A project manager controlling a project by stages is an important concept in PRINCE2 as it is part of management by exception and helps to ensure the ongoing viability of a project.

When using PRINCE2 in an agile environment the project manager should empower the delivery teams to deliver in the best way possible, by being collaborative with work assignment that is based around features and making full use of visual communication channels. Further to this, the use of regular reviews and retrospectives along with setting the appropriate tolerances creates an environment where creativity and responding to change exist in order to best address the customer's needs.

ACKNOWLEDGEMENTS AND FURTHER READING

Esther Derby and Giana Larsen (2006). *Agile Retrospectives: Making Good Teams Great*. Pragmatic Bookshelf.

Norman Kerth (2001). *Project Retrospectives: A Handbook for Team Reviews*. Dorset House Publishing.

Agile retrospective resource wiki: http://retrospectivewiki.org

20

Managing Product Delivery

This chapter covers:

- PRINCE2 guidance on Managing Product Delivery

- Agile ways of working that may already exist

- PRINCE2 Agile guidance on Managing Product Delivery

- Agile concepts and techniques

20 Managing Product Delivery

20.1 PRINCE2 GUIDANCE ON MANAGING PRODUCT DELIVERY

The purpose of the Managing Product Delivery process is to control the link between the project manager and the team manager(s), by placing requirements on accepting, executing and delivering project work.

The role of the team manager(s) is to coordinate an area of work that will deliver one or more of the project's products. They can be internal or external to the customer's organization.

Managing Product Delivery views the project from the team manager's perspective, while the Controlling a Stage process views it from the project manager's perspective.

The team manager ensures that products are created and delivered by the team to the project by:

● Accepting and checking authorized work packages from the project manager.

● Ensuring that interfaces identified in the work package are maintained.

● Ensuring that a team plan is created for the work packages being assigned (this may be done in parallel with the project manager creating the stage plan for the management stage).

● Ensuring that the products are developed in accordance with any development method(s) specified in the work package.

● Demonstrating that each product meets its quality criteria through the quality method(s) specified in the product description – this may include using the PRINCE2 **quality review technique**.

● Obtaining approval for completed products from the authorities identified in the product description.

● Delivering the products to the project manager in accordance with any procedures specified in the work package.

If the project uses external suppliers that are not using PRINCE2, Managing Product Delivery provides a statement of the required interface between the team manager and the PRINCE2 method being used in the project by the project manager. The work package may be part of a contractual agreement. Therefore, the formality of a team plan could vary from simply appending a schedule to the work package, to creating a fully formed plan that is presented in a similar style to a stage plan.

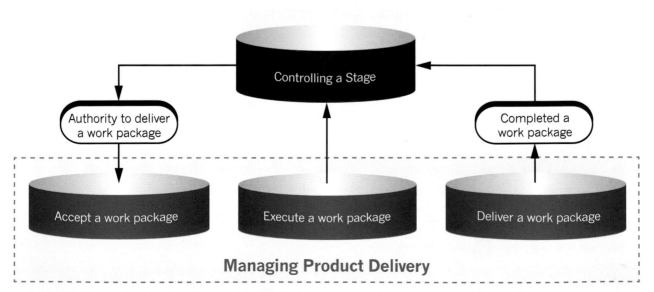

Figure 20.1 Overview of Managing Product Delivery

20.2 AGILE WAYS OF WORKING THAT MAY ALREADY EXIST

The agile way of working focuses very strongly on product delivery and the 'management' of product delivery. There is an abundance of agile concepts, behaviours and techniques that have been created for these, but it should be understood that these are two distinct things.

Approaches such as Scrum focus solely on Managing Product Delivery. However, with Scrum, it is easy to confuse 'Managing Product Delivery' with just 'product delivery'. According to the *Scrum Guide*, Scrum does not contain any engineering or delivery practices so it could be said to 'manage' product delivery as opposed to 'do' product delivery. Equally some agile approaches could be said to be solely delivery practices (such as XP in the software/IT domain) as they have very little that could be described as management practices.

Care needs to be taken to identify agile concepts, behaviours and techniques correctly in terms of what function they perform. Are they delivery practices (sometimes referred to as development or engineering practices) that create products and sub-products, or do they exist at a level above this where they help to organize and control the delivery work? It is possible that they could be doing both.

20.3 PRINCE2 AGILE GUIDANCE FOR MANAGING PRODUCT DELIVERY

When combining PRINCE2 with agile, the Managing Product Delivery process and the use of work packages needs to be seen as a vital interface and linking process. It is the glue that joins together project management (where PRINCE2 provides lots of guidance) with product delivery (where agile provides lots of guidance).

It could be said that this process is more to do with 'managing the interface' between project management and product delivery, as opposed to 'Managing Product Delivery'. The management of one specific work package (and the product or products contained within it) still needs to be carried out, but this is the responsibility of the team manager at the team level inside the agile team.

20.3.1 Work package definition

It is the definition of the work package that is at the heart of this interface. Therefore it needs to blend the complementary styles of PRINCE2 and agile. Blending this will vary according to the project environment, but the main guidance when defining a work package is:

● It should be collaboratively defined by the project manager and the team manager (and the team), perhaps with agreement that there is visibility of both the team plans and the stage plans that they form part of; (this may take place as part of a sprint planning or release planning meeting).

● The formality of reporting arrangements should be agreed (e.g. low-tech burn charts). Checkpoint reports may be done verbally or as a group. Perhaps the same information could be pulled from information on display, or the project manager could attend sprint demos.

● Tolerance with respect to scope and quality could be defined in the work package (as well as in the product description(s)).

● The product description(s) contained in the work package may be defined at a level that clearly describes what the team needs to deliver, whilst at the same time not being too detailed to restrict the team and how they create those products.

● Guidance on the use of appropriate agile behaviours, concepts and techniques may be appropriate if the delivery team would find benefit from this.

● Indicating the level of (internal or external) uncertainty relating to the work package would provide the delivery team with an indication of the levels of risk involved so that they could plan their approach to the work accordingly (e.g. this work package may be classed as complex and it is suggested that a lot of prototyping may be beneficial in this instance).

● Agreement on what the work package may release (if anything) and the preferred size of the timeboxes involved – if there might be more than one.

● Agreement that the team plan will evolve, as it may be based on the self-allocation of work and because empirical forecasting is being used.

- Guidance on the appropriate quality-checking techniques (e.g. using techniques the team is comfortable with or identifying certain reviews that the PRINCE2 quality review technique could be used for).
- Guidance on the impact on external stakeholders (such as operations or the training department) with respect to how the frequent releases may need their involvement.

In some ways the work package is like a handshake, and if this partnership is built correctly it brings the benefits of control in a project environment, whilst at the same time allowing the delivery teams enough room to negotiate the uncertainties they will meet when working at the detailed level.

This process and the use of work packages may not result in significant changes in how agile teams work, but they do need to understand the role they play in a wider PRINCE2 context and also that they need to provide information in the form of reports (e.g. checkpoint reports) and logs (e.g. the quality register) in a timely manner to the project manager to enable the project manager to carry out their duties effectively.

Table 20.1 shows PRINCE2 activities for Managing Product Delivery and how they relate to agile artefacts and events (all product description references for PRINCE2 products are located in Appendix A).

Table 20.1 PRINCE2 Agile activities for Managing Product Delivery

PRINCE2 activities and products	Applicable agile artefacts and events

Accept a work package:
  ○ Create team plan, A.16
  ○ Raise risks against the team plan, A.16
  ○ Update the quality register, A.23
  ○ Approve a work package, A.26
	● Artefacts:
	  ○ Release backlog
	  ○ Sprint backlog
	● Event(s):
	  ○ Release planning
	  ○ Sprint planning

Execute a work package:
  ○ Create specialist products
  ○ Update the quality register, A.23
  ○ Update the configuration item records, A.5
  ○ Update team plan
  ○ Create checkpoint report, A.3
  ○ Raise issues
  ○ Raise risks
  ○ Obtain approval records
	● Artefacts:
	  ○ Sprint backlog (done/not done)
	  ○ Information radiators, burn charts
	  ○ Impediments
	● Event(s):
	  ○ Daily stand-ups

Deliver a work package:
  ○ Update a work package, A.26
  ○ Update team plan
	● Artefacts:
	  ○ Release backlog (done/not done)
	  ○ Sprint backlog (done/not done)
	  ○ Potentially shippable increment
	● Event(s):
	  ○ Sprint review
	  ○ Release review

20.3.2 How to …

There are many behaviours, concepts, frameworks and techniques that are used in agile and referenced throughout this manual. Table 20.2 provides cross-references to some of the most relevant for use during Managing Product Delivery.

Table 20.2 Relevant agile guidance for Managing Product Delivery

	Chapter and section references
Plan releases and sprints	Chapters 12, 27, Appendix H
Planning based around features	Section 25.4, Chapter 27
Using tolerances for scope, quality criteria and work packages	Chapter 6, section 23.1
Define quality criteria and acceptance criteria	Chapter 25
Track progress	Chapter 15
Choose the quality method for a work package	Sections 11.3, 23.1
Use Scrum to help with product delivery	Appendix H
Use Kanban to help with product delivery	Section 20.4.1
Tailor any of the PRINCE2 management products	Chapter 23

20.4 AGILE CONCEPTS AND TECHNIQUES

20.4.1 Kanban and the Kanban method

Kanban is a term that covers the use of **Kanban system**s, which are visual management systems that limit the number of work items in circulation. This creates what is known as a '**pull system**'. Kanban systems exist in a wide variety of forms, and in the late 1940s Taiichi Ohno employed a system of signal cards to deliver the just-in-time element of the Toyota production system. More recently, Kanban boards (see Figure 20.2) have become commonplace when working in an agile way.

As at Toyota, Kanban is usually applied not only to improve flow in the short term but also to create long-lasting and ongoing change to the underlying processes of the organization. With that in mind, David J. Anderson's book, *Kanban – Successful Evolutionary Change for your Technology Business*, documented the principles and practices of the **Kanban method**, to provide a radical new approach to change management. A strong community has grown around the method, and Kanban in general, and both continue to develop with this evolutionary message at heart.

20.4.1.1 Applicability

The first of the Kanban method's foundational principles is 'Start with what you do now'. This means that Kanban should not be regarded as an alternative either to PRINCE2 or to any agile framework. It is better to see it as a way to increase agility through improved day-to-day decision-making (the result of increased transparency), the deferral of commitment (the result of controls on work in progress), and the reduced lead times and increased opportunity for feedback that follow.

Definition: Work in progress (WIP)
Work that has been started but not delivered from the system or timebox.

Kanban becomes applicable with the establishment of a reasonably repeatable workflow. In a PRINCE2 context using agile, this is likely to be found after the project initiation document has been approved and there are discrete work items that can be pulled into a Kanban system. The use of Kanban may then continue after the project's products have been delivered into operational use – a transition that Kanban can help to facilitate.

Tip
AXELOS's ITIL suite of guidance covers all aspects of service management. See 'About AXELOS' at the front of this publication for a list of other AXELOS products.

When using any Kanban concept with PRINCE2 and agile it must be remembered at all times that this is in a project context. Many Kanban examples relate to solving wider organizational problems or typical BAU scenarios such as restructuring a service desk. Within a PRINCE2 context many of the Kanban concepts help to create a more agile environment for PRINCE2, particularly with respect to timeboxes of any length, but this does not mean to say that Kanban is being used to run the project.

20.4.1.2 The basics

The Kanban method is made up of six core practices.

Visualize

By making work visible, teams can easily see how work is progressing, what has been done, what is still to do and what problems exist that are hindering progress. For more information on the benefits of visualization, see section 15.4.2. How the work is physically displayed can vary but it is often a simple grid (or 'ticket', see Figure 20.3) primarily showing the different states a work item passes through and information that will help with prioritization and scheduling (e.g. recording risks associated with the work). The information is usually recorded on cards or sticky notes that are typically updated throughout the day.

> ### Definition: Class of service
> A broadly defined category for different types of work. The classes influence selection decisions in that different classes of service are typically associated with qualitatively different risk profiles, especially with regard to schedule risk and the cost of delay.
> Four generic classes of service are widely recognized: 'standard', 'fixed date', 'expedite' and 'intangible'.

'Swim lanes' can be added to identify similar types of work or 'classes of service'. These would be horizontal rows going across the vertical columns.

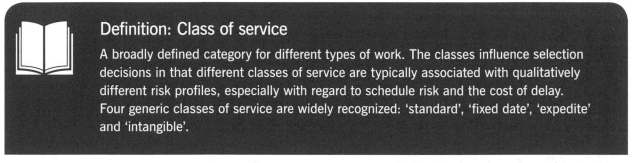

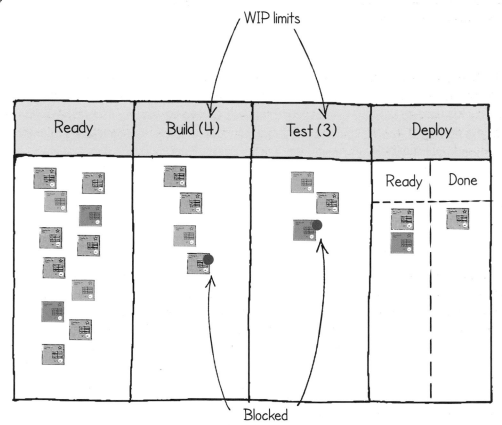

Figure 20.2 An example of how a Kanban board might look

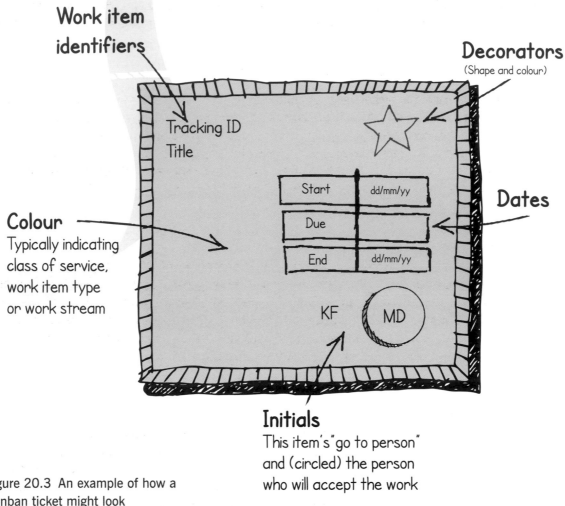

Figure 20.3 An example of how a Kanban ticket might look

A ticket can exist in many forms such as the example shown in Figure 20.3.

Limit 'work in progress' (WIP)

Although this is a fundamental concept in Kanban it appears counterintuitive to many who would be forgiven for thinking that it may slow work down. It is important to understand the reasoning behind limiting WIP as it triggers many events and solves several problems, as illustrated by the following two analogies:

● **Reducing the pressure** Introducing reduced speed limits on motorways and highways speeds up the flow of traffic at busy times

● **Reducing task-switching** Writing a document takes much longer (in terms of actual writing time) if the author is receiving email notifications through a desktop alert, or similar, at the same time. Each email notification breaks the concentration and the current thought processes which then have to be 'reloaded' and restarted.

The actual **WIP limit** is usually shown as a number at the top of a column on the Kanban board, and this denotes the maximum number of sticky notes or cards that are allowed to be present in that column at any one time.

The use of WIP limits underpins the 'pull' system which characterizes the way Kanban avoids scheduling work at specific times (referred to as a '**push system**') and instead pulls work from upstream, when the capacity exists to work on it.

Furthermore, limiting WIP reduces the impact of task-switching and multi-tasking. If a team or individual is working on several things at once, a lot of productive time is wasted when changing between them.

WIP limits effectively produce the visual signals that indicate that work can safely be pulled into a place that has the capacity to deal with it effectively. Conversely, the team can respond when the system appears to be at risk of being overloaded.

Manage the flow

A Kanban system aims to achieve the highest level of performance from the existing way of working in order to deliver something of value as quickly as possible. Therefore the team is constantly looking at ways to maximize flow efficiency and minimize delays (e.g. by removing obstacles). Kanban highlights problems that the team needs to solve. This is a constant team exercise where the objective is to remove waste as quickly as possible. The Kanban board visualizes the work moving through the system and acts like a dashboard which enables the team to see blockers and areas where the flow is not smooth. They can then take immediate remedial action.

Making policies explicit

Even though empowerment, self-organization and trust play a significant role in agile, there still need to be clearly defined boundaries that teams operate within. In the same way as management by exception enables empowerment and autonomy, a team needs to clearly define how it works and make these policies transparent. These could be described as 'rules' and they create an environment that is more objective for decision-making and where scrutiny may be required. Policies (similar to 'working practices' in section 15.4.2) should evolve and be built up collaboratively over time to create a set of guidelines that then become the team norm.

Implement feedback loops

Ultimately, the value being delivered by any process (e.g. a project or a timebox) is judged by the final consumer such as the end customer. Being able to quantitatively assess this is very advantageous as it will directly affect what will subsequently be delivered. Typically there is a long time between a team adding a feature to the to-do list and the team receiving quantitative feedback from the feature being used. Constantly aiming to shorten this feedback loop so that the most valuable work is in the Kanban system is essential in order to deliver the most value (see also section 14.4.1).

The Kanban method contains four types of review to gather feedback (the stand-up meeting, the service delivery review, the operations review and the risk review). The stand-up meeting and the service delivery review can be used within a project context to check what is happening against what was forecast (e.g. for a timebox). Following this, policies can be adjusted as necessary. A risk review can be run at any time to see if there is a pattern to the types of risk that are being identified. The operations review would apply at a higher level than a project (e.g. programme level).

Improve collaboratively, evolve experimentally

The Kanban method embraces the idea that improvement is a collaborative exercise. Its transparency and the ease by which the Kanban system (and thereby the underlying process) can be modified creates the natural conditions for collaborative improvement to occur. The method builds on these advantages in its promotion of experimental improvement.

From observation of the system in action and the capture of key metrics such as lead times and delivery rates, the team is able to form hypotheses of what may be holding the system back and then agree to changes that can be tested experimentally in a **safe-to-fail** manner.

Definition: Safe-to-fail
A safe-to-fail experiment is one that is designed to have only limited impact on the system or the plan in the event of failure.

This practice implies a significant cultural shift for many – it embraces the concept of Kaizen from Toyota's culture – i.e. 'Process improvement is everyone's business every day!' There aren't any process engineers prescribed in Kanban, the point being that everyone focuses on managing the outcome of their process. They see anything that impacts on capability or performance as an issue they themselves need to solve, and not something to delegate to someone else to sort out.

20.4.1.3 Further information

Scrumban

Scrum and Kanban are two of the most popular agile approaches and yet many people get confused regarding the differences between them. They are similar in that they both focus strongly on process improvement, transparency and empiricism. Yet they are different in that Scrum has specific roles, the work is timeboxed and it relates to a specific product; whereas there are no defined roles in Kanban, work is pulled to create a flow and the work may relate to anything.

The very simple structure of Kanban and the fact that it can be applied to any process means that you can apply Kanban to a Scrum environment, although the opposite is not the case. This has led to the creation of a concept known as 'Scrumban' – the application of Kanban where the underlying process (the 'what you do now') is based on Scrum. In its most limited form this may simply involve the use of Kanban systems to manage the work of the sprint. It is more powerful (and increasingly typical) to apply Kanban to a broader workflow that starts upstream of the build process and ends with customer delivery or even post-deployment validation (e.g. using Kanban at a programme or portfolio level).

Work item size and similarity

Kanban systems are able to deal with multiple types of work and/or classes of service. These are typically indicated as tickets of different colour or by organizing the board into horizontal swim lanes. Within such a category, flow will be more predictable if work items are within the same order of magnitude in size, complexity or risk. This is often achieved by policies on work item size, adjusted where necessary for risk. Over time, teams tend to get less tolerant of larger work items as they learn to recognize their disproportionate risk and develop the skills to identify and deliver value in smaller work items.

Experiments

When a team looks to improve how the system works in order to achieve the delivery of more value to the customer, it should do so in a controlled and objective way. There is a lot of data that can be measured and therefore any suggested changes to the way a team is working can be validated quantitatively, empirically and not subjectively. The Kanban method recommends using the 'scientific method' to achieve this. The scientific method is a technique for improving understanding and knowledge by going through a process of several steps such as:

● Ask a question
● Carry out research
● Create a hypothesis
● Carry out experiments
● Analyse the results
● Draw a conclusion.

Cumulative flow diagrams

A common technique used in Kanban is to track work items on a cumulative flow diagram (CFD). This shows the amount of work in each column on a daily basis (see Figure 20.4).

Column counts

Cumulative flow diagram (CFD)

Day	Ready	Build	Test	Ready to deploy	Deployed
8	2	4	4	1	0
9	4	5	3	0	3
10	3	3	5	1	3
11	2	3	4	3	3
12	4	3	4	0	8
13	3	2	5	1	8
14	7	2	4	3	8
15	7	2	4	0	13
16	7	2	5	0	13
17	5	3	5	0	14
18	5	3	4	0	15
19	4	2	5	0	16
20	3	2	3	0	19
21	3	1	1	0	22

■ Ready
■ Build
■ Test
■ Ready to deploy
■ Deployed

Figure 20.4 A cumulative flow diagram

The spreadsheet on the left shows how many work items are in each area of the system and this is represented on the CFD. Reading the spreadsheet from right to left helps when transposing the data vertically onto the CFD (e.g. on day 15, 13 items had been deployed, none were ready to deploy, 4 were in test etc.).

Put more simply, WIP is therefore the vertical difference between the line showing work that is ready and the line showing what has been deployed in Figures 20.4 and 20.5, whereas lead (or cycle) time is the difference horizontally between the two, as shown in Figure 20.5.

Definition: Lead time/cycle time

These two terms are interpreted differently by many in the Kanban community (some see them as representing different things) but in simple terms they refer to how long a work item takes to go through the system or timebox. So although they are often interpreted differently, they are, in effect, the same thing.

Hints that may prove useful

Further to the comments made regarding applicability earlier in this chapter it is important to see Kanban for what it is, and what it offers, and then apply it in a project context in the most appropriate way. A two-week sprint could be planned (to a degree) in advance with a finite amount of work as per Scrum. Alternatively, the sprint could be unplanned (to a degree) and work could be pulled from a list when necessary as per Kanban. The choice will depend on several factors such as the needs of any particular situation, the agile maturity of the team or the preferred working style of the team. It may be appropriate to not use sprints at all and run a three-month stage just using a Kanban system.

If work items in a Kanban system are different in size by a significant order of magnitude, such as when comparing a day to a week, or a week to a month, it may be appropriate to use separate swim lanes for these, as these could represent different 'classes of service'.

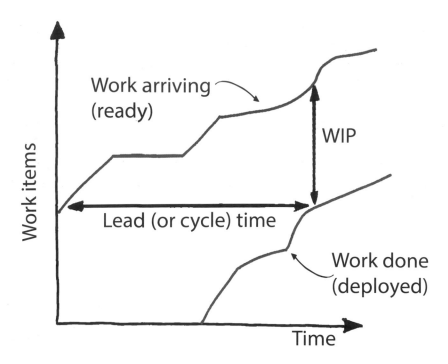

Figure 20.5 A simple view of how to calculate WIP and lead (or cycle) time

Improving flow and delivering value as early as possible (and as much of it as possible) is very much in keeping with the thinking behind flexing what is being delivered. Kanban aims for timeliness and reducing the impact of 'cost of delay' (see Figure 20.6) which can be considerable in many organizations: it is often intangible, as it is not measured. The significance of 'cost of delay' in a project context using agile is that there is a drive to deliver value as early as possible in some form during the project (e.g. a set of features) and a desire that the final product is not ultimately delayed (e.g. by reducing some of what was intended to be delivered).

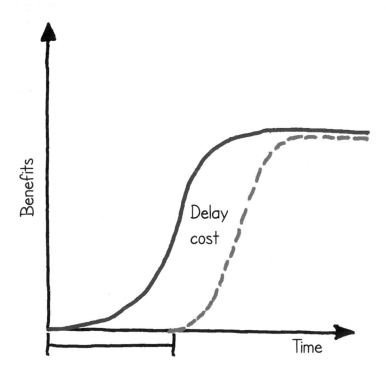

Figure 20.6 The effect of delaying the delivery of a product

If Kanban is being introduced for the first time to a team or it is being used in a specific way for the first time (e.g. it has already been used for stages but not sprints) then Kanban needs to be implemented carefully and gradually. Wholesale changes to existing processes and working practices (i.e. those used for the previous stages or sprints) should be avoided and the team need to agree to gradually change from where they are now and do it collaboratively.

When using Kanban you should always have WIP limits. If you are not using WIP limits then you may still find the use of a Kanban board useful but this would not represent a Kanban system per se.

Take care when someone mentions that they are using Kanban, because quite often all they are using is a Kanban board. Although this is still beneficial, it is the collective power of all of the Kanban practices that enables it to work at its full potential.

Definition: Little's Law

$L = \lambda.W$

In simple terms – the average number of items in a system: L is equal to the average arrival rate, λ, multiplied by the average time an item spends in the system, W (assuming that this is over a long enough period of time and the system is stable).

Little's Law is part of the queueing theory body of knowledge and an adjusted version of it is used to understand the flow of work through a Kanban system. If the nature of the variety of work and the dynamics of the Kanban system remain unchanged in the near future, then data from the recent past can be used to forecast the capability and performance of the Kanban system. This is the primary method of forecasting used in project management when using a Kanban system.

The origin of the term

The word 'Kanban' is used in both Japanese and Chinese, though with different meanings. In Japanese it roughly equates to a 'signal card' or 'sign/visual board'. It is used in inventory control to signal that a particular level of stock has been reached meaning new stock needs to be ordered or pulled from a supplier. It is a physical card or token (see Figure 20.7). In Chinese, it means 'looking at the board'. In Figure 20.7, stock is being taken from the front of the box.

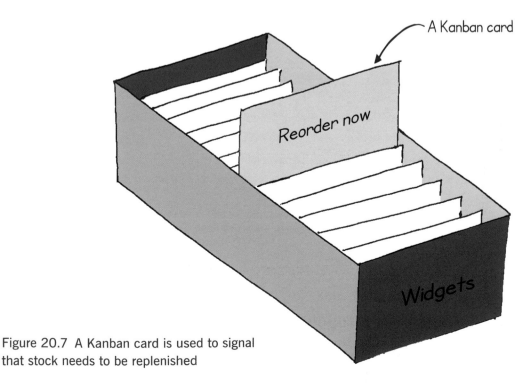

Figure 20.7 A Kanban card is used to signal that stock needs to be replenished

20.4.2 The Lean Startup method

A popular agile publication is *The Lean Startup* by Eric Ries. Lean Startup is a method to grow new businesses, and develop existing ones, through product innovation in uncertain markets. There are many ideas and concepts that can be taken from it that add value when combining PRINCE2 with agile.

The core concepts of Lean Startup that apply to PRINCE2 are:

● Build, measure, learn
● Create a minimum viable product (MVP)
● Fail fast
● **Validated learning**.

Drawing on an approach to developing businesses may not seem to be an obvious parallel to running a project, or even a timebox, but the way that Lean Startup works is to create a simple approach that can be applied to any situation where uncertainty exists, such as a project.

Lean Startup can be used in part or in whole as a source of techniques because it is like PRINCE2 and agile in that it is product-focused and responsive to change.

Time is of the essence nowadays and the customer wants 'as much as they can get in as short a time as possible'. They don't want 'it all in the fullness of time'. A lot of start-up companies are using new technologies, and the pace of change in this area is so fast that they have to use a different management approach, and that approach needs to be an agile one based on the early delivery of value (sometimes this being in the form of 'learnings').

20.4.2.1 Uncertainty still needs to be managed

Lean Startup and PRINCE2 both see the need for a managed process even though Lean Startup is geared to handling uncertainty or looking to innovate. To over-plan and forecast too far ahead wastes effort – but so does a 'just do it' approach. The same thinking is behind combining PRINCE2 with agile.

The guidance on Lean Startup is included in the context of combining PRINCE2 with agile, as some of the core concepts and techniques in Lean Startup are fundamental to the most effective way to deliver a product at the end of a timebox or a project. Lean Startup focuses on uncertainty, learning and handling change.

It should be remembered that Lean Startup in its entirety is not built for projects or timeboxes. It is included in *PRINCE2 Agile* as there are many similarities between creating a successful business and running a successful project in an agile context (e.g. a business needs a business plan and a project needs a business case).

20.4.2.2 Applying Lean Startup to PRINCE2

When applying some of the thinking behind Lean Startup to PRINCE2 it should be seen in the context of a timebox. This timebox could relate to the whole project or just a two-week sprint. Lean Startup is aimed at a group of people such as a delivery team in a sprint creating a product where there is uncertainty. This is the context in which Lean Startup is useful to PRINCE2 as a technique.

At the heart of Lean Startup is the idea that in order to be successful there is a need to focus on learning as this feeds into everything a team is trying to achieve. Understanding the customer's needs and understanding them quickly is vital. The ultimate goals are to get a better understanding of the customer's needs (bearing in mind that they themselves may not know them) and to speed up this learning. Lean Startup refers to this as shortening or accelerating the feedback loop and this is in keeping with the PRINCE2 Agile behaviour of exploration.

20.4.2.3 Measures and validated learnings

Essential to learning is that feedback needs to be measurable. Even if the feedback is subjective it has to be measurable so that it can be quantified (e.g. an opinion could be measured on a scale from 1 to 10). Lean Startup refers to 'vanity metrics' and 'actionable metrics'. The metrics you need to capture are those that directly relate to the business case or a timebox objective. These would be actionable metrics and not vanity metrics. The latter do not relate directly to the business case.

If a tourist attraction is looking to increase revenue:

● Revenue received during a day: actionable metric

● Daily visitors: vanity metric.

How a project is planned has a direct effect on how feedback is received. An early release into operational use of a part of the product will provide feedback. This will have an impact on the rest of the project. The sooner this is received the better. This feedback could turn out to be negative and result in the project being cancelled. Lean Startup is happy with this. If you're going to fail you need to fail as fast as possible ('fail fast, fail quickly' – or put another way, 'learn fast').

One of the key stories described in *The Lean Startup* is that of a company that took six months to build a product and when they launched it the product failed. If they had released a reduced version of the product after one month they would have failed five months earlier and saved a lot of money. The key point that Lean Startup makes about this, and it is at the nucleus of Lean Startup, is that the loss of five months' money is not as important as the loss of five months of learning. After one month they could have responded to what they had learned.

The same applies to a two-week sprint. It may be early in a sprint that a prototype is made and shown to a customer, and immediately rejected. The learning has already started.

20.4.2.4 Build, measure, learn

The three steps of build, measure and learn apply both to releases and interim products (see Figure 20.8). The most important of the three is the final step to do with learning. This then drives a project forward. In Lean Startup terms, if this results in refinements and adjustments this is seen as positive change and is described as 'perseverance' as the solution is becoming more accurate. However, if the feedback is surprising

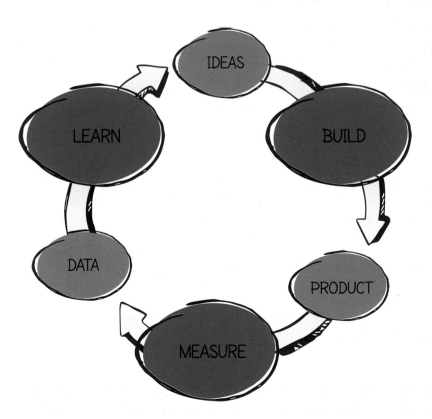

Minimize TOTAL time through the loop

Figure 20.8 The build–measure–learn feedback loop from Lean Startup

or significant and affects the foundations upon which a timebox was built, or more importantly, the project baseline, this may then need the team to take a very substantial change in direction and probably, in PRINCE2 terms, cause an exception. Lean Startup refers to this as a 'pivot' – something major has surfaced and it wasn't expected.

20.4.2.5 Minimum viable product in Lean Startup

The concept of a minimum viable product (MVP) is well known in agile. There are other similar concepts such as minimum marketable feature set (MMFS) and minimum usable subset (MUST) but these are not the same.

The basic idea behind MVP, in Lean Startup terms, is to create the simplest form of the product in order to get feedback. This would typically involve a limited set of features which could then be enhanced throughout the project in accordance with the incoming feedback. However, it is possible that this simple form could also be a paper prototype that could be shown to a customer.

What constitutes an MVP for a project is not easy to define as it depends on the levels of uncertainty that are involved. In very innovative situations it can involve educated guesswork or instincts, but the Lean Startup method forces target measures to be created and then validated as soon as possible by the results.

> ### Definition: Minimum viable product (MVP)
>
> In a PRINCE2 Agile context, the term MVP broadly aligns with the Lean Startup view that it is a 'version of the final product which allows the maximum amount of validated learning with the least effort'. This should not be confused with the viability of the project as a whole. Typically, an MVP would be delivered as early as possible during the project.
>
> It is important to note that an MVP is about learning; it may not go into operational use and may be in the form of a simple experiment or prototype.

Lean Startup could be said to view the MVP concept differently from most agile approaches in that Lean Startup assesses 'minimum viability' based upon 'what is the least that can be done to learn'. Put another way, the team needs to learn as fast as possible or 'learn the most with the least effort'. A common agile view of MVP is about the commercial viability of the product in terms of whether or not it will sell. PRINCE2 Agile does not share this view and defines the MVP based on the Lean Startup definition.

20.4.2.6 Further information

In keeping with Kaizen and continual improvement, Lean Startup sees the need for process when trying to be agile, and the need to continually improve that process. It also sees the need for hard data to scientifically evaluate feedback and learnings. Being flexible and dynamic needs control: 'ad-hocracy' will rarely work, even in the volatile start-up arena. This is why the concepts of Lean Startup can be used to complement PRINCE2 as it believes that to be responsive you need control.

20.4.2.7 Hints that may prove useful

Where there is extreme uncertainty (what Cynefin may describe as 'complex' – see section 17.4.1) Lean Startup is happy for the MVP to have less than the ideal level of quality: i.e. it may contain defects. Lean Startup is comfortable with this, as part of its learning process is to find out from the customer what level of quality they are happy with. In effect this is saying 'let's not guess the quality level – let's find out from the customer's feedback'. This level of quality will need to be defined from the start, as it does not represent the quality level being compromised.

Lean Startup prefers to segment the feedback it receives by groups of users or 'cohorts'. This may not add value if there is a clearly defined user group for a project, but it illustrates why it is important to engage with a representative view of the stakeholders from the customer side. They may have different views on the product or use it in different ways. A single product owner may be a disadvantage if you are using this approach (i.e. segmentation with cohorts).

Lean Startup refers to 'funnel metrics' (e.g. How many enquired about the product? How many asked for a demonstration of the product? How many bought the product?) These all represent data that can be learned from to a degree, but the key metrics (referred to as actionable) need to tie back to the business case to validate the original rationale. A twofold increase in demonstrations isn't great news if there is no increase in sales. However, opportunities to learn about why the number of demonstrations increased, and to hypothesize as to why they are not converting into sales, now exist.

On a PRINCE2 project using agile that is releasing frequently, these funnel metrics may start arriving during the project and may affect how future work is planned and organized (e.g. features may be reprioritized).

20.4.2.8 Reducing uncertainty

It could be said that Lean Startup is at its best when faced with extreme uncertainty and in a project context this level of uncertainty may only apply to a minority of situations. However, uncertainty will always exist to some degree and will vary from project to project and timebox to timebox. This will in turn affect the degree to which the feedback loops are used: i.e. how many and how often. But the goal remains the same in all situations and that is continual feedback to reduce uncertainty and to understand the customer's needs as well as possible.

20.5 SUMMARY

Managing Product Delivery handles the important interface between the project manager and the team manager (and therefore the delivery team who will be working in an agile way). The interface would ideally be collaborative and transparent where there is a collective agreement on what is to be produced and how this will be achieved (as opposed to a situation where instructions are given and followed).

Progress information would be visible and frequently updated by way of the daily activities of working in an agile way. This then makes it easier for the project manager to manage the project at the stage level by having clear and regular information across all of the teams at the delivery level.

ACKNOWLEDGEMENTS AND FURTHER READING

David J. Anderson (2010). *Kanban – Successful Evolutionary Change for your Technology Business.* Blue Hole Press.

Mike Burrows (2014). *Kanban from the Inside.* Blue Hole Press.

Alistair Croll and Benjamin Yoskovitz (2013). *Lean Analytics: Use Data to Build a Better Startup Faster.* O'Reilly Media.

Ash Maurya (2012). *Running Lean: Iterate from Plan A to a Plan that Works.* O'Reilly Media.

Eric Ries (2011). *The Lean Startup: How Constant Innovation Creates Radically Successful Businesses.* Portfolio Penguin.

21

Managing a Stage Boundary

This chapter covers:

- PRINCE2 guidance on Managing a Stage Boundary

- Agile ways of working that may already exist

- PRINCE2 Agile guidance on Managing a Stage Boundary

21 Managing a Stage Boundary

21.1 PRINCE2 GUIDANCE ON MANAGING A STAGE BOUNDARY

The purpose of the Managing a Stage Boundary process is to enable the project board to be provided with sufficient information by the project manager so that it can review the success of the current stage, approve the next stage plan, review the updated project plan, and confirm continued business justification and acceptability of the risks. Therefore, the process should be executed at, or close to the end of, each management stage.

Projects do not always go to plan and in response to an exception report (if the stage or project is forecast to exceed its tolerances) the project board may request that the current stage (and possibly the project) is replanned. The output from replanning is an exception plan which is submitted for project board approval in the same way that a stage plan is submitted for approval.

The Managing a Stage Boundary process is predicated on dividing the project into management stages.

A project, whether large or small, needs to ensure that the products it creates will deliver the benefits being sought, either in their own right or as part of a larger programme. The continuing correct focus of the project should be confirmed at the end of each stage. If necessary, the project can be redirected or stopped to avoid wasting time and money.

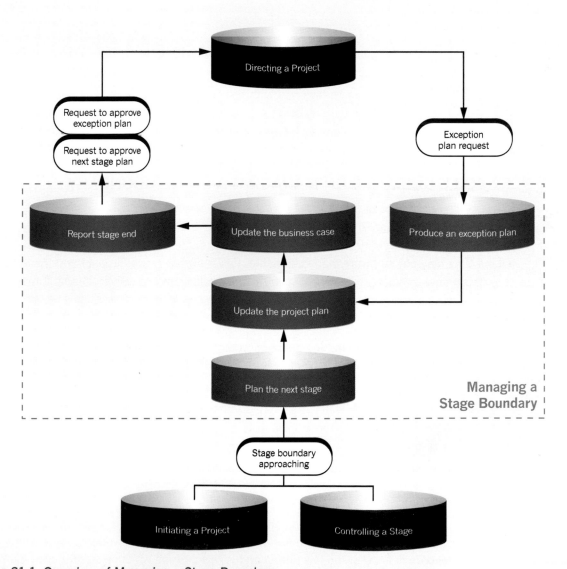

Figure 21.1 Overview of Managing a Stage Boundary

It is also important to recognize that projects can go wrong or can be affected by external factors that invalidate the business justification. An early identifier of potential failure is the project manager's forecast that any of the project or stage tolerances are likely to be exceeded. In such cases it is important to have a mechanism for corrective action in order to bring the project back into the right direction.

A positive decision not to proceed is not failure. However, providing insufficient information that prevents the project board from making an informed decision is itself a failure as it may lead to a wrong decision.

The Managing a Stage Boundary process provides a means by which an exception process can be implemented.

21.2 AGILE WAYS OF WORKING THAT MAY ALREADY EXIST

The Managing a Stage Boundary process is primarily about checking the ongoing viability of a project and stopping the project if this is no longer the case. In agile there is a similar concept of stopping the regular delivery cycle of releases when the value being delivered drops off, becomes marginal to the amount of effort involved or there is an opportunity cost to other work or projects. In agile this is usually determined as and when it happens (e.g. at the end of a sprint or release), whereas in PRINCE2 a stage end and a formal check on ongoing project viability is determined well in advance and the planned delivery of features needs to fit into this.

Tip

The project board should determine how long a stage should last before deciding what goes into it. They may wish to adjust this in a collaborative manner in the light of what is planned, but they should not be driven by this.

There is a similarity between a major review of a release (e.g. one that took three months) and the Managing a Stage Boundary process in that progress can be reviewed with respect to how much value or benefit has been delivered, how the team is performing, how the processes are working, and how the project is progressing with regard to quality and product delivery, planning the next release and assessing the project's exposure to issues and risks.

21.3 PRINCE2 AGILE GUIDANCE ON MANAGING A STAGE BOUNDARY

It is important to use stage boundaries or 'fire-breaks' appropriately when working in an agile way as although the delivery teams may be very content, working to a regular cadence and being very productive, because their focus is on product delivery they may not be aware of the wider context of their work. Their work may be going very well but they may not be aware that a competitor has launched a rival product and the expected benefits of the project are now significantly lower. Despite the good efforts of the delivery teams it may be prudent to cancel the project as it is no longer viable.

Tailoring guidance that may be appropriate is as follows:

● Reviewing how much is being delivered (and the quality of it) compared with what had been planned. This would include comparing the amount of value being delivered with the amount of cost incurred to create that value in order to ascertain if the project is still on track and is still viable.

● What has been released would typically be reviewed. What benefits are being realized?

● The appropriate use of agile could be reviewed in case risks are surfacing in certain areas (e.g. if the level of customer involvement is lower than expected more formality may be required).

● Release planning would typically be reviewed. For example, would it be a good idea to increase the frequency of the releases (if it is possible)? Would it be a good idea to alter the number of sprints (or their lengths) inside each release?

● The efficiency of configuration management and the choice of configuration item records could be assessed with respect to the iterative and incremental nature of the agile way of working. For example, are the configuration item records defined at too low a level and is this causing an unnecessary overhead?

Table 21.1 PRINCE2 Agile activities for Managing a Stage Boundary

PRINCE2 activities and products	Applicable agile artefacts and events

● Plan the next stage:
  ◦ Update the project initiation documentation, A.20
  ◦ Create the stage plan, A.16
  ◦ Create/update configuration item records, A.5
  ◦ Update risk register, A.25
  ◦ Update issue register, A.12
  ◦ Update quality register, A.23
	● Artefacts:
	  ◦ Product backlog (done/not done)
	  ◦ Release backlog (done/not done)
	  ◦ Potentially shippable increment
	● Event(s):
	  ◦ Release planning
	  ◦ Release reviews
	  ◦ Release retrospectives
	  ◦ Note: Sprint planning would typically be too detailed at this point but it may be useful.

● Update the project plan:
  ◦ Update the project plan, A.16
  ◦ Update the issue register, A.12
  ◦ Update the risk register, A.25
	● Artefacts:
	  ◦ Product backlog (done/not done)
	  ◦ Release backlog (done/not done)
	  ◦ Information radiators
	● Event(s):
	  ◦ Release review
	  ◦ Release planning

● Update the business case:
  ◦ Update the business case, A.2
  ◦ Update the benefits review plan, A.1
  ◦ Update the risk register, A.25
  ◦ Update the issue register, A.12
	● Artefacts:
	  ◦ Product backlog (value enabled)
	  ◦ Release backlog (value enabled)
	  ◦ Information radiators
	● Event(s):
	  ◦ Release review
	  ◦ Release planning

● Report stage end:
  ◦ Create end stage report, A.9
  ◦ Create lessons report, A.15
  ◦ Create follow-on action recommendations
	● Artefacts:
	  ◦ Product backlog (done/not done, value enabled)
	  ◦ Release backlog (done/not done, value enabled)
	  ◦ Information radiators
	● Event(s):
	  ◦ Release planning
	  ◦ Release review
	  ◦ Release retrospectives

● Produce an exception plan:
  ◦ Update project initiation documentation, A.20
  ◦ Create exception plan, A.16
  ◦ Create/update configuration item records, A.5
  ◦ Update risk register, A.25
  ◦ Update issue register, A.12
  ◦ Update the quality register, A.23
	● Artefacts:
	  ◦ Product backlog (done/not done)
	  ◦ Release backlog (done/not done)
	  ◦ Impediments from daily stand-ups
	  ◦ Outputs or decisions from a retrospective or a review
	● Event(s):
	  ◦ Sprint planning
	  ◦ Release planning

- Is it worth carrying out a formal workshop to review the stage (perhaps as part of a release review) and then plan the next stage (see Chapter 22, Closing a Project, for how to handle a similar one) or at least a large-scale demo for as many stakeholders as appropriate? (NB: it is unlikely that this event will take place at the very end of a stage – e.g. on the final day.)
- Decide on which of the suggested improvements to the way the teams are working (perhaps created during a release retrospective) can be reasonably expected to be adopted in the next release. Further learnings could be formalized at this point and given to project support so these lessons can help the wider organization.

Table 21.1 shows PRINCE2 activities for Managing a Stage Boundary and how they relate to agile artefacts and events (all product description references for PRINCE2 products are located in Appendix A).

21.3.1 How to …

There are many behaviours, concepts, frameworks and techniques that are used in agile and referenced throughout this manual. Table 21.2 provides cross-references to some of the most relevant for use during Managing a Stage Boundary.

Table 21.2 Relevant agile guidance for Managing a Stage Boundary

	Chapter and section references
Determine value	Section 9.4.1
Plan stages and releases	Chapters 12, 27
Assess and improve team performance	Section 19.4.1
Track progress when using agile	Chapter 15
Define quality criteria and acceptance criteria	Chapter 25
Manage risks and issues	Chapters 13, 14
Assess the risks associated with agile	Chapter 24
Break down requirements and products in a way best suited to agile	Section 25.4
Run workshops	Section 26.4.1
Tailor any of the PRINCE2 management products	Chapter 23

21.4 SUMMARY

In order to keep a project on track and viable PRINCE2 uses stage boundaries as major control points to assess the current status of the project.

Ideally this process should not interrupt the natural flow of a project using agile. Although this is an important point in the project to formalize its continuation, this should still be carried out with as little ceremony as possible because the team interactions and transparency of information will make the situation obvious and therefore the decision easy to make.

Throughout the stage the frequent delivery of products in an iterative and incremental style will mean that it will be clear how many features have been delivered and their level of quality. This will give a clearer indication of progress than information relating to time and cost.

The continual use of 'inspect and adapt' will in turn allow the team to continually and gradually improve how they work with the stage boundary, giving team members the opportunity to consolidate their learnings across the organization as a whole.

Ultimately this gives the project board the confidence to continue on the current successful path or to stop the project and use its resources elsewhere.

22

Closing a Project

This chapter covers:

- PRINCE2 guidance on Closing a Project
- Agile ways of working that may already exist
- PRINCE2 Agile guidance on Closing a Project
- Agile concepts and techniques

22 Closing a Project

22.1 PRINCE2 GUIDANCE ON CLOSING A PROJECT

The purpose of the Closing a Project process (see Figure 22.1) is to provide a fixed point at which acceptance for the project product is confirmed, and to recognize that objectives set out in the original project initiation documentation have been achieved (or approved changes to the objectives have been achieved), or that the project has nothing more to contribute.

One of the defining features of a PRINCE2 project is that it is finite – it has a start and an end. If the project loses this distinctiveness, it loses some of its advantages over purely operational management approaches.

A clear end to a project:

● Is always more successful than a slow drift into use as it is a recognition by all concerned that:
  ● The original objectives have been met (subject to any approved changes)
  ● The current project has run its course
  ● Either the operational regime must now take over the products from this project, or the products become inputs into some subsequent project or into some larger programme
  ● The project management team can be disbanded
  ● Project costs should no longer be incurred

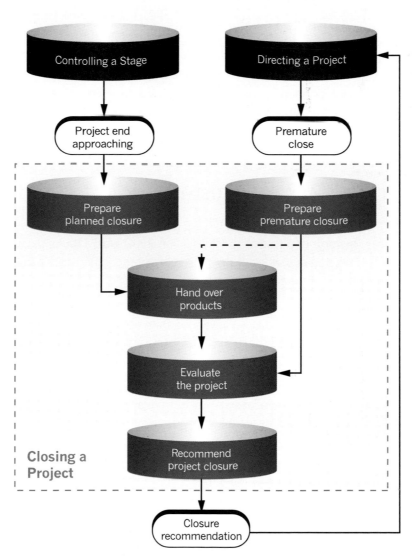

Figure 22.1 Overview of Closing a Project

- Provides an opportunity to ensure that all unachieved goals and objectives are identified so that they can be addressed in the future
- Transfers ownership of the products to the customer and terminates the responsibility of the project management team.

Closure activities should be planned as part of the stage plan for the final management stage. When Closing a Project, work is required to prepare input to the project board in order to obtain its authorization to close the project. Subsequently, the executive should also notify corporate or programme management that the project has closed.

It is also possible that the project board may wish to trigger a premature closure of the project under some circumstances (for example, if the business case is no longer valid). If the project is being brought to a premature close, this process will still need to be executed but may have to be tailored to the actual project situation.

A number of actions specific to the project's products may be required after the project, and these should be documented and planned for as follow-on action recommendations. These may have different audiences and therefore may need to be issued individually. The needs of the recipient will determine the format and content – some may want a formal report, some a log entry on a system, and others a meeting.

22.2 AGILE WAYS OF WORKING THAT MAY ALREADY EXIST

It is possible in some agile environments that there aren't many defined processes with respect to closing down a project, although mature agile environments will have these in place. This is primarily because:

- Regular handovers (preferably carried out collaboratively) into operational use (or near operational use) reduce some of the need to formalize certain activities at the end, as they have become second nature (e.g. process reviews, updating operational documentation, getting sign-off/acceptance).
- Ending a piece of work is often decided upon at the time (when added value has become marginal) as opposed to in advance, or when acceptance criteria become satisfied.

Due to the iterative and incremental nature of agile, the frequency of the delivery of product into operational use, and ease of delivery, are usually good indicators of the level of maturity of agile within an organization.

22.3 PRINCE2 AGILE GUIDANCE ON CLOSING A PROJECT

Tailoring guidance that may be appropriate is as follows:

- Project closure may take the form of a workshop (see section 22.4) where the original baseline is checked in relation to the final outputs and outcomes of the project, and preparation for closure authorization can take place. This may include a review of the final release.
- Benefits may have already been enabled and be delivering value.
- End-of-project activities should already be in an advanced state of completeness due to frequent releases gradually improving how project closure is done and populating information. For example:
  - Project/process evaluation should be ongoing through the frequent use of retrospectives.
  - Continual use of 'inspect and adapt' would mean that the lessons report has been created as the project has gone along, and many of the lessons would have already been actioned and evaluated from retrospectives at both the project and delivery levels.
  - User acceptance would be happening regularly, although care should be taken to ensure that user acceptance is not too informal when closing the project in order to ensure that the customer's quality expectations and acceptance criteria have been met.
  - Operational handovers (and acceptance) are likely to have happened many times due to the incremental delivery of products, so the final handover should be a routine event.
  - Training and technical documentation would be finalized, as it would have been created iteratively and incrementally throughout the project.

Table 22.1 shows PRINCE2 activities for Closing a Project and how they relate to agile artefacts and events (all product description references for PRINCE2 products are located in Appendix A).

Table 22.1 PRINCE2 Agile activities for Closing a Project

PRINCE2 activities and products	Applicable agile artefacts and events

● Prepare planned closure:
  ● Update project plan, A.16
  ● Create product status account, A.18
	● Artefacts:
	  ● Project vision
	  ● Product backlog (done/not done)
	  ● (Final) release backlog (done/not done)
	  ● Potentially shippable increment
	  ● Information radiators
	● Event(s):
	  ● Release review
	  ● Release retrospective

● Prepare premature closure:
  ● Update issue register, A.12
  ● Update project plan, A.16
  ● Create product status account, A.18
  ● Create additional work estimates
	● Artefacts:
	  ● Outstanding impediments
	  ● Project vision
	  ● Product backlog (done/not done)
	  ● (Final) release backlog (done/not done)
	  ● Potentially shippable increment (or part thereof, if shippable)
	  ● Information radiators
	● Event(s):
	  ● Release review
	  ● Release retrospective

● Hand over products:
  ● Create/update follow-on action recommendations
  ● Update configuration item records, A.5
  ● Update benefits review plan, A.1
  ● Obtain acceptance record
	● Artefacts:
	  ● Potentially shippable increment
	  ● Product backlog (done/not done and value enabled)
	● Event(s):
	  ● Release review (or subsequently)

● Evaluate the project:
  ● Create end project report, A.8
  ● Create the lessons report, A.15
	● Artefacts:
	  ● Project vision
	  ● Product backlog (done/not done, value enabled)
	  ● Release backlog (done/not done, value enabled)
	  ● Information radiators
	● Event(s):
	  ● (Final) release review
	  ● Project/release retrospective

● Recommend project closure:
  ● Close issue register, A.12
  ● Close the risk register, A.25
  ● Close the quality register, A.23
  ● Close the lessons log, A.14
  ● Prepare draft project closure notification
	● Artefacts:
	  ● Product backlog (done/not done, value enabled)
	  ● Decisions from the (final) release review or project retrospective

22.3.1 How to …

There are many behaviours, concepts, frameworks and techniques that are used in agile and referenced throughout this manual. Table 22.2 provides cross-references to some of the most relevant for use during Closing a Project.

Table 22.2 Relevant agile guidance for Closing a Project

	Chapter and section references
Evaluate the project	Sections 26.4.1, 19.4.1
Manage releases	Chapter 27
Assess value	Section 9.4.1
Define quality criteria and acceptance criteria	Chapter 25
Use the definition of 'done'	Section 11.4, Appendix H
Close a project that has been using agile	Section 22.4
Tailor any of the PRINCE2 management products	Chapter 23

22.4 AGILE CONCEPTS AND TECHNIQUES

22.4.1 An example of how to close a PRINCE2 Agile project

An ideal way to close a project would be with a workshop involving all of the key project stakeholders. Ideally this would be independently facilitated and use information from project-level information radiators that have been used throughout the project. It may even take place in the room or area where the project took place and the project management team worked.

The whole project team should be present (e.g. the project board, project assurance) along with other stakeholders such as those who will make the final product operational (or the final release of the product operational), those who will maintain and support it, and those from the strategic level who will be interested in the project outcome from a programme perspective.

The following is an example of how a workshop could be structured:

- **Final product demo** In order to achieve sign-off from the customer. This would not be a 'big event' as it would be the last in a regular and frequent series of demonstrations. There shouldn't be any surprises here and it will not be a 'big reveal' due to the constant customer involvement throughout the project that has resulted in a lot of transparency and interaction.

- **Follow-on actions** These could be assigned to people formally or verbally or even by handing them a sticky note from an information radiator. Collectively the workshop participants could decide if unfinished work could be moved over to an appropriate BAU backlog, or handed over to the strategic/programme level as potentially a new project. Correctly addressing outstanding actions is most effectively done when the parties affected are in attendance and can discuss the relative merits of the options available.

- **Checking against the baseline** The final project-level information radiators and a demonstrable product could be compared with the original vision and baseline information, along with other supporting documentation that the project was justified against. The information radiators would typically show the project product description, the business case and the project plan and would have dynamically displayed this information throughout the project.

- **Reviewing the use of agile** This would involve assessing how well the delivery teams, and the project management team as a whole, used retrospectives to address issues and risks as they went along. Further to this, the use of the Agilometer should be checked to see if it had been assessed correctly and to determine if lessons about the use of agile on this project, and how the associated risks were handled, could be used on other projects. Ideally, project support would be in attendance to capture these learnings.

- **Closing the event** Perhaps the executive (depending on personal style), who would be there to look at the final costs, could thank the team and celebrate the end in some form such as a team meal. When a project has involved high levels of collaboration and teamwork, and the team is disbanded, it can result in a degree of 'mourning' for the team members, so this should be anticipated and ideas suggested as to how to reduce this.

22.4.2 Premature close

If the project has closed prematurely, it could have been triggered by a fail fast/learn fast situation caused by the correct use of management by exception (for example, a stage boundary was reached and the project was no longer viable, or tolerances were forecast to be exceeded and it was not worth taking remedial action). Many agile techniques are designed to help with this, such as timeboxing or empirical forecasting, which forces the 'bad' news to surface in a transparent way.

If a project is going to fail it is best that failure arrives as quickly as possible. Many agile techniques and ways of working can contribute to this, but the following are the most significant:

- Empirical forecasting
- Transparency
- Timeboxing
- Sprint (or release) demonstrations, reviews and retrospectives
- Shortening the feedback loop to the customer
- Frequent customer interaction
- Experimentation, prototyping and spiking
- Early enablement of benefits that did not accrue.

All of these concepts and techniques create or force a clear understanding of what is being attempted and can therefore highlight that a project or stage will take too long, cost too much, will fail to work or the project objectives have not been set correctly.

22.5 SUMMARY

PRINCE2 uses the Closing a Project process in order to clearly confirm that the project has ended and that the purpose for it has been met and accepted by the customer.

When using agile this is still likely to be a formal event but an event in which most of the information is already known and most of the work already done due to the iterative and incremental nature of the agile way of working. Examples of this would be that benefits are already being accrued, most of the project's products are in operational use and documentation is almost complete and just needs to be finalized.

This then allows for a smooth and efficient closure of the project and helps the project manager and project board to do this with the minimum of effort thereby enabling them to move on to other work and other projects without delay.

23

Summary of tailoring guidance for the PRINCE2 products

This chapter covers:

- Baseline products
- Record products
- Report products

23 Summary of tailoring guidance for the PRINCE2 products

All products can exist in a wide range of formats from the very formal (e.g. a bound document) to the very informal (e.g. an email or a conversation). They all need to exist in some form even if only a sentence or a paragraph within another product. It should not be assumed that each product is a document.

PRINCE2 identifies three types of management product (baseline, record and report). They are used by the PRINCE2 processes so that certain roles can take actions and/or make decisions.

All of the product descriptions defined by PRINCE2 can be used without any changes: see Appendix A for the full list of PRINCE2 products. The following guidance describes some tailoring and advice that may be appropriate depending on the needs of the project.

23.1 BASELINE PRODUCTS

Baseline products are subject to change control. In Table 23.1, the numbered baseline products refer to the numbers used in the PRINCE2 manual for the PRINCE2 management products (see also Table 16.2).

Table 23.1 Tailoring baseline products

Baseline products	Overview of the tailoring required and further considerations
1. Benefits review plan	There is likely to be an emphasis on how frequent releases have been planned in order to enable benefits during the course of a project. This may lead to the early delivery of actual benefits to the customer. The way these are planned will have an impact on the ongoing viability of the project. It would be likely that a significant amount of benefits are planned to be delivered (or at least enabled) before the project end date.
2. Business case	This needs to be expressed in a way that allows for flexing of the amount being delivered. The MVP would need to be identified so that an exception can be raised if this is forecast to be delivered later than expected (see Chapter 9, Business Case theme, for more details).
4. Communication management strategy	It is essential that there is a clearly understood and agreed strategy regarding the common techniques and concepts that agile uses to communicate (e.g. informal interactions, daily stand-ups, modelling, prototyping, visualization and workshops). See also Chapter 25.
	This applies to all levels of the project and would define approaches to such things as how a sprint review will take place and how the delivery teams will communicate with the project manager through checkpoint reports.
6. Configuration management strategy	The iterative and incremental nature of agile means that there will naturally be several versions of products and that change is inevitable; therefore this should be embraced and supported accordingly. In environments where automation and frequent releases into operational use occur, specific tools may exist and their use should be clearly defined.
	The level at which configuration management takes place needs to take into account that project- or stage-level change may affect the agreed baseline, whereas detailed change is likely not to.
16. Plan (project, stage and team)	Agile plans tend to be informal or low-tech at the delivery level and this can be highly effective even though they may be no more than to-do lists or backlogs. However, there may be more formality as the level of planning goes higher. Release plans may also be created to complement the planning at the stage plan level.
	Agile plans are likely to show features (or sets of features) and their order and their dependencies, and are likely to have been created collaboratively by those who will carry out the planned work.
	Product-based planning can still be used at all levels of the project (including product delivery).
17. Product description	Product descriptions can be used interchangeably with user stories (and sometimes epics). Both product descriptions and user stories can be product backlog items. They describe the 'who, what and why'. A product description can contain more information than a user story. Product descriptions can be used in tandem with user stories by defining the higher level of understanding with product descriptions and the lower levels of understanding with user stories.
	The format of a product description could be an index card or a document.
	See Figure 25.1 for mapping product descriptions, requirements, epics and user stories.

Table continues

Table 23.1 continued

Baseline products	Overview of the tailoring required and further considerations
19. Project brief	Although this is an important product in PRINCE2 it may have an informal format and presentation when working with agile.
	The project definition in an agile context is preferably more outcome-based than solution-based and is also likely to outline the areas of scope and quality criteria that have flexibility in the sense that they can be prioritized.
	The project approach will contain an agile element describing the use of agile, which techniques and approaches have been selected, and how the agile element will benefit the project.
	The delivery-level roles in the project management team structure will have more detail and may be included.
	Due to the desire for incremental delivery of benefits there will probably be more detailed information on the impact this may have on areas such as operations and maintenance.
20. Project initiation documentation	The guidance provided for the project brief is also appropriate for this product although the understanding of the project will now have evolved further.
	In an agile context the project initiation documentation should be created with the view of 'enough and no more'. That is to say it should be complete, but it needs to be as concise as possible and at the appropriate level of detail. Otherwise its role as a form of communication will suffer.
	This product (or parts of it) may exist on an information radiator if appropriate for the project environment.
21. Project product description	In alignment with the business case this is likely to focus on defining a product with a close link to a desired outcome in preference to just defining a solution. It may be created as part of a workshop (e.g. a visioning workshop). The purpose of this product should be clearly visible to all irrespective of the project environment (e.g. it should be clearly displayed on a wall or clearly displayed on the intranet).
	It is an important product when combining PRINCE2 with agile in that it defines the ultimate output (the final product) and the outcome, which needs to be clear and precise so that the iterative and incremental nature of agile does not go off track.
	The 'composition' field will either contain the highest level of product descriptions or product groupings and their respective priorities. Either way these will be similar to epics.
22. Quality management strategy	The agile way of working needs to be incorporated into the strategy for ensuring that the quality level is maintained. Some agile concepts exist in order to protect the level of quality (e.g. by delivering fewer requirements in order to ensure that the quality reviewing is not compromised). Agile behaviours will need to be part of the strategy, as they need to be assured.
	There may be occasions when the quality level will be set at a low level due to the uncertainty of the work involved (e.g. the project could be highly innovative). The audience for this may be **early adopters** who are more interested in utilizing the product and do not mind some deficiencies in terms of robustness or stability.
24. Risk management strategy	Any way of working has risks associated with it, and the risks associated with using agile need to be managed. An agile risk assessment is used to help with this (see Chapter 24). There is likely to be more focus on the risks associated with the agile behaviours than with other areas of agile because this is where many of the benefits of using agile are found. There may be a significant impact on the project should the behaviours break down.
	In terms of roles and responsibilities, the agile way of working relies on everyone looking out for risks and raising them quickly (see also Chapter 13).

Baseline products	Overview of the tailoring required and further considerations
26. Work package	How work packages are specified has a very significant impact on successfully combining PRINCE2 with agile. Although it is a formal interface this would typically be carried out in a collaborative way and negotiated by the project manager and the team manager and perhaps with the delivery team as well.
	One or more work packages may be collaboratively defined as the output from a sprint planning meeting.
	A work package should be defined in such a way as to create a safe boundary of control, whilst at the same time creating the space for the delivery team to create the product (or products) in the most effective way through self-organizing.
	A customer subject matter expert (CSME) is likely to help with prioritizing the work involved.
	A work package may include one or more releases and one or more sprints. Alternatively, it could contain just one sprint or just one user story. Therefore it is essential from the start to get clarity on how work packages will be designed and how they will operate on a project.

23.2 RECORD PRODUCTS

Records are dynamic management products that maintain information regarding project progress. In Table 23.2, the numbered records refer to the numbers used in the PRINCE2 manual for the PRINCE2 management products (see also Table 16.2).

Table 23.2 Tailoring record products

Records	Overview of the tailoring required and further considerations
5. Configuration item records	These may need to cater for high degrees of change due to the regular iteration of products under configuration management. Operational stakeholders may wish to be involved or consulted with respect to this.
7. Daily log	The project manager can use this to store information, as there may be a lot of informal communications such as those taking place face-to-face.
12. Issue register	May be informal or low-tech (e.g. on a wall).
14. Lessons log	Continual process improvement is a prominent agile concept and therefore this may be very conspicuous – perhaps on the wall in a team room (or a virtual version of this). This may be used quickly to create working agreements and may take place during a retrospective.
23. Quality register	On some occasions this may be low-tech.
25. Risk register	May be informal or low-tech. May contain risks identified by the agile risk assessment (see Chapter 24).

23.3 REPORT PRODUCTS

Reports are management products providing a snapshot of the status of certain aspects of the project. In Table 23.3, the numbered reports refer to the numbers used in the PRINCE2 manual for the PRINCE2 management products (see also Table 16.2).

Table 23.3 Tailoring report products

Reports	Overview of the tailoring required and further considerations
3. Checkpoint report	An important product that would typically be in the form of an information radiator and/or a burn chart (see Figure 15.1). Could be replaced by a daily stand-up or Scrum meeting with the agreement of the delivery team but would need to avoid being seen as a 'reporting to' mechanism. If the information is transparent then this can be extracted (or 'pulled') by the project manager when required.
8. End project report	An assessment of the use of agile is likely to be included in this with reference to the judgements made when using the Agilometer.
9. End stage report	May be built incrementally throughout a stage depending on the frequency of timeboxes or releases. May be part of a release review.
10. Exception report	Most likely to occur due to the expected amount to be delivered being forecast to exceed tolerance. This could be triggered by a burn chart (at the sprint or release level) showing how progress has gone outside tolerance. This may result in an immediate meeting where options are discussed before raising it with the project board.
11. Highlight report	An important product that may contain additional information on releases (e.g. what has been released and what benefits have been enabled). May be delivered verbally.
	Could be in the form of an information radiator and/or a burn chart. If the information is transparent then this can be extracted (or 'pulled') by the project board when required.
13. Issue report	May be low-tech and produced or updated during a sprint review or release review.
15. Lessons report	May be low-tech and handed to project support informally.
18. Product status account	These may need to cater for high degrees of change due to the regular iteration of products under configuration management.

Image 23.1 Adapting and reworking the PRINCE2 products

PART III

AREAS OF PARTICULAR FOCUS FOR PRINCE2 AGILE

24

The Agilometer

This chapter covers:

- What is it: when and how to assess suitability
- Responding to and monitoring the assessment
- Evolving the Agilometer

24 The Agilometer

24.1 PURPOSE

The purpose of this focus area is to describe how to assess the agile environment in order to tailor PRINCE2 in the most effective way. Every project situation is different in some form due to factors such as the level of trust between the customer and the supplier, the technology being used or the level of uncertainty. Therefore it is important to decide in advance how to address these advantages and disadvantages in order to run a project in the most effective way from an agile perspective.

In order to receive the most benefit from using a method or approach it is essential to adjust and adapt it to suit the context and conditions it is operating in. PRINCE2 is no exception to this rule and it provides a lot of guidance on how to tailor PRINCE2 for any project situation. The aim of the Agilometer is to provide further guidance (with respect to agile considerations) that will create a level of control and predictability, without becoming overly prescriptive.

Take the analogy of driving a car. A typical car provides a mode of transport and has many features to help make a journey in a safe manner (e.g. engine, lights, wipers); however, it still needs a driver to make decisions and use those features to control the car appropriately. On a regular car journey the route and the destination may not change but the conditions do. This is why a driver drives differently in snow and on ice compared with driving on a dry road on a sunny day. Importantly, assessing the conditions before the journey commences helps improve the chances of carrying out the journey in the safest and most effective way.

24.2 WHEN TO ASSESS SUITABILITY

Agile suitability is assessed throughout the project (e.g. during retrospectives). It is specifically assessed during pre-project and again, in a more detailed way, during the initiation stage. The results of these assessments would appear in the project brief and the project initiation documentation in order to provide the project board with information to help shape its decision to authorize any work. It is important that the project board has enough awareness of agile in general, so that it can understand what the assessment is saying and make an informed decision about such things as potential areas of risk or benefit.

As an example, a situation may occur where a project is assessed as being ideal for a highly agile approach, but the project board is concerned that the approach is susceptible to certain risks (e.g. the customer is unable to sustain its involvement) and therefore requests that more governance is put in place in this area. Further to this example, another scenario may involve a project being assessed as 'neutral' or 'average' in terms of how much agile can be used, but the project board realizes that too much formal reporting has been put in place and the business case is not viable unless more frequent deliveries of benefits take place (e.g. it needs the earlier realization of benefits or earlier customer feedback, and therefore is happy to receive reports in a much more informal manner or by other means).

These examples show that all the project team members need to understand the risks and benefits associated with agile in order to get the most from it. It is not something that is only relevant at the delivery level or to the project manager.

24.3 HOW SUITABILITY IS ASSESSED (THE AGILOMETER)

It is the project manager's role to facilitate the agile assessment, as this will affect how the project is managed.

In order to tailor PRINCE2 in the best way possible it is important to assess the context that a project exists in with regard to the environment and the working relationships. To achieve this PRINCE2 Agile has an assessment tool called the Agilometer (see Figure 24.1) to answer the question of 'How agile can we be on this project?'

The Agilometer looks at six key areas, and the project manager is responsible for canvassing the key stakeholders involved in the project as to what values to give each category. Each category is represented on the figure by a slider. Each slider is described in more detail in section 24.7.

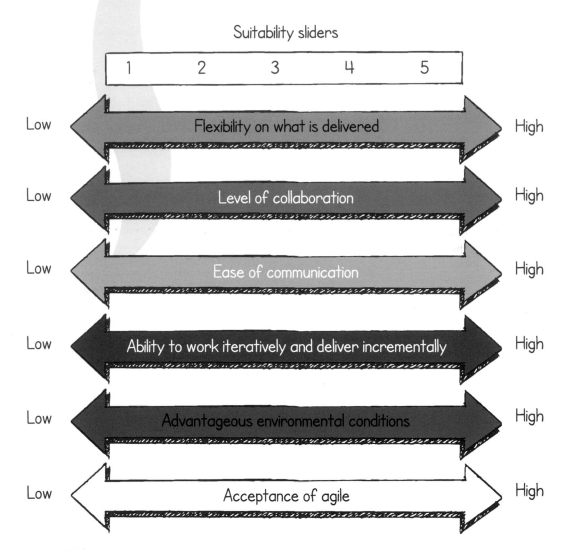

Figure 24.1 The Agilometer

When using the Agilometer it is important to see it as a guide to help you make an informed decision. The Agilometer itself does not make a decision or offer any recommendations. Further to this it is important to see each slider in isolation and not to create an average score across all areas.

The Agilometer shows where there are risk areas with using agile. It also shows the opposite: i.e. where there are benefits with using agile

An example of using the Agilometer *correctly* would be a response such as 'The collaboration slider is quite low: what can we do to improve it?'

An example of how to use it *incorrectly* would be the statement 'The average score across all of the sliders is 3.9, so the context is favourable to the agile way of working.'

The Agilometer illustrates areas that are favourable or may present risks. Averaging out the sliders can obscure this information.

24.4 RESPONDING TO THE ASSESSMENT

After using the Agilometer to create an assessment, the next step is to see what can be done to improve the sliders and shift them further to the right. Here are some simple examples of how to move a slider:

> **Tip**
> 'Must' is a level of priority for a requirement (or user story) that 'must' be satisfied because without it, either the output from a timebox won't work or it is not worth delivering the output.

24.4.1 The 'flexibility on what is delivered' slider

- The customer may be unaware of why there is a need to be flexible with what is delivered. Therefore training and education may be appropriate.
- Are there too many requirements that are 'musts'? Can they (or the assumptions behind them) be challenged to see if the priority is too high?

24.4.2 The 'level of collaboration' slider

- Get people together and break down any barriers.
- Investigate reasons why people may be reluctant to collaborate. Have they been let down in the past? Political baggage?

24.4.3 The 'ease of communication' slider

- Bridge any physical gaps by arranging visits for a day or a week.
- Use video-conferencing and plan around different time zones.
- Co-locate the team.
- Improve the use of tactile and/or low-tech solutions when presenting information.

24.4.4 The 'ability to work iteratively and deliver incrementally' slider

- Challenge the team to think of partial deliveries that will be 'of use' in some form or another.
- What could go into a first release?
- Something 'of use' can have many forms (e.g. a quick win, technical proof of concept, getting the hardest work out of the way first).
- Try to calculate the value of delivering something early.

24.4.5 The 'advantageous environmental conditions' slider

- Would new tools help? Can you do more to protect the team from outside disturbances? Would some training help?
- Can 'the commercials' be adjusted to align more with the agile way of working? Do third parties need awareness about their role on a project using agile? Can you draw on other people's experiences?

24.4.6 The 'acceptance of agile' slider

- Would training help? Would a more informal workshop approach get over key messages?
- Can you direct people to helpful information on your knowledge base about agile (e.g. the company intranet)?
- Can you get key personnel (e.g. at project board level) to help explain agile to key stakeholders?
- Make it clear to the key stakeholders what the benefit is for them.

24.5 MONITORING THE ASSESSMENT

The assessment can be reviewed at various times throughout the project – for example, at stage end or after a release – to see if the settings on the Agilometer are happening as predicted. Any deviation between the prediction and reality as perceived by the team would result in a change to the project management or delivery process. A slider that is much further left than predicted is likely to mean that an area of risk has been created. A slider much further to the right than predicted could mean that less governance or control is needed in certain areas.

24.6 EVOLVING THE AGILOMETER

From a wider organizational or programme-level viewpoint, it is important to see the Agilometer (as it appears in this manual) as only a starting point. Organizations need to evolve their own Agilometer as they may need to include factors that are specific to themselves, representing significant areas of risk and benefit to working in an agile way. It is best to keep this concept relatively simple. Too many sliders can cloud the information needed to answer reasonably simple questions, such as 'How agile can we be on this project?' 'What are the risks and benefits that are likely to happen?' As each project uses the Agilometer, continual improvement can be used to tune it to suit future projects.

24.6.1 Apply appropriately

Agile needs to be applied appropriately to the context and the conditions of a project. It will be highly unlikely that you can apply it in the same way when building a nuclear submarine as you would when you are producing a new chocolate bar. PRINCE2 Agile highlights the factors that need to be addressed, and advises on possible courses of action. Tailoring is essential on all projects, as no two projects are identical.

It is possible that the prevailing conditions are just too risky for the use of agile to any significant degree, so the Agilometer would highlight that it may be worth using another approach instead. This could even happen during the project, in which case it would need to go into exception.

Ultimately the most important point to understand when tailoring the approach to a project is that the result will always be a case of 'How much agile can we use?' as opposed to a yes/no decision. In PRINCE2 there is no such thing as an 'agile project' or a 'non-agile project'. How agile you can be on a project is like a spectrum; it is always a matter of degree.

24.7 THE AGILOMETER SLIDER DEFINITIONS

(Only Level 5 is discussed – this indicates the highest and most preferred condition.)

24.7.1 Flexibility on what is delivered

Definition of Level 5: Stakeholders are very comfortable with the fact that change is inevitable and needs to happen in order to converge on an accurate product. They are also very comfortable with the role they need to play in prioritizing the work, and they understand that the scope of the work and the quality criteria are being flexed in order to protect the level of quality and the deadline for what is being delivered.

Example behaviours:

- Stakeholders are 'change friendly'.
- It is accepted that the detail will change; however, significant changes need to be controlled.
- Everything is prioritized, using techniques such as MoSCoW.
- It is understood by all that flexing what is being delivered will protect deadlines and quality, and specifically that this will prevent quality-checking and testing from being squeezed.
- De-scoping and prioritization will be a team exercise but is customer driven.
- Embracing change at the detail level produces more accurate products.

24.7.2 Level of collaboration

Definition of Level 5: There is a very high level of collaboration amongst all parties involved. This is typified by a one-team culture and excellent working relationships both internally and externally. High levels of trust exist and a desire to be helpful is prevalent.

Example behaviours:

- There is a 'one-team' culture in the project team.
- There is a partnership approach between the customer and the supplier.
- There is an absence of 'silos' and 'turf'.
- There is an absence of 'baggage' associated with events from the past.
- Trust and listening epitomize the behaviour of the people involved.
- People work quickly, are helpful and look out for each other.
- There is an absence of a blame and 'cc: email' culture.
- There is an acceptance that mistakes will happen due to some communications being informal.

24.7.3 Ease of communication

Definition of Level 5: Communication is very easy amongst all parties involved. The environment is 'communication rich' where there is a lot of face-to-face interaction, and visual information is readily available in such forms as prototypes and models. Retrieval of information is also easy in order to reference knowledge, information or data that is either historical or current.

Example behaviours:

- There are high levels of visibility and transparency (e.g. plans on walls).
- A lot of information is managed in a 'low-tech' and/or tactile way.
- There are high levels of co-location.
- Where there is a less than ideal situation (e.g. the team is physically dispersed), measures have been taken to reduce the impact (e.g. video-conferencing).
- There is a lot of informal communication, face-to-face and over the phone.
- There is a limited amount of formal reporting.

24.7.4 Ability to work iteratively and deliver incrementally

Definition of Level 5: It is very easy to deliver benefit to the customer by regular partial deliveries of the final product. It is also very easy to work iteratively in the sense that products and understanding can be refined interactively by the frequent delivery of formal and informal deliverables. There is a desire to learn, experiment and explore (and fail!) as well as an overarching feeling of 'think big; start small'.

Example behaviours:

- The team is happy to experiment and be creative.
- It is understood that things are rarely right first time.
- The project can be broken down into chunks that can deliver benefits early.
- Learning and validation are seen as an ongoing process.
- 'Little and often' is seen as a safe way of delivering and a good way of staying in control.
- Incrementalism is seen as good for 'real' feedback and gives confidence to the customer as they see things being delivered.

24.7.5 Advantageous environmental conditions

Definition of Level 5: The overall working environment is very supportive of working in an agile way. Personnel are assigned full-time to their work; they are appropriately skilled; they have very efficient platforms to work from (e.g. tooling, communications). Contractual frameworks and compliance considerations are not seen as restrictive.

Example behaviours:

● People are dedicated to the project and the team is stable.

● Team personnel are experienced in their trades.

● Any third parties are comfortable with working in an agile way.

● Commercial and contractual details do not inhibit the agile way of working and delivering.

● The environment and tooling are conducive to agile.

24.7.6 Acceptance of agile

Definition of Level 5: All stakeholders closely involved are fully aware of the behaviours, concepts and techniques of working in an agile way. They have been trained and have experience. They are not only happy to work in this way but they prefer it and understand the advantages that it brings. Peripheral stakeholders are also aware of the need to carry out their roles in an 'agile friendly' way.

Example behaviours:

● Everyone accepts the agile philosophy and understands the difference from a traditional way of working.

● People have been trained to an appropriate level.

● There are no blockers to using agile from peripheral areas such as procurement or quality assurance (i.e. they understand the philosophy too).

FURTHER READING

DSDM project approach questionnaire: http://www.dsdm.org/product/project-approach-questionaire-paq

25

Requirements

This chapter covers:

- Requirements definition and product descriptions
- Requirements decomposition, granularity and prioritization
- Agile concepts and techniques

25 Requirements

25.1 PURPOSE

The purpose of this focus area is to describe how to define and prioritize requirements (or user stories), so that they are in a form that is conducive to working in an agile way (where the requirements are subject to the inevitability of change – see also Chapter 14, Change theme).

25.1.1 Requirements terminology

There are many terms that are used to describe what a product does or how well it does it. In PRINCE2 Agile the conventions in Table 25.1 are used.

Table 25.1 Requirements and equivalent terms

Approximate level of detail	Preferred PRINCE2 Agile terms	Possible equivalent terms
The highest	Project product description	Vision
High level	Product group	Epic, feature, function, theme, scope
	Project product description composition	
	High-level requirement	
Intermediate level	Product description	Epic, feature, function, coarse-grained user story
	Intermediate-level requirement	
Low level	Product description	User story, fine-grained user story
	Sub-product	
	Low-level or detailed requirement	

25.1.1.1 Further clarification

The following lists some of the ways requirements are treated in PRINCE2 Aglle:

- In order to meet a requirement or produce a product it may be necessary to carry out one or more 'tasks'. These could appear on a team plan or sprint backlog (not referred to as requirements by PRINCE2 Agile).
- Requirements fall into two types: functional (what it does) and non-functional (how well it does it).
- Throughout the PRINCE2 and the agile communities, many of these terms are used interchangeably (e.g. function, feature, user story, requirement) although they are not necessarily referring to the same thing. Table 25.1 provides the view of PRINCE2 Agile and how it refers to these terms.
- Throughout this manual, the terms 'requirements', 'product descriptions' and 'user stories' are often used interchangeably, as most of the time they are referring to the same thing. The choice of term will depend on which term best suits the context.

25.1.2 The role of requirements

Requirements have a special role in an agile context. They represent the 'currency' an agile team deals in. Managing and trading requirements becomes a focal point of the way an agile team works, as less focus needs to be applied to other constraints such as managing time and cost.

Defining a requirement is one thing, defining it well is another! It is essential that requirements are defined well, as this gives a level of precision that actually defines the end product. However, to do this requires the relevant technical skills and the use of good techniques such as interviewing skills and process modelling.

Take, as an example of the importance of requirements, the delivery of a new kitchen. This is what the customer wants and what the project must deliver, as described in the project product description. A business case would have been created in order to justify this. But how does the customer define what they mean by 'a kitchen'? Does the new kitchen have a dishwasher and an ice-maker? How important are these features? Requirements describe what the customer means by 'a kitchen'.

25.2 REQUIREMENTS DEFINITION

One of the most powerful techniques in PRINCE2 is that of product-based planning (see Appendix D). This technique shifts the emphasis from activity-based planning to a more black-and-white form of planning focused on the end state of a product or sub-product (i.e. is it complete and 100% finished, or is it still a work in progress?) agile works in the same way as with the definition of 'done' in Scrum (see Appendix H) and 'acceptance criteria' in the glossary.

25.3 DEFINING PRODUCT DESCRIPTIONS

It is important when using PRINCE2 with agile to define product descriptions at the correct level of detail at the right time and then allow them to evolve. Too much detail will stifle the dynamic and responsive nature of agile because agile refines the detailed understanding of a product as it evolves. Equally, too little detail creates room for misunderstanding, as requirements would be too vague. This would then need further clarification or rework, causing delays and probably frustration.

25.4 REQUIREMENTS DECOMPOSITION AND GRANULARITY

Essential to the success of using PRINCE2 with agile is to ensure that requirements are defined at the appropriate level of understanding during each stage of a project. This normally involves a simple three-step process (see Table 25.2 and Figure 25.1), although this may be done in two steps on smaller projects where the processes of Starting up a Project and Initiating a Project may have been combined.

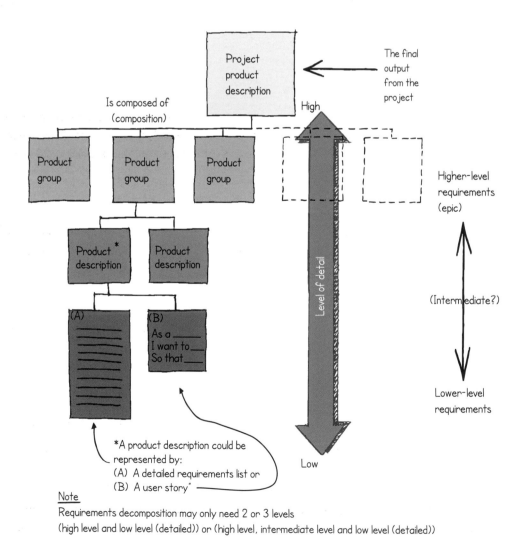

Figure 25.1 Possible requirements decomposition and equivalent terminology

This could be likened to JIT (just-in-time) inventory management in that just enough detail needs to be available at the right time. The 'Level of requirement' column in Table 25.2 is only a very general guide and is included to give at least some idea of scale, but this should not be seen as anything more than a rudimentary rule of thumb. If a team is prioritizing 200 user stories it should not be in the pre-project stage!

The 'Metaphor' column is intended to provide help with visualizing the need to take requirements and break them down through the duration of the project. Too much detail early on can obscure the bigger picture.

Table 25.2 Typical levels of requirements decomposition

Project stage	Level of requirement and a possible guide as to how many	Metaphor	Possible format
Pre-project	High level (possibly less than 10)	Boulders	Key objectives of the project in bullet point form – perhaps listed under the project product description as 'composition' or defined as product groupings
Initiation stage	Intermediate level (possibly more than 10 but less than 100)	Rocks	Product descriptions, epics
Delivery stage(s)	Detail level (possibly more than 100)	Gravel	Detailed requirements/user stories relating to the product descriptions defined in the initiation stage

From an estimation point of view (in the form of time, cost or benefits), the margin of error at each of these stages could be as follows:

● Pre-project, 50% to 100%

● Initiating stage, 20% to 40%

● Delivery stage(s), 10% to 20%.

Again, this should only be seen as a guide and for illustrative purposes as this will vary according to such things as industry sector, organization and experience. It is sometimes referred to as the 'cone of uncertainty'. The real margin of error will vary from project to project depending on each project's conditions and level of uncertainty.

25.5 REQUIREMENTS PRIORITIZATION

Requirements prioritization is an essential part of using PRINCE2 in an agile environment and is at the heart of how it works. Continual prioritization of what is being delivered and the work being done enables deadlines to be hit and the quality level to be protected.

25.5.1 Approaches to prioritization

With respect to product delivery, there are two approaches to prioritization that are frequently used when working in an agile way:

● MoSCoW

● Ordering (1,2,3,…,n).

It is important to use the correct approach in the correct situation because these do not work in the same way.

MoSCoW typically works at higher levels and over longer timescales where requirements may be grouped by function and dependencies exist between these functions.

Ordering primarily works at a lower level (or task level) where certain technical activities are taking place.

The choice of approach will be dictated by the level of uncertainty of the work being undertaken. Generally speaking MoSCoW would be the default approach, as it specifically addresses situations where work is time-bound and finite such as when working on a project, or in a timebox.

25.5.2 Definition of MoSCoW

This acronym is used to categorize items such as requirements or tasks into one of the four following levels of how they relate to a deadline (see Table 25.3):

● Must have
● Should have
● Could have
● Won't have for now.

Table 25.3 MoSCoW priorities

Priority with respect to the timebox*	Description
Must have	Must be satisfied because without it, either the output from the timebox won't work or it is not worth delivering the output
Should have	Should be satisfied because it is highly desirable or very important, but it is not a must have
Could have	Could be satisfied because it is still desirable or important, but not as much as a should have
Won't have for now	Won't be satisfied before the deadline

* Where the timebox could relate to a project, a stage, a release or a low-level timebox (e.g. a sprint).

25.5.3 What happens if they are all 'musts'?

It is a very natural and common concern that, when prioritizing using MoSCoW, everything will turn out to be a 'must'. Typically, this is rarely true.

Tip
MoSCoW always relates to a deadline.

25.5.4 Is the requirement essential?

One technique for checking if a requirement really is a 'must' is to ask the question: 'Would you put the product into operational use without this?' In other words, is the output from the project still viable in accordance with the rationale and justification for the project, without satisfying this requirement? For example:

● Would you sell a car without wheels or an engine?
● Would you sell a car without satellite navigation?
● Would you sell a car without electric windows?

Although the example is a simplistic analogy, it highlights that some features of a car are essential and others are not. Also, those features that are not essential may have satisfactory alternatives such as a manual winder for the windows.

Further to this, the analogy also highlights the need to understand the overall objective for the project (as defined in the project product description), as the MoSCoW priorities would be different if the objective was to produce a luxury car as opposed to a budget car.

25.5.5 Can the requirement be decomposed?

Another technique which can be used to reduce the amount of effort needed for the 'musts' is to break the requirement down into more detail. It is normal for a high-level requirement that has been prioritized as a 'must' to be broken down into sub-requirements that comprise several musts, shoulds and coulds, thereby creating contingency in the form of shoulds and coulds.

Take, for example, the search function of a customer relationship management system that must be able to search for customer details. The sub-requirements or musts, shoulds and coulds of such a function include:

- Must be able to search by customer name
- Could be able to search on parts of the customer name
- Must be able to search by customer account number
- Should be able to search by address
- Could be able to search by date of birth.

> **Tip**
> If ever you need to quickly demonstrate prioritization with MoSCoW, a simple ballpoint pen can be a useful prop (see Figure 25.2). It can also be used to illustrate decomposition and how a 'must' can exist within a 'could'.

25.5.6 Ordering

There are situations when the best way to prioritize is to use a simple list where the most important item is at the top and the least important is at the bottom. This could be achieved using a basic scoring system from 1 to 5 for each item in the list, and then ordering all the 5s relative to one another and then so on with the 4s and 3s etc. This approach to prioritization is most appropriate when there is little dependency among the items on the list (i.e. they are broadly independent of one another) and the items on the list do not naturally group together so that they can be worked on at the same time.

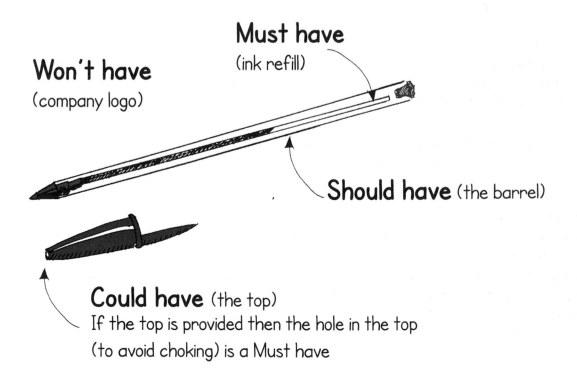

Figure 25.2 'MoSCoWing' a pen

Kanban and Scrum tend to use ordering rather than MoSCoW. However, this approach may not work as well as MoSCoW if a list of requirements has natural groupings and/or dependencies, as the following example shows.

25.5.6.1 Example

You are building a luxury house that must be finished by a certain date. You cannot lower the level of quality and you cannot use additional resources to get it finished on time.

The best prioritization approach to use in this situation is MoSCoW, as you would plan a series of high-level deliverables based around activities that can be grouped together and dependencies that need to be met. For example:

● Clear the site, lay the foundations and install services (e.g. electricity and water).
● Build the main house (so that you can live somewhere).
● Build the garage.
● Create the garden (after most of the construction vehicles have left).

You may feel that the most important part of the whole project is the roof on the main house, but you wouldn't start with this. You may also feel that the garden is more important to you than the garage, but you would deliver this after the garage because the process of building the garage may ruin the garden. When using MoSCoW, you do not necessarily deliver all of the 'musts' first. In cases where you have many features that are dependent on each other, this will rarely happen.

If your plan for the garden involves creating several features – such as a pond, a patio, planting trees, creating flowerbeds, building a greenhouse, creating a sandpit and installing a bird table – then this part of the project may lend itself more to ordering than MoSCoW because the features are reasonably independent of each other and do not naturally group together. You would then complete as many of these as you could before the deadline.

25.5.7 What can be prioritized?

When using agile, prioritization is used constantly and in many forms. The most obvious area where prioritization happens is with respect to the requirements of the project, and this covers those that are both functional and non-functional. Using a camera as an example, its functional and non-functional requirements could include that:

● It MUST take a photograph (functional).
● Its shutter MUST work in cold temperatures (non-functional).

Many other areas could be prioritized, such as the tasks that need to be completed to satisfy a requirement. One especially useful area that could be prioritized is the quality criteria relating to a particular requirement or product description. Following on from the example above:

● The shutter MUST work at –5°C
● The shutter SHOULD work at –20°C
● The shutter COULD work at –35°C.

Quality review activities could also be prioritized in order to target testing and checking more effectively, as it is rare that there is enough time to check everything.

It is important that the correct prioritization approach is used in the appropriate circumstance. This is affected by the level of the requirements and their dependency on one another.

25.5.8 Handling change with prioritization

Change is inevitable on any project and PRINCE2 Agile refers to two types of change: detail and baseline (see also Chapter 14, Change theme).

25.5.8.1 Detail change

If the customer changes their mind on a requirement or comes up with a new requirement but this does not affect the project product description, then this would be seen as creating a more accurate final product and therefore would be seen as something positive.

25.5.8.2 Baseline change

If on the other hand a change to a requirement, or a new requirement, means that there needs to be a change to a product description, then this would be seen as a change to the baseline of the project and would therefore mean the rationale and justification of the project would need to be revisited.

A problem often cited on projects is that of 'scope creep'. PRINCE2 does not see refining the detailed requirements as they evolve as scope creep, whereas if there are changes to the higher-level requirements then this needs the appropriate level of governance. The tolerances used to define requirements can help with this along with defining the quality criteria more as a spectrum, rather than a binary condition.

25.5.9 Dynamic change with prioritization

PRINCE2 Agile is structured around flexing what is delivered as outlined in Chapter 6. Due to this, change can be handled very dynamically, if the change is of the detailed type outlined previously. When change of this type occurs there are two questions that need to be answered with respect to prioritization:

- What is the priority of the new requirement?
- Which requirement, or requirements, will be de-scoped to make way for the new requirement? This is sometimes referred to as 'trading', or 'swapping', requirements.

Although answering these questions may involve discussions with various stakeholders including representatives of the supplier side, ultimately it needs to be driven from the customer side.

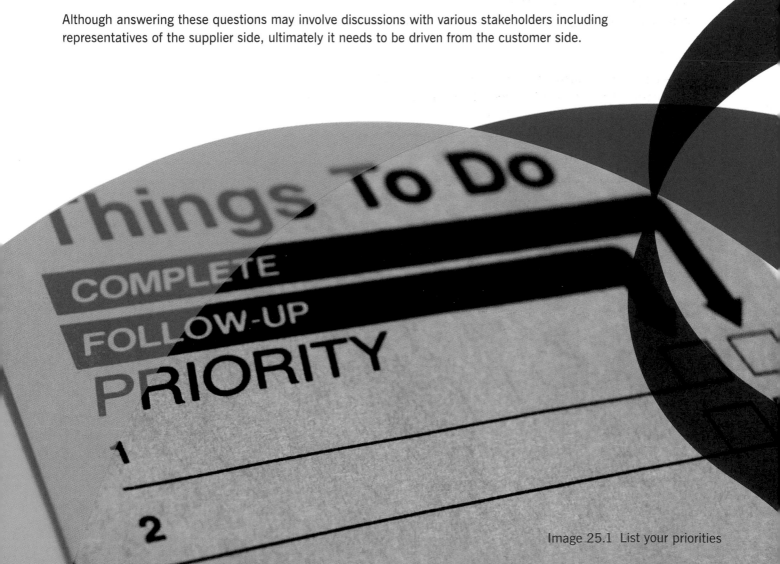

Image 25.1 List your priorities

Hints that may prove useful:

- See the list of requirements as dynamic – embrace change at the detailed level.
- Remember 'Archimedes' law of displacement' – it also applies to new requirements or tasks: if new ones are coming in then some of the existing ones need to make way. This will be carried out by removing requirements or tasks that are of a similar level of effort.
- One of the first reactions to a delay, or an issue, of a project manager using agile in a PRINCE2 environment should be to think 'I need the customer to de-scope something or at least flex the quality criteria on something.'
- Are the tolerance levels flexible enough to allow for a reasonable amount of de-scoping or flexing of the quality criteria, or are they too narrow and causing off-specs and requests for change?

25.5.10 The reason for prioritization

Prioritizing requirements or user stories is a regular and fundamental activity when using agile, but the reasons for this are sometimes overlooked. If you are prioritizing and in effect 'maximizing the amount of work you are not doing' then you will be able to hit deadlines, protect the quality of the products being delivered and respond to changes in order to provide a more accurate final product.

25.6 AGILE CONCEPTS AND TECHNIQUES

25.6.1 User stories

User stories are a very popular technique used throughout agile. The thinking behind user stories is quite simple and if some basic guidelines are followed correctly their use can be quite effective. This simplicity only goes so far and user stories need to be complemented by a degree of rigour to gain the most benefit from this technique.

25.6.1.1 The basics

The exact format can vary but will be based on describing 'who, what and why?'

25.6.1.2 As a <role>, I want to <function>, so that <benefit>

Originally the above heading would have been physically written on a card or sticky note (see Figure 25.3 for an example of a well-written user story) but capturing this electronically (e.g. on a spreadsheet) now also takes place. However, there is more visibility and transparency if it is hand written (or printed off) and this is the preferred approach if possible.

Additional information is needed to evolve the user story – one important area being the addition of acceptance criteria (in the same way as with quality criteria for a PRINCE2 product description) in order to be able to test the user story. Sometimes this is called acceptance criteria or the definition of 'done'. Further to this the user story should also contain at some point an idea of the effort involved in creating it and an idea of the value that it is worth to the customer. These two values could be relative or actual (see section 12.4.1).

PRINCE2 sees user stories as broadly similar to a requirement (which may be a product description or contained within a product description (see section 25.1.1 for information on how to map these terms). A user story does have its own style in that it is often low-tech (i.e. it is very simple in form) and is often a physical thing (such as an index card).

It is essential to avoid the common mistake made when using user stories, which is to see them for more than what they are. They are not fully or partially defined requirements: they are a starting point.

The purpose of a user story is to enable discussion and communication to take place in order to arrive at a thorough understanding of what the customer needs. The card provides interesting information but it is the conversation around it that is vital. Mike Cohn (verbal communication) describes it as 'a token for a conversation'.

Further to this point it could be argued that the information on a user story is deliberately insufficient in order to necessitate a conversation with the customer.

25.6.1.3 Further information

The 'Three Cs' technique (created by Ron Jeffries) distils this into three steps:

- **Card** Writing the story card
- **Conversation** The ongoing discussion involving the card
- **Confirmation** Writing the acceptance test.

The INVEST mnemonic (created by Bill Wake) is used by many as a simple checklist to create a well-written user story in that it should be:

- **I** – Independent
- **N** – Negotiable
- **V** – Valuable
- **E** – Estimable
- **S** – Small
- **T** – Testable.

In terms of managing the user stories (e.g. for planning purposes), making each user story 'independent' from one another means that someone can work on that user story without overlapping with or being dependent on someone else's work. Making them 'small' further helps with planning and the quicker delivery of value.

'Negotiable' refers to the collaborative working between the customer and the team delivering the product.

The thinking behind making the user story 'valuable', 'estimable' and 'testable' focuses the customer and the team to be clear on what they are really trying to achieve. If these three cannot be achieved then there is more to do before work commences.

The SMART abbreviation can also be used in this way (i.e. Specific, Measurable, Agreed, Realistic, Timed).

25.6.1.4 Epics

Embryonic customer requirements can initially be quite large or vague. This has given rise to a different type of user story known as an epic. In effect this is a high-level or 'super-user' story that will over time be broken down into user stories at a level of granularity that the delivery teams can work on. One approach to deriving the user stories is to walk through the process which relates to the epic.

Epics can appear on a product backlog but they would not appear towards the top, as they would not be written in sufficient detail.

25.6.1.5 Hints that may prove useful

User stories should be seen as summarizing key information about a requirement. Therefore it would usually be the case that other supporting information or documentation would need to be referenced in order to fully understand all of the detail behind a user story. This supporting information could have many forms such as a more detailed written specification, figures and models or reference material such as standards and guidelines. These cross-references would be included as part of the user story.

People sometimes refer to epics as coarse-grained user stories that break down into fine-grained user stories.

If the user story clearly shows the information regarding effort and value, it can make prioritization easier. A high-value feature with a low amount of effort will stand out as a priority.

User stories evolve as understanding increases. This is why in an agile environment there is little desire to define them in detail in the early stages of a project.

Acceptance criteria are often harder to write than they may first appear. One approach is to frame the acceptance criteria in the form of user-focused questions. For example, if you are setting acceptance criteria for a coffee mug, the following may be appropriate:

> *Can I put boiling-hot water into the mug and drink from it within five minutes by holding the mug by the handle?*

Just specifying the criterion that 'it will need to hold boiling-hot water' doesn't help with what the user actually wants to do (as the handle may be too hot to touch). Equally, specifying a thickness measurement in respect of the width of the mug (e.g. 2 mm) still doesn't relate directly to the user's need.

25.6.1.6 Creating user stories requires some skill

Creating user stories is often a lot harder than it appears. Creating good user stories and requirements are skills that can take a long time to master. Specialist roles such as requirements engineers and business analysts can add a lot of value in this area.

On projects that normally require more than one customer representative, the need for technical specialization in the area of writing user stories and requirements may become necessary.

It is one thing to write a user story, but another thing altogether to write a good one (see Figure 25.3).

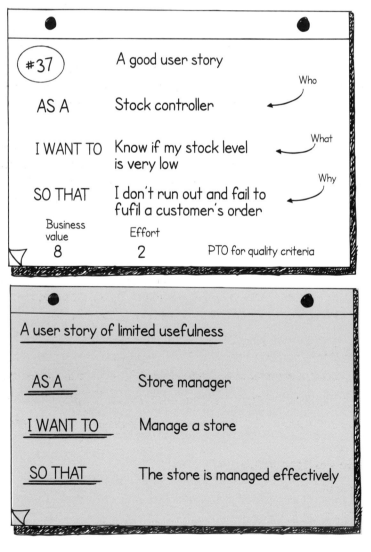

Figure 25.3 A good user story and a poor one

25.6.1.7 Definition of 'ready'

Although not as common as using the definition of 'done' or using acceptance criteria, the use of the definition of 'ready' is a practice used by many in the agile community. This is, in effect, the opposite of 'Are we done?', as it means 'Are we ready?' For example, a definition of 'ready' could be created for a user story so that a delivery team knows that it can start working on it.

For example, in order for a user story (in this case prior to sizing/estimation) to be considered 'ready', it must:

- Contain all three fields describing the who, what and why
- Be understood by the delivery team
- Have a benefit that is measurable
- Have a function that does not contain a solution
- Adhere to the INVEST guidelines
- Have acceptance criteria that are understood by the team
- Define the user as a role
- Identify any supporting documents that are relevant.

25.6.1.8 Technical stories

User stories, as the name implies, focus on the people and roles that interact with the product. This works well when we are describing what something does and what function it needs to perform. However, it doesn't work so well when we are describing how the product works in terms of such things as performance or speed. Further to this, when a customer is describing how the product needs to work, this often applies to many features. In other words this kind of requirement can cut across several user stories.

These kinds of requirements are often described as 'non-functional' and they need to be handled carefully when working in an agile environment. Fitting them into the standard user story format is possible (e.g. refer to the 'user' as 'the system') but treating them slightly differently and referring to them as technical stories is also an option.

An example of a technical story may be when work needs to be completed on the underlying quality of the product (often called refactoring in agile) or experiments and investigations need to take place (often called prototyping or spiking in agile). Sometimes this kind of story or requirement can be included in the definition of 'done', but these types of story are still important as normal user stories though they may be captured in a slightly different way.

25.6.1.9 A means to an end

User stories are an effective technique when using agile. They are easy to manage, they stimulate collaboration and ultimately, when used correctly, improve communication. But always remember it is what happens around the user story that is far more important than the user story itself.

ACKNOWLEDGEMENTS AND FURTHER READING

Dai Clegg and Richard Barker (2004). *Case Method Fast-Track: A RAD Approach*. Addison Wesley.

Mike Cohn (2004). *User Stories Applied: For Agile Software Development*. Addison Wesley.

Lance B. Coleman, Sr. (2015). *The Customer-Driven Organization: Employing the Kano Model*. Apple Academic Press.

Kent Beck: http://www.threeriversinstitute.org/blog

Ron Jeffries: http://ronjeffries.com/

26

Rich communication

This chapter covers:

- Forms of communication
- The PRINCE2 Agile approach to communication
- Agile concepts and techniques

26 Rich communication

26.1 PURPOSE

The purpose of this focus area is to help avoid many of the communication problems that can occur on a project, and explain the various ways in which information and knowledge can pass between project stakeholders in the most effective way.

'Communication problems' are regularly cited as a difficulty faced by people working on projects. This can often be the most significant problem encountered. Because effective communication is so important when a group of people come together to create something, it needs to be proactively addressed and managed throughout a project.

Effective communication is fundamental to the agile way of working but it won't just happen; it needs to be made to happen.

26.2 FORMS OF COMMUNICATION

Communication can take place in many ways and can operate at many levels. An email could contain the start and end time for a meeting, and a conversation could involve strong views and emotions about an individual's poor performance.

Communication can take on many forms such as data, information, knowledge and wisdom (the DIKW hierarchy), and it can be communicated in many ways, such as a document, a phone call, a video-conference or a face-to-face conversation. Further to this, it could be taking place between two people, or two groups of people or even several groups of people.

In order to achieve the most effective and productive communication possible on a project, it is vital to interact in the most appropriate way, at the most appropriate time and using the most appropriate method.

Communication is everywhere on a project. It could be said to be the oxygen that a project needs to survive.

26.3 THE PRINCE2 AGILE APPROACH TO COMMUNICATION

Communication on a project will always be difficult to some degree. It is often noted that a small team located in the same room and working on one product can be highly effective. Part of the reason for this is that the communication between the team members is so fast and clear.

A married couple who have been together for 50 years can still have misunderstandings and communication problems, so if a new project team is assembled to work on something demanding and with lots of uncertainty, communication problems are inevitable.

PRINCE2 Agile focuses on this situation because in order to succeed with PRINCE2 in an agile environment effective communication is essential. When communication breaks down in an agile context it can be very damaging.

26.3.1 Choosing the most appropriate channel

One of the most effective ways to improve communication is to use the right vehicle for conveying a message at the right time. Teams communicate in many different ways such as:

● Using the written word in the form of documents, emails or instant messaging
● Using visualizations in the form of figures or pictures
● Verbally by telephone
● Verbally face-to-face (perhaps by webcam).

People working on a project will be using some or all of these channels at some point and often mixing them together.

To run a project in the most effective way and to get the most effective use of PRINCE2 it is very important to move the communication traffic to the most effective channels, and one of the best ways to do this is to use as much face-to-face communication as possible, ideally accompanied by visualization. This is why a team room, where everyone is co-located, having lots of information readily available on the walls, is seen as an ideal situation.

However, projects have complexity and they may involve several people and involve many teams – this is far from ideal with respect to the ease of communication.

Even so, it is still essential to move the communication traffic to the faster, clearer channels. The phone should be favoured over email, and face-to-face should be favoured over the phone.

Technology should be assessed with respect to making communication easier and more effective. Webcams and collaboration tools can help build a multi-faceted approach to communication.

The type and frequency of communication need to be agreed by the project management team and the level of formality agreed. It needs to be understood when informal channels are appropriate (e.g. a regular one-to-one meeting that is not recorded) and when there is a need to formally record decisions (e.g. that may be needed for auditing purposes). This should be recorded in the communications management strategy, which itself could be an informal document in that it is displayed as part of an information radiator.

26.3.2 The difficulties with the written word

The biggest problem with communication lies in the fact that human beings find it relatively difficult to process large amounts of information in the form of the written word. Communicating between two people, or two groups of people, with a document containing many pages of text has many disadvantages – for example, parts of it might not be read or the reader might be unable to interact with the document.

Tip

Why do many people use emoticons in an email or text message? Because it is easier to convey feelings than it is without them and makes the message more accurate and less prone to being misunderstood.

Typical emoticons: ☺ ☹ :D

This is not to say that there isn't a role for the written word. The opposite is the case. It can provide clarification and is ideal for relaying factual or uncontentious information. It can also allow the writer time to reflect and compose something that is carefully thought out. However, when communication involves opinions or emotions, the written word is not as effective as a phone call or a face-to-face conversation. Potentially, over-reliance on the written word can be counter-productive.

A characteristic of the agile way of working is the way team members will try to shift the communication traffic to the more effective channels (see Figure 26.1). But this takes effort and a desire to work this way. It is usually a lot easier to send an email than to meet with someone to discuss a problem. However, a face-to-face discussion is very likely to achieve a lot more in a very short space of time.

A significant point often missed with respect to face-to-face meetings or even phone calls is the emotional bonding and buy-in to a discussion or decision. Email and the written word are somewhat sterile and therefore this is harder to achieve.

An important point for anyone with a leadership or management role on a project is to be fully aware of how a team is communicating. A vibrant and interactive team using a lot of visualization should be easy to identify. Somewhat harder to identify is when a team, or some members of it, are relying too heavily on such things as email.

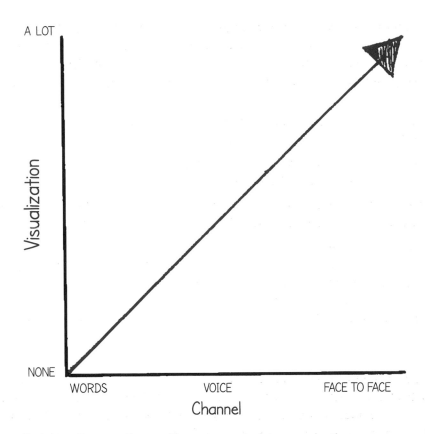

Figure 26.1 Factors that may improve the quality and speed of communication

One particular example of a communication problem that can be very damaging for a project is when a project manager (or team manager) primarily manages a team using email. On the surface this will cause communication to be slow and open to misinterpretation. However, there is a much more serious problem that is likely to emerge with this form of communication, and that is that it takes the energy out of a team as people spend more time on email than interacting with one another. Ultimately, this has the potential to destroy the 'heart and soul' of a team.

26.3.3 Getting the right blend

Effective communication needs to be organized and planned. PRINCE2 is also very clear about the need to document only when necessary. It also describes management products as 'information sets' and not documents. This mind-set should be built on by developing a blend of communication techniques that work when using agile.

When people interact face-to-face, they convey meaning with the words they use, the way they say them and the body language they use when saying them.

It is important to see communication in an agile environment as a shift in emphasis, because an agile team needs to work at much quicker speeds due to the iterative and responsive nature of agile. This is why agile makes extensive use of workshops, face-to-face meetings, visualizations in the form of models and prototypes, and video. But this does not mean there isn't a place for email or written documents (which need to be used to record decisions and actions); it just means that some, or most, of this needs to be moved to the faster, clearer channels whenever possible. It is also worth mentioning that a team whose members are not co-located may have a greater need for email and written documents than a co-located team.

26.4 AGILE CONCEPTS AND TECHNIQUES

26.4.1 Workshops

In agile terms a workshop is generally regarded as an activity where several people come together in order to achieve an objective by harnessing the interactions and creativity of the participants. Typically, a workshop would last from two or three hours to a whole day, but the principles behind the technique can be applied to any timescale (e.g. running a 15-minute retrospective).

The ideal way to run a workshop is by using a neutral facilitator who has no stake in the outcome. Without a facilitator the group will need to police itself, which will be difficult because participants will be concentrating on creating the content to achieve the objective of the workshop.

26.4.1.1 The basics

In simple terms the thinking behind the workshop technique is that it is better to consolidate the understanding of many people by listening to them at the same time, as opposed to consolidating this understanding having listened to them separately. In a workshop, different viewpoints (and their explanations) can be seen immediately by everyone involved; however, the interaction needs to be managed to ensure that everyone can contribute fairly.

Image 26.1 Agile makes extensive use of workshops

Preparation is essential for a successful workshop, and this can take as long as the workshop itself. Typical steps would include:

● **Workshop objective** Why is the workshop taking place? What is it looking to achieve?
● **Attendees** Who should attend to ensure that the workshop objective is met?
● **Agenda** What steps should take place during the workshop and in what order?
● **Logistics** Covering areas such as venue, room layout, refreshments and equipment
● **Pre-reading** What information do the participants need to know in advance to enable a workshop to run as smoothly as possible?

An experienced facilitator would be familiar with these steps, and this is another reason why it is preferable to use a facilitator who can work with the person authorizing the workshop (known as the workshop owner), to structure the workshop in the most appropriate way.

When creating an agenda for a workshop a variety of tools and techniques are available that can be used to address certain problems and situations. Again, an experienced facilitator would be conversant with many of these (see Table 26.1).

26.4.1.2 Example workshop technique 1: group work

At some points during a workshop it may be a good idea to break the whole group into smaller sub-groups. This can enable more areas to be covered and perhaps allow for quieter members of the group to contribute more freely.

Table 26.1 Possible workshop techniques

SWOT analysis	Focuses on the four areas of strengths, weaknesses, opportunities and threats for a given situation.
Impact/effort grids	A two-by-two (four box) grid that allows items to be positioned against two criteria on the x and y axes (e.g. cost versus effort, impact versus probability).
Rich pictures	Using visualization to convey messages (often feelings) in a form that can use metaphors and humour.
Prioritization with dots	The use of sticky dots or marker pen dots to quickly vote on a set of options.
Gap analysis	A three-step technique used to describe how something (e.g. an organization or a project) can get from one state or situation to another. The first step is to describe where it is now. Step two describes where it needs to be, and step three describes what actions need to happen in order to get from the 'now' state to the 'to be' state.
Brainstorming	A way of generating ideas, which normally involves sticky notes so that all ideas are initially produced without being affected by other people. Ideas are then discussed, perhaps grouped and then developed further.
Visioning	Creating shared goals or objectives, often using visualization. Defining the overall 'why?'
The five whys (repeatedly asking 'why?')	A questioning technique to get to the root of a problem or request.
Dr Edward de Bono's Six Thinking Hats	A technique to help people think in six different ways: ● The White Hat calls for information known or needed. ● The Yellow Hat symbolizes brightness and optimism. ● The Black Hat is judgement – the devil's advocate or why something may not work. ● The Red Hat signifies feelings, hunches and intuition. ● The Green Hat focuses on creativity. ● The Blue Hat is used to manage the thinking process.

26.4.1.3 Example workshop technique 2: sticky notes

The use of sticky notes provides many advantages such as: they make people concise, they are somewhat anonymous, they help the group create output quickly, they are movable and they are visual.

26.4.1.4 Further information

Workshops can be used whenever needed and at any point in a project. They are often used during the early stages but it would be a mistake to limit their use to just this area. The reason for this is that the technique can be very helpful in several situations such as:

- Planning and estimating
- Reviewing
- Problem-solving
- Requirements-gathering
- Project kick-offs
- Carrying out a stakeholder analysis
- Identifying and analysing risk.

Tools and techniques, and how they are used, play a significant part in workshops but perhaps the most important area to get right is the group dynamics. Strong personalities and conflicting views need to be managed, and this is where a neutral facilitator is perhaps most valuable.

A simple intervention by a facilitator when one person talks over another can give a clear signal to the group that everyone's views will be heard.

26.4.1.5 Hints that may prove useful

Groups can use workshops without a facilitator, but this would normally require the group to have established and agreed its own working norms. This often takes time to establish and typically exists in teams that have been together for a significant period of time.

A workshop is quite a significant event that takes a lot of time and resources to set up and run. Therefore, it is always advisable to question whether a workshop is really necessary or if there could be another way of achieving the objective (e.g. a small meeting).

With some workshops it is a good idea to create something collectively as a group (e.g. a plan); whereas at other times it is better for specific individuals to create something and then have it reviewed as a group (e.g. a business case).

26.4.1.6 Run workshops well

Workshops are a very powerful tool. When run correctly they can create high-quality outputs in short spaces of time through motivated individuals collaborating and communicating effectively. This in turn creates clarity, consensus and ownership.

ACKNOWLEDGEMENTS AND FURTHER READING

Marshall B. Rosenberg (2003). *Nonviolent Communication: a Language of Life*. Puddle Dancer Press.

Zachman Framework (i.e. the who, what, when, where, why and how): http://www.zachman.com/about-the-zachman-framework

27

Frequent releases

This chapter covers:
- The importance of frequent releases to agile
- Releasing early and frequently

27 Frequent releases

27.1 PURPOSE

The purpose of this focus area is to describe the importance of frequent releases when using agile. It also describes what considerations to take into account when planning releases and planning the project as a whole. This focus area also addresses what to do when a release cannot go directly into the operational environment.

This focus area is closely linked to the Plans theme (see Chapter 12) and configuration management.

A fundamental concept of any agile method or approach is to frequently deliver something of use. There are many advantages associated with this such as:

● It enables an early delivery of benefit to the customer.
● It allows for feedback.
● It is likely to reduce risk (e.g. of delivering the wrong product).
● It gives confidence about how the project is proceeding through visibility and evidence.
● It fosters engagement with project stakeholders.
● It makes releasing easier and perhaps second nature.

The strategy for delivering frequently and how to plan for this needs careful consideration as there are many trade-offs that have to be taken into account.

27.2 RELEASING EARLY AND FREQUENTLY

Traditionally, many projects have delivered the final product using a serial, or Waterfall, approach whereby there are a series of technical phases (such as analysis, design, build, test, implement) leading to the whole product being delivered at the end of the project (see Figure 2.2).

Even when working in this way, the project can still be broken down into chunks to allow for an earlier delivery of parts of the final product. This is sometimes referred to as 'phased Waterfall' as each chunk is still planned around technical phases. But this is still not an agile way of working.

Agile looks at this in a completely different way. It does not base its plans upon technical phases; it bases them on features and requirements instead. As part of the initiation stage of a project PRINCE2 Agile looks at how the final product can be broken down into coherent chunks and what parts of the final product can be delivered early to achieve the advantages outlined previously.

27.2.1 How releases fit in with the PRINCE2 process

Releases can be planned using product-based planning, and individual product descriptions can have their quality criteria defined to allow for different product 'states' (to reflect releases). Release backlogs would then sit under these. An alternative to this is to avoid using 'states' and assign products to a release backlog when appropriate. This is likely to be more appropriate if there are many releases and a high degree of change as to what is going into each release. It will be easier to use product-based planning this way as well.

Release planning needs to be incorporated into the PRINCE2 plans. A project plan would need to clearly show how many releases were expected throughout the project, when they will take place and what features are intended to be released. The same applies to a stage plan, albeit with a shorter horizon (see Figure 12.3).

The different levels of plan would need to be synchronized with respect to release planning. An example of this would be where the project board would like to establish a stage boundary in order to manage by exception. It would need to balance out its own needs to set a timescale with the needs of the customer or the delivery teams, who will have a view on what releases they would like to happen and at what time.

What is being released, and when, should not be seen as a minor or incidental part of a plan. How a product is released, gradually over time, will have a direct effect on how benefits are realized and can have a significant effect on whether or not the project can continue to be justified. It is possible that a project needs to realize early benefits in order to fund later parts of the project. The project board needs to be fully aware of the significance of release planning. It is not something that just concerns the people working at the delivery level.

Some of the fundamentals of the Lean Startup approach involve releasing a product in such a way that it maximizes the viability of the product and enables it to fail fast if it is going to fail. A well-crafted release plan can prove significantly beneficial to an organization. It can create feedback that can be responded to at the earliest opportunity.

How frequently and regularly releases take place (in terms of creating a regular cadence or 'heartbeat') needs to be collectively decided by the key stakeholders involved on the project (e.g. the help desk or the training department). In some situations products and sub-products can be delivered too quickly for the customer to absorb them efficiently. This could result in disruption from an operational point of view.

27.2.2 Releasing into operational use

To benefit from all of the advantages of frequent delivery, the ideal situation is for any release to go into the operational environment. However, this is not always possible or desirable. If a release does not go into operational use, it is unlikely to generate any benefits or 'real' customer feedback.

Tip

It is possible to release features too quickly! So you need to involve the right stakeholders.

A lot depends on how much control over releasing into operational use a project has. If the necessary stakeholders are on the project and they can dictate whether or not a release goes into operational use, and they are responsible for the impact of the release, then this is the ideal situation. This would be seen as 'very agile'. However, if another company or department is responsible for the release process and the impact a release may have, then they may have other factors to consider such as contractual obligations or the needs of other stakeholders. This does, to a degree, limit the agile way of working.

27.2.3 Not releasing into operational use

Even though feedback from real customers and some form of benefits realization would be missing, there are still many advantages to delivering something into a staging area before going into operational use: for example, the opportunity to assess progress and the levels of quality being achieved. A significant customer demo could take place in order to receive feedback on how the product is developing, along with how the project processes and team behaviours have helped with that specific delivery.

Tip

It may be appropriate to populate a list of FAQs for when the product goes into operational use.

Unfortunately there is a significant limitation with respect to agile's desire for regular, frequent (even continual) delivery when some form of staging area is involved. Typical reasons for inclusion of a staging area are regulatory compliance checking, integration testing or any other form of validation and verification process. The problem is that when an error is picked up and a change needs to be made, further work may have already taken place on the current state of the product, which would have been baselined at the point of delivery into the staging area.

The agile way of working is compromised to a degree when this happens because the problem cannot typically be solved by flexing what is being delivered. Whether or not a product is compliant with a safety standard is usually a yes or no, pass or fail condition. It is unlikely that you could 'drop a little bit out of compliance'!

The problem will always remain, however, that when products are delivered into staging areas, their rework will need to be accommodated and planned for in advance. This will affect configuration management and version control so that the current state of the product can be efficiently resynchronized back to one version.

27.3 SUMMARY

There are significant advantages of frequently releasing products and sub-products. This is an essential part of the iterative and incremental nature that differentiates agile from more traditional approaches to product development. Approaches such as Kanban and Lean Startup relentlessly pursue frequent delivery to the customer in as short a time as possible, in order to gain these advantages. The ultimate goal is to release continually if conditions allow and the benefits of doing so are realized.

28

Creating contracts when using agile

This chapter covers:

- Traditional contracts
- Structuring an agile contract
- The role of the supplier in an outcome-based contract

28 Creating contracts when using agile

Many of the fundamental concepts of agile do not sit easily with the way that contracts between a customer and a supplier are typically structured. Agile is a collaboration where a customer and a supplier work together and share risk. A contract is usually an adversarial mechanism which describes 'legal remedies' for when things go wrong. Any project using PRINCE2 Agile needs to choose between using existing practices or using a different underlying structure that is more amenable to working in an agile way.

28.1 TRADITIONAL CONTRACTS

In simple terms a typical contract (sometimes referred to as a 'traditional' contract) would involve the customer engaging the supplier to deliver a specific solution or output that is defined by a set of specific requirements. These requirements would usually be several in number and may be quite detailed. Along with this there would usually be a deadline and a price.

Projects are difficult and face uncertainty; therefore the detailed requirements are likely to change over the course of the project, as well as the understanding of how long the work will take.

The principal issue with the traditional structure of a contract is that the requirements and the understanding of the work involved will inevitably change over time, and someone will need to pay for that change, or at least factor this into the contract in the form of a contingency (e.g. the supplier adds 20% to the price).

In an agile context this structure is counter-productive because agile is 'change friendly' and works on the basis that modifications will inevitably happen; it is not necessarily a negative situation if changes ultimately result in something that is more closely aligned with the customer's real needs and potentially delivers more value than originally intended.

In an agile context the customer and the supplier need to work together to optimize the solution in order to achieve the best possible outcome in terms of value to the customer. Focusing the contract on the solution is less likely to produce this effect.

28.2 PRIMARY CONSIDERATIONS WHEN STRUCTURING AN AGILE CONTRACT

When looking to structure a contract in a way that is more conducive to working with agile, the most important area to address first is to understand the level of trust and collaboration between the customer and the supplier. Trust is a difficult area to cover in a contract, as many elements of a contract concern the problems that may occur. Therefore a contract needs to support collaborative ways of working (e.g. by containing incentives and levels of commitment).

A customer and supplier may have worked together for several years and the trust and collaboration between them may be very high. Alternatively, if a supplier is new to a customer, levels of trust and collaboration might be unknown and difficult to assess.

The reason this is so important is because it will determine the amount of risk that is shared between the customer and the supplier. The risk relates to the uncertainties of the project. A former United States Secretary of Defense used the phrases 'known unknowns' and 'unknown unknowns' and these exist on any project. When these unknowns surface during a project, who 'pays' for the change: the supplier because they should have anticipated it, or the customer because they should have specified it?

Alternatively, should the 'cost' of the change be shared because both parties know that there is uncertainty and 'unknowns'? The more trust and collaboration that exist between a customer and supplier, the less is the likelihood of:

● The supplier adding a contingency premium to the price of the contract in relation to the amount of risk involved

● The customer going into too much detail when initiating a project in the belief that they are removing uncertainty (sometimes referred to as 'the illusion of certainty').

28.3 GUIDANCE ON HOW TO STRUCTURE AN AGILE CONTRACT

Structuring a contract that is suitable when working with agile does not necessarily involve creating a completely new type of contract. Existing contract frameworks currently being used by organizations may still be suitable to a large extent (e.g. as a master agreement). However, change will be needed at the lower levels in order to work in a more agile way (e.g. in a statement of work (or SOW), which may apply to a period of time, such as a sprint or a release).

When using agile, structuring a contract according to the following guidelines is likely to be more beneficial to both parties than using a traditional style of contract:

● If possible, make the focus of what is being delivered 'outcome-based' in preference to 'output-based'. An output focus is typically about a product or solution that either is, or is not, as specified. An outcome focus relates to the benefits and value that a project enables. This allows the customer and supplier to work together to create an output (or product) that can be changed and adjusted throughout the course of the project, in order to deliver something more valuable if the opportunity arises. There is a difficulty with outcome-based contracts in that outcomes can be hard to define objectively (see section 9.4.1, Defining value) and if this is the case, then a middle ground between outcome and output is to use such things as service levels or throughputs (e.g. velocity), whilst still allowing the customer and supplier to respond to change in order to optimize the value delivered.

● Define the level of customer involvement needed during the project. This would take the form of how much time would be committed to the project by the customer so that the supplier can benefit from the collaborative working relationship. This is likely to take the form of named individuals from a variety of levels with clearly defined roles and responsibilities. When working in an agile way, a collaborative relationship between the customer and supplier is an essential ingredient that helps with many things such as speed of decision-making, accuracy of deliverables and ultimately the ownership of the products delivered. Agreeing the level of commitment in advance and clearly defining responsibilities increase the chance that this collaboration will happen.

● Create several time-based deliveries as part of the main agreement (e.g. based around sprints or releases), which can be used to monitor the overall project against an agreed baseline that relates to the value the project should deliver. This may, or may not, be put into operational use, but it will show how much is being delivered by the supplier, and it can be measured according to, for example, value, velocity or story points. This allows the customer to see how the project is progressing. In effect the customer is buying amounts of time (or a throughput of work) from the supplier. It may be appropriate to create an initial delivery that goes into more detail of what the project intends to achieve (e.g. this may include requirements-gathering and/or a prototype).

● Allow for the project to be stopped at any time by the project board. This allows the customer to stop a project if feedback from early deliveries indicates that the project as a whole is no longer viable. This will not be seen by the supplier as breaking an agreement, as this is always a possibility with this form of contract and the supplier is fully aware of it from the start. Further to this, most existing contracts have early termination clauses anyway. This does not preclude the contract from being fixed-price, although the full price will only be relevant if the project runs to completion.

Tip

Sometimes sprint zero (or early sprints) can be used for the initial delivery. (Also referred to as iteration zero or discovery.)

● Incentives can be linked to the amount delivered. If the supplier delivers everything that was intended during a particular timeframe, then they receive 100% (or even 100%+) of the remuneration agreed. Lesser deliveries could then be on a sliding scale as shown in Table 28.1.

Table 28.1 Sliding-scale incentives

Delivery target	Amount received	Customer credit
90% or greater	100% (or more)	0%
80% to 90%	90%	10%
70% to 80%	80%	20%
60% to 70%	70%	30%

Table 28.2 Levels of trust and incentives

Level of trust	Composition of the incentive scheme
Very high	No need to incentivize.
High	Incentives for amount delivered and shortfalls used as credits for use on future work (see column 3 in Table 28.1).
Moderate	Incentives acting more as penalty clauses (although the supplier may be happy with this arrangement).

The composition of an incentive scheme would depend on the level of trust and collaboration between the customer and supplier, which may take the form of schemes shown in Table 28.2.

An incentive scheme can be seen as a penalty clause depending on the nature of the relationship. If the incentives are linked to throughput (e.g. velocity) this can create a mutually beneficial situation; although trust plays an important part here as throughput can be manipulated (e.g. the supplier inflates the story points used for estimation or delivers more features by focusing on easier, less critical ones – sometimes this is referred to as 'gaming'). If the incentives are related to outcomes and value delivered, the risk of 'gaming' is reduced.

● Requirements will be defined in the contract at a high or intermediate level, but not in detail. If the requirements are not specified in detail from the start, this allows for the correct products to emerge during the course of the project without the need to control and change the baseline created during project Initiation, which may form part of the contract.

● Requirements need to be prioritized so that the most important in terms of value are delivered, and the least important can be used as contingency in order to protect the quality of what is delivered and also to meet deadlines. A minimum viable product (MVP) is also likely to be described. The level of trust is important with respect to the MVP as this may represent a 'material breach' and a failure to deliver. Alternatively, it could still be classed as 'best endeavours', in that what the customer and supplier set out to achieve did not actually turn out to be possible.

● Requirements change is handled by 'trading' new ones for existing ones (see section 25.5); for example, any new requirements discovered during the project can be added to the requirements list, but the effort needed to satisfy the new requirement will be at the expense of other requirements that are either given a lower place in the order of priorities or removed from the list altogether.

● Depending on the level of trust between the customer and the supplier, it may be agreeable to create a contract using as few clauses as possible and then add clauses when needed (in effect this represents a 'minimum viable contract'). This is counter to the usual approach of starting with many clauses and removing the ones that aren't needed. However, it is the quality of the clauses that is the most important consideration and not the quantity (e.g. specification of who owns the intellectual property of the output).

In summary, the guidelines for structuring a contract for use in an agile context are as follows:

● Focus on outcomes or throughput in preference to outputs

● Define the amount of customer involvement required in order to collaborate with the supplier in the best way

● Buy amounts of time relating to timeboxes with deliverables

● Allow for a premature end to the project

● Relate incentives to the amount delivered (value or throughput)

- Avoid including detailed requirements
- Prioritize the requirements and identify an MVP
- Handle changing requirements by trading out the less important ones
- If preferred, build a contract up from the 'minimum' to start with.

28.4 THE ROLE OF THE SUPPLIER IN AN OUTCOME-BASED CONTRACT

An outcome cannot be achieved by the supplier alone, whereas an output can. This means that the supplier will need to estimate the amount of work they can achieve (e.g. by calculating their expected velocity) and then work with the customer to agree how they commit to this, and how the risk is shared.

Typically, the delivery rate is what goes into the contract, as this is under the control of the supplier. It is possible for the outcome or the benefits delivered to go into the contract instead, or as well, but this will depend on how much risk each party wants to share.

28.5 SUMMARY

A contract based on outcomes or throughput needs collaboration between the customer and the supplier.

In simple terms an agile contract should create the right behaviours; moving from a solution-based view to a view based around throughput or outcomes is more likely to produce those beneficial behaviours.

Structuring a contract to align with the agile way of working is advantageous when using PRINCE2 Agile because the customer and supplier should be constantly responding to change in order to deliver the highest value possible in the defined timescale. This therefore needs a contract that supports the objective of delivering value and allowing for change.

Ultimately, the contract should be seen as a safety net and not a weapon.

ACKNOWLEDGEMENTS AND FURTHER READING

www.flexiblecontracts.com

APPENDICES

A

Product description outlines

Appendix A Product description outlines

The product descriptions in this appendix are shortened versions of those in Appendix A of the PRINCE2 manual (*Managing Successful Projects with PRINCE2*).

A.1 BENEFITS REVIEW PLAN

A.1.1 Purpose

A benefits review plan is used to define how and when a measurement of the achievement of the project's benefits, expected by the senior user, can be made. The plan is presented to the executive during the Initiating a Project process, updated at each stage boundary, and used during the Closing a Project process to define any post-project benefits reviews that are required.

The plan has to cover the activities to find out whether the expected benefits of the products have been realized and how the products have performed when in operational use. Each expected benefit has to be assessed for the level of its achievement and whether any additional time is needed to assess the residual benefits. Use of the project's products may have brought unexpected side-effects, either beneficial or adverse. Time and effort have to be allowed to identify and analyse why these side-effects were not foreseen.

If the project is part of a programme, the benefits review plan may be contained within the programme's benefits realization plan and executed at the programme level. Post-project, the benefits review plan is maintained and executed by corporate or programme management.

A.1.2 Composition

- The scope of the benefits review plan covering what benefits are to be measured
- Who is accountable for the expected benefits
- How to measure achievement of expected benefits, and when they can be measured
- What resources are needed to carry out the review work
- Baseline measures from which the improvements will be calculated
- How the performance of the project's product will be reviewed.

A.2 BUSINESS CASE

A.2.1 Purpose

A business case is used to document the justification for the undertaking of a project, based on the estimated costs (of development, implementation and incremental ongoing operations and maintenance costs) against the anticipated benefits to be gained and offset by any associated risks. It should outline how and when the anticipated benefits can be measured.

The outline business case is developed in the Starting up a Project process and refined by the Initiating a Project process. The Directing a Project process covers the approval and re-affirmation of the business case.

The business case is used by the Controlling a Stage process when assessing impacts of issues and risks. It is reviewed and updated at the end of each management stage by the Managing a Stage Boundary process, and at the end of the project by the Closing a Project process.

A.2.2 Composition

- **Executive summary** Highlights the key points in the business case, which should include important benefits and the return on investment (ROI)
- **Reasons** Defines the reasons for undertaking the project and explains how the project will enable the achievement of corporate strategies and objectives

- **Business options** Analysis and reasoned recommendation for the base business options of: do nothing, do the minimum or do something
- **Expected benefits** The benefits that the project will deliver expressed in measurable terms against the situation as it exists prior to the project. Benefits should be both qualitative and quantitative. They should be aligned to corporate or programme benefits. Tolerances should be set for each benefit and for the aggregated benefit. Any benefits realization requirements should be stated
- **Expected dis-benefits** Outcomes perceived as negative by one or more stakeholders. Dis-benefits are actual consequences of an activity whereas, by definition, a risk has some uncertainty about whether it will materialize. For example, a decision to merge two elements of an organization onto a new site may have benefits (e.g. better joint working), costs (e.g. expanding one of the two sites) and dis-benefits (e.g. drop in productivity during the merger). Dis-benefits need to be valued and incorporated into the investment appraisal
- **Timescale** Over which the project will run (summary of the project plan) and the period over which the benefits will be realized. This information is subsequently used to help timing decisions when planning (project plan, stage plan and benefits review plan)
- **Costs** A summary of the project costs (taken from the project plan), the ongoing operations and maintenance costs and their funding arrangements
- **Investment appraisal** Compares the aggregated benefits and dis-benefits to the project costs (extracted from the project plan) and ongoing incremental operations and maintenance costs. The analysis may use techniques such as cash flow statement, ROI, net present value, internal rate of return and payback period. The objective is to be able to define the value of a project as an investment. The investment appraisal should address how the project will be funded
- **Major risks** Gives a summary of the key risks associated with the project together with the likely impact and plans should they occur.

A.3 CHECKPOINT REPORT

A.3.1 Purpose

A checkpoint report is used to report, at a frequency defined in the work package, the status of the work package.

A.3.2 Composition

- **Date** The date of the checkpoint
- **Period** The reporting period covered by the checkpoint report
- **Follow-ups** From previous reports, for example action items completed or issues outstanding
- **This reporting period:**
  - The products being developed by the team during the reporting period
  - The products completed by the team during the reporting period
  - Quality management activities carried out during the period
  - Lessons identified
- **Next reporting period:**
  - The products being developed by the team in the next reporting period
  - The products planned to be completed by the team in the next reporting period
  - Quality management activities planned for the next reporting period
- **Work package tolerance status** How execution of the work package is performing against its tolerances (e.g. cost/time/scope actuals and forecast)
- **Issues and risks** Update on issues and risks associated with the work package.

A.4 COMMUNICATION MANAGEMENT STRATEGY

A.4.1 Purpose

A communication management strategy contains a description of the means and frequency of communication to parties both internal and external to the project. It facilitates engagement with stakeholders through the establishment of a controlled and bi-directional flow of information.

A.4.2 Composition

- **Introduction** States the purpose, objectives and scope, and identifies who is responsible for the strategy
- **Communication procedure** A description of (or reference to) any communication methods to be used. Any variance from corporate or programme management standards should be highlighted, together with a justification for the variance
- **Tools and techniques** Refers to any communication tools to be used, and any preference for techniques that may be used, for each step in the communication process
- **Records** Definition of what communication records will be required and where they will be stored (for example, logging of external correspondence)
- **Reporting** Describes any reports on the communication process that are to be produced, including their purpose, timing and recipients (for example, performance indicators)
- **Timing of communication activities** States when formal communication activities are to be undertaken (for example, at the end of a stage) including performance audits of the communication methods
- **Roles and responsibilities** Describes who will be responsible for what aspects of the communication process, including any corporate or programme management roles involved with communication
- **Stakeholder analysis:**
  - Identification of the interested party (which may include accounts staff, user forum, internal audit, corporate or programme quality assurance, competitors etc.)
  - Current relationship
  - Desired relationship
  - Interfaces
  - Key messages
- **Information needs for each interested party:**
  - Information required to be provided from the project
  - Information required to be provided to the project
  - Information provider and recipient
  - Frequency of communication
  - Means of communication
  - Format of the communication.

A.5 CONFIGURATION ITEM RECORD

A.5.1 Purpose

To provide a record of such information as the history, status, version and variant of each **configuration item**, and any details of important relationships between them.

The set of configuration item records for a project is often referred to as a configuration library.

A.5.2 Composition

The composition of a configuration item record will be defined in the project's configuration management strategy.

There follows a suggested list of components for each configuration item record (note that the first three uniquely identify the configuration item):

- **Project identifier** A unique reference. It will typically be a numeric or alpha-numeric value
- **Item identifier** A unique reference. It will typically be a numeric or alpha-numeric value
- **Current version** Typically an alpha-numeric value
- **Item title** The description of the item (for a product this should be as it appears in the product breakdown structure)
- **Date of last status change**
- **Owner** The person or group who will take ownership of the product when it is handed over
- **Location** Where the item is stored
- **Copy-holders (if relevant)** Who currently has the product?
- **Item type** Component, product, release
- **Item attributes** As defined by the configuration management strategy. These are used to specify a subset of products when producing a product status account, such as the management stage in which the product is created, the type of product (e.g. hardware/software), product destination etc.
- **Stage** When the product will be developed
- **Users** The person or group who will use the item
- **Status** As defined by the configuration management strategy, e.g. pending development, in development, in review, approved or handed over
- **Product state (if used)** As defined by the product description, e.g. dismantled machinery, moved machinery, reassembled machinery
- **Variant (if used)** For example, language variants
- **Producer** The person or team responsible for creating or obtaining the item
- **Date allocated** To the producer
- **Source** For example, in house, or purchased from a third-party company
- **Relationship with other items** Those items that:
  - Would be affected if this item changed
  - If changed, would affect this item
- **Cross-references:**
  - Issues and risks
  - Documentation that defines requirements, design, build, production and verification for the item (specifically this will include the product description).

A.6 CONFIGURATION MANAGEMENT STRATEGY

A.6.1 Purpose

A configuration management strategy is used to identify how, and by whom, the project's products will be controlled and protected.

It answers the questions:

- How and where the project's products will be stored
- What storage and retrieval security will be put in place
- How the products and the various versions and variants of these will be identified

- How changes to products will be controlled
- Where responsibility for configuration management will lie.

A.6.2 Composition

- **Introduction** States the purpose, objectives and scope, and identifies who is responsible for the strategy
- **Configuration management procedure** A description of (or reference to) the configuration management procedure to be used. Any variance from corporate or programme management standards should be highlighted, together with a justification for the variance. The procedure should cover activities such as planning, identification, control (including storage/retrieval, product security, handover procedures etc.), status accounting, and verification and audit
- **Issue and change control procedure** A description (or reference to) the issue and change control procedures to be used. Any variance from corporate or programme management standards should be highlighted, together with a justification for the variance. The procedure should cover activities such as capturing, examining, proposing, deciding and implementing
- **Tools and techniques** Refers to any configuration management systems or tools to be used and any preference for techniques that may be used for each step in the configuration management procedure
- **Records** Definition of the composition and format of the issue register and configuration item records
- **Reporting** Describes the composition and format of the reports that are to be produced (issue report, product status account), their purpose, timing and chosen recipients. This should include reviewing the performance of the procedures
- **Timing of configuration management and issue and change control activities** States when formal activities (for example, configuration audits) are to be undertaken
- **Roles and responsibilities** Describes who will be responsible for what aspects of the procedures, including any corporate or programme management roles involved with the configuration management of the project's products. Describes whether a change authority and/or change budget will be established
- **Scales for priority and severity** For prioritizing requests for change and off-specifications and for determining the level of management that can make decisions on severity of issue.

A.7 DAILY LOG

A.7.1 Purpose

A daily log is used to record informal issues, required actions or significant events not caught by other PRINCE2 registers or logs. It acts as the project diary for the project manager.

It can also be used as a repository for issues and risks during the Starting up a Project process if the other registers have not been set up.

There may be more than one daily log as team managers may elect to have one for their work packages, separate from the project manager's daily log.

A.7.2 Composition

A daily log is in free form but likely to include:

- Date of entry
- Problem, action, event or comment
- Person responsible
- Target date
- Results.

A.8 END PROJECT REPORT

A.8.1 Purpose

An end project report is used during project closure to review how the project performed against the version of the project initiation documentation used to authorize it. It also allows the passing on of:

- Any lessons that can be usefully applied to other projects
- Details of unfinished work, ongoing risks or potential product modifications to the group charged with future support of the project's products in their operational life.

A.8.2 Composition

- **Project manager's report** Summarizing the project's performance
- **Review of the business case** Summarizing the validity of the project's business case:
  - Benefits achieved to date
  - Residual benefits expected (post-project)
  - Expected net benefits
  - Deviations from the approved business case
- **Review of project objectives** Review of how the project performed against its planned targets and tolerances for time, cost, quality, scope, benefits and risk. Review the effectiveness of the project's strategies and controls
- **Review of team performance** In particular, providing recognition for good performance
- **Review of products:**
  - Quality records listing the quality activities planned and completed
  - Approval records listing the products and their requisite approvals
  - Off-specifications listing any missing products or products that do not meet the original requirements, and confirmation of any concessions granted
  - Project product handover: confirmation (in the form of acceptance records) by the customer that operations and maintenance functions are ready to receive the project's product
  - Summary of follow-on action recommendations: request for project board advice about who should receive each recommended action. The recommended actions are related to unfinished work, ongoing issues and risks, and any other activities needed to take the products to the next phase of their life
- **Lessons report** (see section A.15) A review of what went well, what went badly, and any recommendations for corporate or programme management consideration (and if the project was prematurely closed, then the reasons should be explained).

A.9 END STAGE REPORT

A.9.1 Purpose

An end stage report is used to give a summary of progress to date, the overall project situation and sufficient information to ask for a project board decision on what to do next with the project.

The project board uses the information in the end stage report in tandem with the next stage plan to decide what action to take with the project: for example, authorize the next stage, amend the project scope or stop the project.

A.9.2 Composition

- **Project manager's report** Summarizing the stage performance
- **Review of the business case** Summarizing the validity of the project's business case:

- Benefits achieved to date
- Residual benefits expected (remaining stages and post-project)
- Expected net benefits
- Deviations from approved business case
- Aggregated risk exposure
- **Review of project objectives** Review of how the project has performed to date against its planned targets and tolerances for time, cost, quality, scope, benefits and risk. Review the effectiveness of the project's strategies and controls
- **Review of stage objectives** Review of how the specific stage performed against its planned targets and tolerances for time, cost, quality, scope, benefits and risk
- **Review of team performance** In particular, providing recognition for good performance
- **Review of products:**
  - Quality records listing the quality activities planned and completed in the stage
  - Approval records listing the products planned for completion in the stage and their requisite approvals
  - Off-specifications listing any missing products or products that do not meet the original requirements, and confirmation of any concessions granted
  - Phased handover (if applicable): confirmation by the customer that operations and maintenance functions are ready to receive the release
  - Summary of follow-on action recommendations (if applicable): request for project board advice for who should receive each recommended action. The recommended actions are related to unfinished work, ongoing issues and risks, and any other activities needed to take the products handed over to the next phase of their life
- **Lessons report** (if appropriate – see section A.15) A review of what went well, what went badly, and any recommendations for corporate or programme management consideration
- **Issues and risks** Summary of the current set of issues and risks affecting the project
- **Forecast** The project manager's forecast for the project and next stage against planned targets and tolerances for time, cost, quality, scope, benefits and risk.

Where the end stage report is being produced at the end of the initiation stage, not all of the above content may be appropriate or necessary.

A.10 EXCEPTION REPORT

A.10.1 Purpose

An exception report is produced when a stage plan or project plan is forecast to exceed tolerance levels set. It is prepared by the project manager in order to inform the project board of the situation, and to offer options and recommendations for the way to proceed.

A.10.2 Composition

- **Exception title** An overview of the exception being reported
- **Cause of the exception** A description of the cause of a deviation from the current plan
- **Consequences of the deviation** What the implications are if the deviation is not addressed for:
  - The project
  - Corporate or programme management
- **Options** What are the options that are available to address the deviation and what would the effect of each option be on the business case, risks and tolerances?
- **Recommendation** Of the available options, what is the recommendation, and why?
- **Lessons** What can be learned from the exception, on this project or future projects?

A.11 HIGHLIGHT REPORT

A.11.1 Purpose

A highlight report is used to provide the project board (and possibly other stakeholders) with a summary of the stage status at intervals defined by them. The project board uses the report to monitor stage and project progress. The project manager also uses it to advise the project board of any potential problems or areas where the project board could help.

A.11.2 Composition

- **Date** The date of the report
- **Period** The reporting period covered by the highlight report
- **Status summary** An overview of the status of the stage at this time
- **This reporting period:**
  - Work packages – pending authorization, in execution, and completed in the period (if the work packages are being performed by external suppliers, this information may be accompanied by purchase order and invoicing data)
  - Products completed in the period
  - Products planned but not started or completed in the period (providing an early-warning indicator or potential breach of time tolerance)
  - Corrective actions taken during the period
- **Next reporting period:**
  - Work packages – to be authorized, in execution, and to be completed during the next period (if the work packages are being performed by external suppliers, this information may be accompanied by purchase order and invoicing data)
  - Products to be completed in the next period
  - Corrective actions to be completed during the next period
- **Project and stage tolerance status** How execution of the project and stage are performing against their tolerances (e.g. cost/time actuals and forecast)
- **Requests for change** Raised, approved/rejected and pending
- **Key issues and risks** Summary of actual or potential problems and risks
- **Lessons report** (if appropriate – see section A.15) A review of what went well, what went badly, and any recommendations for corporate or programme management consideration.

A.12 ISSUE REGISTER

A.12.1 Purpose

The purpose of the issue register is to capture and maintain information on all of the issues that are being formally managed. The issue register should be monitored by the project manager on a regular basis.

A.12.2 Composition

For each entry in the issue register, the following should be recorded:

- **Issue identifier** Provides a unique reference for every issue entered into the issue register. It will typically be a numeric or alpha-numeric value
- **Issue type** Defines the type of issue being recorded, namely:
  - Request for change
  - Off-specification
  - Problem/concern

- **Date raised** The date on which the issue was originally raised
- **Raised by** The name of the individual or team who raised the issue
- **Issue report author** The name of the individual or team who created the issue report
- **Issue description** A statement describing the issue, its cause and impact
- **Priority** This should be given in terms of the project's chosen categories. Priority should be re-evaluated after impact analysis
- **Severity** This should be given in terms of the project's chosen scale. Severity will indicate what level of management is required to make a decision on the issue
- **Status** The current status of the issue and the date of the last update
- **Closure date** The date the issue was closed.

A.13 ISSUE REPORT

A.13.1 Purpose

An issue report is a report containing the description, impact assessment and recommendations for a request for change, off-specification or a problem/concern. It is only created for those issues that need to be handled formally.

The report is initially created when capturing the issue, and updated both after the issue has been examined and when proposals are identified for issue resolution. The issue report is later amended further in order to record what option was decided upon, and finally updated when the implementation has been verified and the issue is closed.

A.13.2 Composition

- **Issue identifier** As shown in the issue register (provides a unique reference for every issue report)
- **Issue type** Defines the type of issue being recorded, namely:
  - Request for change
  - Off-specification
  - Problem/concern
- **Date raised** The date on which the issue was originally raised
- **Raised by** The name of the individual or team who raised the issue
- **Issue report author** The name of the individual or team who created the issue report
- **Issue description** A statement describing the issue in terms of its cause and impact
- **Impact analysis** A detailed analysis of the likely impact of the issue. This may include, for example, a list of products impacted
- **Recommendation** A description of what the project manager believes should be done to resolve the issue (and why)
- **Priority** This should be given in terms of the project's chosen scale. It should be re-evaluated after impact analysis
- **Severity** This should be given in terms of the project's chosen scale. Severity will indicate what level of management is required to make a decision on the issue
- **Decision** The decision made (accept, reject, defer or grant concession)
- **Approved by** A record of who made the decision
- **Decision date** The date of the decision
- **Closure date** The date that the issue was closed.

A.14 LESSONS LOG

A.14.1 Purpose

The lessons log is a project repository for lessons that apply to this project or future projects. Some lessons may originate from other projects and should be captured on the lessons log for input to the project's strategies and plans. Some lessons may originate from within the project – where new experience (both good and bad) can be passed on to others via a lessons report.

A.14.2 Composition

For each entry in the lessons log, the following should be recorded:

- **Lesson type** Defines the type of lesson being recorded:
  - Project – to be applied to this project
  - Corporate or programme – to be passed on to the corporate or programme management
  - Both project and corporate or programme management
- **Lesson detail** The detail may include:
  - Event
  - Effect (e.g. positive/negative financial impact)
  - Causes/trigger
  - Whether there were any early-warning indicators
  - Recommendations
  - Whether it was previously identified as a risk (threat or opportunity)
- **Date logged** The date on which the lesson was originally logged
- **Logged by** The name of the person or team who raised the lesson
- **Priority** In terms of the project's chosen categories.

A.15 LESSONS REPORT

A.15.1 Purpose

The lessons report is used to pass on any lessons that can be usefully applied to other projects.

The purpose of the report is to provoke action so that the positive lessons become embedded in the organization's way of working, and that the organization is able to avoid any negative lessons on future projects.

A lessons report can be created at any time in a project and should not necessarily wait until the end. Typically it should be included as part of the end stage report and end project report. It may be appropriate (and necessary) for there to be several lessons reports specific to the particular organization (e.g. user, supplier, corporate or programme).

The data in the report should be used by the corporate group that is responsible for the quality management system, in order to refine, change and improve the standards. Statistics on how much effort was needed for products can help improve future estimating.

A.15.2 Composition

- Executive summary
- Scope of the report (e.g. stage or project)
- A review of what went well, what went badly and any recommendations for corporate or programme management consideration. In particular:

- Project management method (including the tailoring of PRINCE2)
- Any specialist methods used
- Project strategies (risk management, quality management, communications management and configuration management)
- Project controls (and the effectiveness of any tailoring)
- Abnormal events causing deviations
- A review of useful measurements such as:
  - How much effort was required to create the products
  - How effective was the quality management strategy in designing, developing and delivering fit-for-purpose products (for example, how many errors were found after products had passed quality inspections?)
  - Statistics on issues and risks
- For significant lessons it may be useful to provide additional details on:
  - Event
  - Effect (e.g. positive/negative financial impact)
  - Causes/trigger
  - Whether there were any early-warning indicators
  - Recommendations
  - Whether the triggered event was previously identified as a risk (threat or opportunity).

A.16 PLAN

A.16.1 Purpose

A plan provides a statement of how and when objectives are to be achieved, by showing the major products, activities and resources required for the scope of the plan. In PRINCE2, there are three levels of plan: project, stage and team. Team plans are optional and may not need to follow the same composition as a project plan or stage plan.

An exception plan is created at the same level as the plan that it is replacing.

A project plan provides the business case with planned costs, and it identifies the management stages and other major control points. It is used by the project board as a baseline against which to monitor project progress.

Stage plans cover the products, resources, activities and controls specific to the stage and are used as a baseline against which to monitor stage progress.

Team plans (if used) could comprise just a schedule appended to the work package(s) assigned to the team manager.

A plan should cover not just the activities to create products but also the activities to manage product creation – including activities for assurance, quality management, risk management, configuration management, communication and any other project controls required.

A.16.2 Composition

- **Plan description** Covering a brief description of what the plan encompasses (i.e. project, stage, team, exception) and the planning approach
- **Plan prerequisites** Containing any fundamental aspects that must be in place, and remain in place, for the plan to succeed
- **External dependencies** That may influence the plan
- **Planning assumptions** Upon which the plan is based

- **Lessons incorporated** Details of relevant lessons from previous similar projects, which have been reviewed and accommodated within this plan
- **Monitoring and control** Details of how the plan will be monitored and controlled
- **Budgets** Covering time and cost, including provisions for risks and changes
- **Tolerances** Time, cost and scope tolerances for the level of plan (which may also include more specific stage- or team-level risk tolerances)
- **Product descriptions** (see section A.17) Covering the products within the scope of the plan (for the project plan this will include the project's product; for the stage plan this will be the stage products; and for a team plan this should be a reference to the work package assigned). Quality tolerances will be defined in each product description
- **Schedule** Which may include graphical representations of:
  - Gantt or bar chart
  - Product breakdown structure (see Appendix D for an example)
  - Product flow diagram (see Appendix D for an example)
  - Activity network
  - Table of resource requirements – by resource type (e.g. four engineers, one test manager, one business analyst)
  - Table of requested/assigned specific resources – by name (e.g. Nikki, Jay, Francesca).

A.17 PRODUCT DESCRIPTION

A.17.1 Purpose

A product description is used to:

- Understand the detailed nature, purpose, function and appearance of the product
- Define who will use the product
- Identify the sources of information or supply for the product
- Identify the level of quality required of the product
- Enable identification of activities to produce, review and approve the product
- Define the people or skills required to produce, review and approve the product.

A.17.2 Composition

- **Identifier** Unique key, probably allocated by the configuration management method and likely to include the project name, item name and version number
- **Title** Name by which the product is known
- **Purpose** This defines the purpose that the product will fulfil and who will use it. Is it a means to an end or an end in itself? It is helpful in understanding the product's functions, size, quality, complexity, robustness etc.
- **Composition** This is a list of the parts of the product. For example, if the product were a report, this would be a list of the expected chapters or sections
- **Derivation** What are the source products from which this product is derived? Examples are:
  - A design is derived from a specification
  - A product is bought in from a supplier
  - A statement of the expected benefits is obtained from the user
  - A product is obtained from another department or team
- **Format and presentation** The characteristics of the product – for example, if the product were a report, this would specify whether the report should be a document, presentation slides or an email

- **Development skills required** An indication of the skills required to develop the product or a pointer to which area(s) should supply the development resources. Identification of the actual people may be left until planning the stage in which the product is to be created

- **Quality criteria** To what quality specification must the product be produced, and what quality measurements will be applied by those inspecting the finished product? This might be a simple reference to one or more common standards that are documented elsewhere, or it might be a full explanation of some yardstick to be applied. If the product is to be developed and approved in different states (e.g. dismantled machinery, moved machinery and reassembled machinery), then the quality criteria should be grouped into those that apply for each state

- **Quality tolerance** Details of any range in the quality criteria within which the product would be acceptable

- **Quality method** The kinds of quality method – for example, design verification, pilot, test, inspection or review – that are to be used to check the quality or functionality of the product

- **Quality skills required** An indication of the skills required to undertake the quality method or a pointer to which area(s) should supply the checking resources. Identification of the actual people may be left until planning the stage in which the quality inspection is to be done

- **Quality responsibilities** Defining the producer, reviewer(s) and approver(s) for the product.

A.18 PRODUCT STATUS ACCOUNT

A.18.1 Purpose

The product status account provides information about the state of products within defined limits. The limits can vary. For example, the report could cover the entire project, a particular stage, a particular area of the project, or the history of a specific product. It is particularly useful if the project manager wishes to confirm the version number of products.

A.18.2 Composition

- **Report scope** Describing the scope of the report (e.g. for the entire project, by stage, by product type, by supplier etc. The product's attribute can be used to select the subset of products for the report)
- **Date produced** The date the report was generated
- **Product status** For each product within the scope of the report, the report may include:
  - Product identifier and title
  - Version
  - Status and date of status change
  - Product state
  - Owner
  - Copy-holders
  - Location
  - User(s)
  - Producer and date allocated to producer
  - Planned and actual date product description was baselined
  - Planned and actual date product was baselined
  - Planned date for the next baseline
  - List of related items
  - List of related issues (including changes pending and approved) and risks.

A.19 PROJECT BRIEF

A.19.1 Purpose

A project brief is used to provide a full and firm foundation for the initiation of the project and is created in the Starting up a Project process.

In the Initiating a Project process, the contents of the project brief are extended and refined in the project initiation documentation, after which the project brief is no longer maintained.

A.19.2 Composition

- **Project definition** Explaining what the project needs to achieve. It should include:
  - Background
  - Project objectives (covering time, cost, quality, scope, risk and benefit performance goals)
  - Desired outcomes
  - Project scope and exclusions
  - Constraints and assumptions
  - Project tolerances
  - The user(s) and any other known interested parties
  - Interfaces
- **Outline business case** (see section A.2) Reasons why the project is needed and the business option selected. This will later be developed into a detailed business case during the Initiating a Project process
- **Project product description** (see section A.21) Including the customer's quality expectations, user acceptance criteria, and operations and maintenance acceptance criteria
- **Project approach** To define the choice of solution that will be used within the project to deliver the business option selected from the business case, taking into consideration the operational environment into which the solution must fit
- **Project management team structure** A chart showing who will be involved with the project
- **Role descriptions** For the project management team and any other key resources identified at this time
- **References** To any associated documents or products.

A.20 PROJECT INITIATION DOCUMENTATION

A.20.1 Purpose

The purpose of the project initiation documentation is to define the project, in order to form the basis for its management and an assessment of its overall success. The project initiation documentation gives the direction and scope of the project and (along with the stage plan) forms the 'contract' between the project manager and the project board.

The three primary uses of the project initiation documentation are to:

- Ensure that the project has a sound basis before asking the project board to make any major commitment to the project
- Act as a base document against which the project board and project manager can assess progress, issues and ongoing viability questions
- Provide a single source of reference about the project so that people joining the 'temporary organization' can quickly and easily find out what the project is about, and how it is being managed.

The project initiation documentation is a living product in that it should always reflect the current status, plans and controls of the project. Its component products will need to be updated and re-baselined, as necessary, at the end of each stage, to reflect the current status of its constituent parts.

The version of the project initiation documentation that was used to gain authorization for the project is preserved as the basis against which performance will later be assessed when closing the project.

A.20.2 Composition

There follows a contents list for the project initiation documentation. Note that the first two items (project definition and project approach) are extracted from the project brief.

- **Project definition** Explaining what the project needs to achieve. It should include:
  - Background
  - Project objectives and desired outcomes
  - Project scope and exclusions
  - Constraints and assumptions
  - The user(s) and any other known interested parties
  - Interfaces
- **Project approach** To define the choice of solution that will be used in the project to deliver the business option selected from the business case, taking into consideration the operational environment into which the solution must fit
- **Business case** (see section A.2) Describing the justification for the project based on estimated costs, risks and benefits
- **Project management team structure** A chart showing who will be involved with the project
- **Role descriptions** For the project management team and any other key resources
- **Quality management strategy** (see section A.22) Describing the quality techniques and standards to be applied, and the responsibilities for achieving the required quality levels
- **Configuration management strategy** (see section A.6) Describing how and by whom the project's products will be controlled and protected
- **Risk management strategy** (see section A.24) Describing the specific risk management techniques and standards to be applied, and the responsibilities for achieving an effective risk management procedure
- **Communication management strategy** (see section A.4) To define the parties interested in the project and the means and frequency of communication between them and the project
- **Project plan** (see section A.16) Describing how and when the project's objectives are to be achieved, by showing the major products, activities and resources required on the project. It provides a baseline against which to monitor the project's progress stage by stage
- **Project controls** Summarizing the project-level controls such as stage boundaries, agreed tolerances, monitoring and reporting
- **Tailoring of PRINCE2** A summary of how PRINCE2 will be tailored for the project.

A.21 PROJECT PRODUCT DESCRIPTION

A.21.1 Purpose

The project product description is a special form of product description that defines what the project must deliver in order to gain acceptance. It is used to:

- Gain agreement from the user on the project's scope and requirements
- Define the customer's quality expectations
- Define the acceptance criteria, method and responsibilities for the project.

The product description for the project product is created in the Starting up a Project process as part of the initial scoping activity, and is refined during the Initiating a Project process when creating the project plan. It is subject to formal change control and should be checked at stage boundaries (during Managing a Stage Boundary) to see if any changes are required. It is used by the Closing a Project process as part of the verification that the project has delivered what was expected of it, and that the acceptance criteria have been met.

A.21.2 Composition

- **Title** Name by which the project is known
- **Purpose** This defines the purpose that the project's product will fulfil and who will use it. It is helpful in understanding the product's functions, size, quality, complexity, robustness etc.
- **Composition** A description of the major products to be delivered by the project
- **Derivation** What are the source products from which this product is derived? Examples are:
  - Existing products to be modified
  - Design specifications
  - A feasibility report
  - Project mandate
- **Development skills required** An indication of the skills required to develop the product, or a pointer to which area(s) should supply the development resources
- **Customer's quality expectations** A description of the quality expected of the project's product and the standards and processes that will need to be applied to achieve that quality. They will impact on every part of the product development, and thus on time and cost. The quality expectations are captured in discussions with the customer. Where possible, expectations should be prioritized
- **Acceptance criteria** A prioritized list of criteria that the project's product must meet before the customer will accept it – i.e. measurable definitions of the attributes that must apply to the set of products to be acceptable to key stakeholders (and, in particular, the users and the operational and maintenance organizations). Examples are: ease of use, ease of support, ease of maintenance, appearance, major functions, development costs, running costs, capacity, availability, reliability, security, accuracy or performance
- **Project-level quality tolerances** Specifying any tolerances that may apply for the acceptance criteria
- **Acceptance method** Stating the means by which acceptance will be confirmed. This may simply be a case of confirming that all the project's products have been approved or may involve describing complex handover arrangements for the project's product, including any phased handover of the project's products
- **Acceptance responsibilities** Defining who will be responsible for confirming acceptance.

A.22 QUALITY MANAGEMENT STRATEGY

A.22.1 Purpose

A quality management strategy is used to define the quality techniques and standards to be applied, and the various responsibilities for achieving the required quality levels, during the project.

A.22.2 Composition

- **Introduction** States the purpose, objectives and scope, and identifies who is responsible for the strategy
- **Quality management procedure** A description of (or reference to) the quality management procedure to be used. Any variance from corporate or programme management quality standards should be highlighted, together with a justification for the variance. The procedure should cover:
  - Quality planning
  - Quality control: the project's approach to quality control activities. This may include:

- Quality standards
- Templates and forms to be employed (e.g. product description(s), quality register)
- Definitions of types of quality methods (e.g. inspection, pilot)
- Metrics to be employed in support of quality control

● Quality assurance: the project's approach to quality assurance activities. This may include:
- Responsibilities of the project board
- Compliance audits
- Corporate or programme management reviews

● **Tools and techniques** Refers to any quality management systems or tools to be used, and any preference for techniques which may be used for each step in the quality management procedure

● **Records** Definition of what quality records will be required and where they will be stored, including the composition and format of the quality register

● **Reporting** Describes any quality management reports that are to be produced; their purpose, timing and recipients

● **Timing of quality management activities** States when formal quality management activities are to be undertaken – for example, audits (where this may involve reference to the quality register)

● **Roles and responsibilities** Defines the roles and responsibilities for quality management activities, including those with quality responsibilities from corporate or programme management.

A.23 QUALITY REGISTER

A.23.1 Purpose

A quality register is used to summarize all the quality management activities that are planned or have taken place, and provides information for the end stage reports and end project report. Its purpose is to:

● Issue a unique reference for each quality activity

● Act as a pointer to the quality records for a product

● Act as a summary of the number and type of quality activities undertaken.

A.23.2 Composition

For each entry in the quality register, the following should be recorded:

● **Quality identifier** Provides a unique reference for every quality activity entered into the quality register. It will typically be a numeric or alpha-numeric value

● **Product identifier(s)** Unique identifier(s) for the product(s) that the quality activity relates to

● **Product title(s)** The name(s) by which the product(s) is known

● **Method** The method employed for the quality activity (e.g. pilot, quality review, audit etc.)

● **Roles and responsibilities** The person or team responsible for the quality management activities (e.g. auditor or, for quality reviews, presenter, reviewer(s), chair, administrator)

● **Dates** Planned, forecast and actual dates for:
- The quality activity
- Sign-off that the quality activity is complete

● **Result** The result of the quality activity. If a product fails a quality review, then any re-assessment should be listed as a separate entry in the register, as the original quality activity has been completed (in deciding that the result is a 'fail')

● **Quality records** References to the quality inspection documentation, such as a test plan or the details of any actions required to correct errors and omissions of the products being inspected.

A.24 RISK MANAGEMENT STRATEGY

A.24.1 Purpose

A risk management strategy describes the specific risk management techniques and standards to be applied and the responsibilities for achieving an effective risk management procedure.

A.24.2 Composition

- **Introduction** States the purpose, objectives and scope, and identifies who is responsible for the strategy
- **Risk management procedure** A description of (or reference to) the risk management procedure to be used. Any variance from corporate or programme management standards should be highlighted, together with a justification for the variance. The procedure should cover activities such as:
  - Identify
  - Assess
  - Plan
  - Implement
  - Communicate
- **Tools and techniques** Refers to any risk management systems or tools to be used, and any preference for techniques which may be used for each step in the risk management procedure
- **Records** Definition of the composition and format of the risk register and any other risk records to be used by the project
- **Reporting** Describes any risk management reports that are to be produced, including their purpose, timing and recipients
- **Timing of risk management activities** States when formal risk management activities are to be undertaken – for example, at end stage assessments
- **Roles and responsibilities** Defines the roles and responsibilities for risk management activities
- **Scales** Defines the scales for estimating probability and impact for the project to ensure that the scales for cost and time (for instance) are relevant to the cost and timeframe of the project. These may be shown in the form of probability impact grids giving the criteria for each level within the scale, e.g. for 'very high', 'high', 'medium', 'low' and 'very low'
- **Proximity** Guidance on how proximity for risk events is to be assessed. Proximity reflects the fact that risks will occur at particular times and the severity of their impact will vary according to when they occur. Typical proximity categories will be: imminent, within the stage, within the project, beyond the project
- **Risk categories** Definition of the risk categories to be used (if at all). These may be derived from a risk breakdown structure or prompt list. If no risks have been recorded against a category, this may suggest that the risk identification has not been as thorough as it should have been
- **Risk response categories** Definition of the risk response categories to be used, which themselves depend on whether a risk is a perceived threat or an opportunity
- **Early-warning indicators** Definition of any indicators to be used to track critical aspects of the project so that if certain predefined levels are reached, corrective action will be triggered. They will be selected for their relevance to the project objectives
- **Risk tolerance** Defining the threshold levels of risk exposure, which, when exceeded, require the risk to be escalated to the next level of management. (For example, a project-level risk tolerance could be set as any risk that, should it occur, would result in loss of trading. Such risks would need to be escalated to corporate or programme management.) The risk tolerance should define the risk expectations of corporate or programme management and the project board
- **Risk budget** Describing whether a risk budget is to be established and, if so, how it will be used.

A.25 RISK REGISTER

A.25.1 Purpose

A risk register provides a record of identified risks relating to the project, including their status and history. It is used to capture and maintain information on all of the identified threats and opportunities relating to the project.

A.25.2 Composition

For each entry in the risk register, the following should be recorded:

- **Risk identifier** Provides a unique reference for every risk entered into the risk register. It will typically be a numeric or alpha-numeric value
- **Risk author** The person who raised the risk
- **Date registered** The date the risk was identified
- **Risk category** The type of risk in terms of the project's chosen categories (e.g. schedule, quality, legal etc.)
- **Risk description** In terms of the cause, event (threat or opportunity) and effect (description in words of the impact)
- **Probability, impact and expected value** It is helpful to estimate the inherent values (pre-response action) and residual values (post-response action). These should be recorded in accordance with the project's chosen scales
- **Proximity** This would typically state how close to the present time the risk event is anticipated to happen (e.g. imminent, within stage, within project, beyond project). Proximity should be recorded in accordance with the project's chosen scales
- **Risk response categories** How the project will treat the risk in terms of the project's chosen categories. For example:
  - For threats: avoid, reduce, fallback, transfer, accept, share
  - For opportunities: enhance, exploit, reject, share
- **Risk response** Actions to resolve the risk, and these actions should be aligned to the chosen response categories. Note that more than one risk response may apply to a risk
- **Risk status** Typically described in terms of whether the risk is active or closed
- **Risk owner** The person responsible for managing the risk (there can be only one risk owner per risk)
- **Risk actionee** The person(s) who will implement the action(s) described in the risk response. This may or may not be the same person as the risk owner.

A.26 WORK PACKAGE

A.26.1 Purpose

A work package is a set of information about one or more required products collated by the project manager to pass responsibility for work or delivery formally to a team manager or team member.

A.26.2 Composition

Although the content may vary greatly according to the relationship between the project manager and the recipient of the work package, it should cover:

- **Date** The date of the agreement between the project manager and the team manager/person authorized
- **Team manager or person authorized** The name of the team manager or individual with whom the agreement has been made
- **Work package description** A description of the work to be done
- **Techniques, processes and procedures** Any techniques, tools, standards, processes or procedures to be used in the creation of the specialist products

- **Development interfaces** Interfaces that must be maintained while developing the products. These may be people providing information or those who need to receive information

- **Operations and maintenance interfaces** Identification of any specialist products with which the product(s) in the work package will have to interface during their operational life. These may be other products to be produced by the project, existing products, or those to be produced by other projects (for example, if the project is part of a programme)

- **Configuration management requirements** A statement of any arrangements that must be made by the producer for: version control of the products in the work package; obtaining copies of other products or their product descriptions; submission of the product to configuration management; any storage or security requirements; and who, if anyone, needs to be advised of changes in the status of the work package

- **Joint agreements** Details of the agreements on effort, cost, start and end dates, and key milestones for the work package

- **Tolerances** Details of the tolerances for the work package (the tolerances will be for time and cost but may also include scope and risk)

- **Constraints** Any constraints (apart from the tolerances) on the work, people to be involved, timings, charges, rules to be followed (for example, security and safety) etc.

- **Reporting arrangements** The expected frequency and content of checkpoint reports

- **Problem handling and escalation** This refers to the procedure for raising issues and risks

- **Extracts or references** Any extracts or references to related documents, specifically:

  - **Stage plan extract** This will be the relevant section of the stage plan for the current management stage or will be a pointer to it

  - **Product description(s)** This would normally be an attachment of the product description(s) for the products identified in the work package (note that the product description contains the quality methods to be used)

- **Approval method** The person, role or group who will approve the completed products within the work package, and how the project manager is to be advised of completion of the products and work package.

There should be space on the work package to record both its initial authorization and its acceptance and return as a completed work package. This can be enhanced to include an assessment of the work and go towards performance appraisal.

Projects with common controls across all work packages may simply cross-reference the controls defined in the project plan or stage plan.

B

Roles and responsibilities

Appendix B Roles and responsibilities

In PRINCE2 there are nine roles which are defined with specific responsibilities. They relate to project direction, project management and project delivery, although in the case of project delivery, PRINCE2 only refers to the team manager and not the members of the delivery team.

Appendix C of *Managing Successful Projects with PRINCE2* includes comprehensive descriptions for these roles and they are summarized here in Table B.1.

Table B.1 PRINCE2 roles

Role	Summary
Project board	The project board is accountable to corporate or programme management for the success of the project, and has the authority to direct the project within the remit set by corporate or programme management as documented in the project mandate.
	The project board is also responsible for the communications between the project management team and stakeholders external to that team (e.g. corporate and programme management).
	According to the scale, complexity, importance and risk of the project, project board members may delegate some project assurance tasks to separate individuals. The project board may also delegate decisions regarding changes to a change authority.
Executive	The executive is ultimately responsible for the project, supported by the senior user and senior supplier. The executive's role is to ensure that the project is focused throughout its life on achieving its objectives and delivering a product that will achieve the forecast benefits. The executive has to ensure that the project gives value for money, ensuring a cost-conscious approach to the project, balancing the demands of the business, user and supplier.
	Throughout the project, the executive is responsible for the business case.
	The project board is not a democracy controlled by votes. The executive is the ultimate decision maker and is supported in the decision-making by the senior user and senior supplier.
Senior user(s)	The senior user(s) is responsible for specifying the needs of those who will use the project's products, for user liaison with the project management team, and for monitoring that the solution will meet those needs within the constraints of the business case in terms of quality, functionality and ease of use.
	The role represents the interests of all those who will use the project's products (including operations and maintenance), those for whom the products will achieve an objective or those who will use the products to deliver benefits. The senior user role commits user resources and monitors products against requirements. This role may require more than one person to cover all the user interests. For the sake of effectiveness, the role should not be split between too many people.
	The senior user(s) specifies the benefits and is held to account by demonstrating to corporate or programme management that the forecast benefits which were the basis of project approval have in fact been realized. This is likely to involve a commitment beyond the end of the life of the project.
Senior supplier(s)	The senior supplier represents the interests of those designing, developing, facilitating, procuring and implementing the project's products. This role is accountable for the quality of products delivered by the supplier(s) and is responsible for the technical integrity of the project. If necessary, more than one person may be required to represent the suppliers.
	Depending on the particular customer/supplier environment, the customer may also wish to appoint an independent person or group to carry out assurance on the supplier's products (for example, if the relationship between the customer and supplier is a commercial one).
Project manager	The project manager has the authority to run the project on a day-to-day basis on behalf of the project board within the constraints laid down by them.
	The project manager's prime responsibility is to ensure that the project produces the required products within the specified tolerances of time, cost, quality, scope, risk and benefits. The project manager is also responsible for the project producing a result capable of achieving the benefits defined in the business case.
Team manager	The team manager's prime responsibility is to ensure production of those products defined by the project manager to an appropriate quality, in a set timescale and at a cost acceptable to the project board. The team manager role reports to, and takes direction from, the project manager.

Table continues

Table B.1 continued

Role	Summary
Change authority	The project board may delegate authority for approving responses to requests for change or off-specifications to a separate individual or group, called a change authority. The project manager could be assigned as the change authority for some aspects of the project (e.g. changing baselined work packages if it does not affect stage tolerances).
Project assurance	Project assurance covers the primary stakeholder interests (business, user and supplier).
	Project assurance has to be independent of the project manager; therefore the project board cannot delegate any of its assurance activities to the project manager.
Project support	The provision of any project support on a formal basis is optional. If it is not delegated to a separate person or function it will need to be undertaken by the project manager.
	One support function that must be considered is that of configuration management. Depending on the project size and environment, there may be a need to formalize this and it may become a task with which the project manager cannot cope without support.
	Project support functions may be provided by a project office or by specific resources for the project. Refer to OGC's guidance Portfolio, Programme and Project Offices (2008) for further information on the use of a project office.

In *PRINCE2 Agile* a set of delivery roles have been defined so that they can be used if appropriate, or they can be used to understand what may be expected of a delivery team using agile. These are described in Table B.2.

It should be noted that roles are not the same as job titles. A role on a project is temporary and is carried out by one or more individuals. Someone could be carrying out several roles on several projects. A job title is different from this in that it is usually defined by a job description and represents a person's role in an organization (e.g. engineer, administrator, tester, designer etc.)

Table B.2 PRINCE2 Agile delivery roles

Role	Description
Customer subject matter expert	A customer subject matter expert (CSME) is assigned to the delivery team and plays an active part by acting as a representative of all of the customer stakeholders with a responsibility for ensuring that the project's products are understood and are correct at the detailed level. The person carrying out this role probably wants, or needs, the final product and is motivated for the project to succeed as they are impacted or helped by it.
	Responsibilities include:
	● Making appropriate and timely decisions on behalf of the customer at the detailed level
	● Explaining and helping to define the detailed requirements of the customer
	● Ensuring that the detailed requirements are consistent with the higher-level requirements agreed by the senior user
	● Prioritization of requirements at the detailed level
	● Ensuring that products have been reviewed appropriately and are fit for purpose from a customer perspective
	● Collaborating and communicating with other customer stakeholders (such as customer representatives) in order to ensure that all views and needs relevant to the project are understood and addressed.
	Competencies include:
	● Open-minded
	● Facilitative
	● Gives attention to detail
	● Respected
	● Decisive
	● Empowered.

Role	Description
Customer representative	A customer representative is partially assigned to the delivery team or the senior user in order to contribute, or to be canvassed about, specific information that may be of use to the project. This is a consultative role that provides general or detailed information relating to specific areas of the project that may be involved or impacted. Responsibilities may include: ● Defining requirements for their own specific area of interest ● Highlighting any areas that the project may impact directly or indirectly ● Working with the customer SME(s) to provide a wider and more representative picture of the customer view ● Providing support to reviewing the project's products where relevant. Competencies include: ● Knowledgeable about their own area ● Empowered ● Decisive ● Collaborative.
Supplier subject matter expert	A supplier subject matter expert (SSME) is assigned to the delivery team and provides the appropriate technical skills to build and initially quality check the project's products. They should be working collaboratively with the customer SME(s) and other customer representatives to evolve the products so that they deliver what is required in order to ultimately achieve the highest value possible for the customer. Responsibilities include: ● Creating the project's specialist products ● Being aware of the wider technical view of the products that are evolving ● Carrying out initial technical assurance to check that the specialist products have been produced correctly ● Liaising with the customer to refine initial understanding of the requirements ● Explaining what alternatives there are to satisfy individual requirements ● Ensuring that work is compliant with any organizational or project standards. Competencies include: ● Multi-skilled to some degree ● Customer-focused ● Creative ● Technical excellence.
Supplier representative	A supplier representative is partially assigned to the delivery team or to the senior supplier to contribute, or to be canvassed about, specific technical or specialist information that may be of use to the project. This is a consultative role that provides general or detailed technical information relating to specific areas of the products being delivered. Responsibilities may include: ● Providing technical guidance on specific areas where appropriate (e.g. design, performance, releasing into operational use, ongoing support) ● Communicating technical standards and guidance on areas such as technical compliance ● Highlighting any areas that the project may impact directly or indirectly from a technical perspective. Competencies include: ● Technical excellence ● Proactive ● Inquisitive.

Table continues

Table B.2 continued

Role	Description
Delivery team quality assurance	This role is responsible for independently checking that the project's products are fit for purpose from a customer and supplier perspective at the delivery level. This should be carried out collaboratively by engaging with the customer SME(s) and the supplier SME(s) in an iterative style of working as the products and the understanding of them evolve. Customer and supplier quality assurance can be carried out by two separate roles if appropriate. Responsibilities include: ● Ultimately responsible for ensuring that products have met their quality criteria from both a customer and supplier perspective ● Advising and supporting the rest of the delivery team on how the products will be assured in order to make the process as transparent and as easy as possible ● Engaging with other stakeholders (customer or supplier) in order to check that nothing is overlooked from the wider view of the project. Competencies include: ● Excellence in quality assurance ● Thorough ● Approachable ● Pragmatic ● Independent.

C

Health check – PRINCE2 Agile version

Appendix C Health check – PRINCE2 Agile version

This appendix contains checklists that can be used at any time during a project to assess how well the project is going from an agile perspective. This is not a replacement for the PRINCE2 health check, which should be used as well.

A positive response to any of the following statements would usually indicate that agile is working well in that respect. Each answer in isolation means relatively little but, in totality, the health check will give a general indication of the health of the project in agile terms. A simple rating system of 'yes or no' should be sufficient, but this can be elaborated further if desired.

C.1 IS THE FOLLOWING HAPPENING?

C.1.1 Behaviours

Statement	Rating
Collaboration, trust and a no-blame culture exist.	
Self-organization is predominant and is supported by the project management team.	
There is a culture of inspect and adapt and continual improvement.	
Transparency prevails.	
Teams are regularly talking about the delivery of value and benefits.	
There is an attitude of keeping things simple.	
All stakeholders impacted by the project are being kept up to date.	
The product board is frequently interacting with the people involved on the project.	
Planning and work assignment are being carried out collaboratively.	
The Pastor of Fun is well-organized.	

C.1.2 Environment

Statement	Rating
People are happy and work is enjoyable.	
The team is stable, ring-fenced and working well together.	
The project is responsive to change and is change friendly.	
The customer is involved and engaged at all levels.	
A blended view prevails that takes into account the diverse views of the customer on a project.	
The desired outcome, as well as the desired output, is clear to everyone.	
There is a thirst for feedback and a collective desire to find out what the customer really wants.	
Agile learnings are being moved around the organization (e.g. by project support).	
Communication is very good and fast-moving.	
Control has a light touch and people are empowered.	
Musts really are musts.	
The project management team and the delivery teams are 'understanding agile' and not just 'doing agile'.	
The overriding mind-set of the people on the project is an agile one.	
Frequent releases are happening that are ideally put into operational use (or a staging area if the live environment is not ready).	
The five targets of what to fix and what to flex are understood by all.	
Significant events become routine because they happen frequently (e.g. stage boundaries or release reviews).	
All roles are clearly defined and understood (and this is taking into account that the mapping of the agile roles to PRINCE2 is not necessarily straightforward).	
PRINCE2 is seen as agile.	

C.1.3 Process

Statement	Rating
Management by exception is working fully.	
The level of control is appropriate to the level of uncertainty.	
The work package interface is happening well. It is smooth, has clarity and is not a source of communication problems.	
Requirements and user stories are explored and not just followed blindly.	
The way of working is typically iterative and incremental, and benefits are being delivered at several points throughout the project.	
There are clear definitions of 'done' and 'ready', and working agreements are transparent.	
Planning and work are feature-focused and timeboxed.	
The MVP is clear to everyone, and it is understood that its role on the project is to help with learning.	
Quality checking and testing includes independent quality checking and testing.	
Quality checking is happening as you go and sometimes even drives the building of the products.	
Planning is happening well in relation to all planning horizons (i.e. short term, medium term and long term) and with respect to the appropriate level of uncertainty.	
A lot of planning is being done empirically.	
Early requirements are based at a level that avoids unnecessary detail.	
Project assurance is adding value from an agile perspective.	

C.1.4 Techniques

Statement	Rating
Prioritization is happening continually, and timeboxes are not being extended or having people added to them.	
Information is very visible (e.g. on the walls) and is kept up to date.	
When prioritizing, teams are looking at both scope and quality criteria.	
Acceptance criteria always exist and are well written.	
Estimation is a team-based activity.	
Documentation is Lean, and the right channels are being used for each type of message.	
Demos take place frequently.	
Some risks are being mitigated by the use of spikes, prototypes and experiments.	
Burn charts are being widely used and progress is clear to see.	
User stories are being used to stimulate conversation and communication.	
When Kanban is used, a holistic approach is adopted – not just a Kanban board.	
Workshops are a regular occurrence and are being used appropriately.	
Stand-ups are happening daily and are taking place quickly (i.e. lasting 15 minutes or less, perhaps 10).	
People are clear on terms like 'requirement', 'user story', 'feature' and 'epic'.	
Product descriptions have been written at the appropriate level and with flexibility as to quality criteria.	

D

Product-based planning
example

Appendix D Product-based planning example

D.1 SCENARIO

A project is required to organize and run a conference for between 80 and 100 delegates. The date and subject matter are set, and the focus of the conference is to bring members of a particular profession up to date on recent developments in professional procedures and standards. The project team will need to identify a venue, and check its availability, facilities and price before booking it. They will also need to identify suitable speakers and book them, before producing a detailed agenda and programme. A mailing list of delegates is available, and once the venue has been booked, the project team will need to issue a press release based on the agreed programme. Part of the project will involve producing 100 delegate handouts, with a cover reflecting the selected subject matter. These handouts must contain a printed agenda covering the agreed programme, copies of slides and notes used by the speakers, and a feedback form to capture attendee reviews. Booking arrangements for attending the conference, including details of the programme and venue, must be sent out in the mail-shot. The team will need to regularly update the attendance list based on responses to the mail-shot, and make arrangements to recruit staff to help on the day, based on the final attendance list.

D.2 EXAMPLE OF A PROJECT PRODUCT DESCRIPTION

Title	Annual conference
Purpose	The conference is the annual showcase of the profession and provides its members with an opportunity to learn about the latest developments in professional procedures and standards, and to network with fellow members.
Composition	<ul><li>Conference venue</li><li>Attendees</li><li>Speakers</li><li>Publicity</li><li>Delegate handouts</li><li>Conference logistics.</li></ul>
Derivation	<ul><li>Selected subject matter</li><li>Mailing list</li><li>Previous conference lessons and materials</li><li>Agreed date.</li></ul>
Development skills required	<ul><li>Conference management</li><li>Marketing</li><li>Public relations.</li></ul>
Customer's quality expectations	Priority 1: The conference must be<ul><li>Professional in style, funded by attendees and address the needs of the range of members (from beginners to experienced professionals)</li><li>The event will provide a forum for networking</li><li>Repeat attendance at future conferences is generated from satisfied members</li></ul>Priority 2:<ul><li>The speakers will be chosen on the basis of their knowledge, experience and expertise. They are not delivering a 'sales pitch' to the members</li><li>The conference will be interactive in style</li><li>The conference will be held at a central location, therefore minimizing travel.</li></ul>

Table continues

Project product description continued

Title	Annual conference
Acceptance criteria and project-level quality tolerances	In priority order: ● The cost of the conference must be covered by the attendance fees ● Minimum of 80 and maximum of 100 people attend the conference ● More than 50% of the presentations are interactive (tutorials rather than lectures) ● The speakers and programme are approved by the editorial board representing the interests of the members ● The attendees' satisfaction survey indicates that >75% will attend next year's conference and/or recommend it to colleagues ● The hotel venue is within three miles of a main-line train station.
Acceptance method	As the conference cannot be rerun should it prove to be unacceptable, the project board will grant: ● Preliminary acceptance – based on approval of the agreed programme by the editorial board and independent assurance that the attendee numbers and conference costs are forecast to be acceptable ● Final acceptance – based on the end project report providing evidence that the acceptance criteria were met.
Acceptance responsibilities	● The senior user and executive are responsible for confirming acceptance.

D.3 EXAMPLES OF A PRODUCT BREAKDOWN STRUCTURE

PRINCE2 does not specify the format in which a product breakdown structure is drawn. Three example formats are provided for the conference project:

● Hierarchy chart (Figure D.1)

● Mindmap (Figure D.2)

● Indented list.

Product breakdown structure in the form of an indented list

Conference

1 Venue

    1.1 Venue requirements

    1.2 Candidate venues

    1.3 Venue assessments

    1.4 Selected and booked venue

2 Attendees

    2.1 Mailing list (external)

    2.2 Responses (external)

    2.3 Booking arrangements

    2.4 Final attendee list

3 Speakers

    3.1 Speaker options

    3.2 Speaker invitations

    3.3 Booked speakers

4 Publicity

    4.1 Mail-shot

    4.2 Press release

5 Delegate handouts

    5.1 Covers

    5.2 Printed agenda

    5.3 Slides and notes

    5.4 Satisfaction survey form

6 Conference logistics

    6.1 Selected subject matter (external)

    6.2 Agreed date (external)

    6.3 Agreed programme

    6.4 On-the-day staff

7 Previous conference lessons and materials (external).

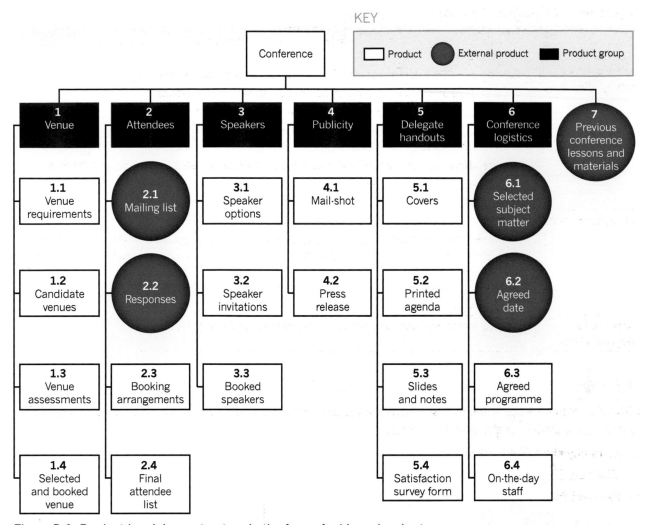

Figure D.1 Product breakdown structure in the form of a hierarchy chart

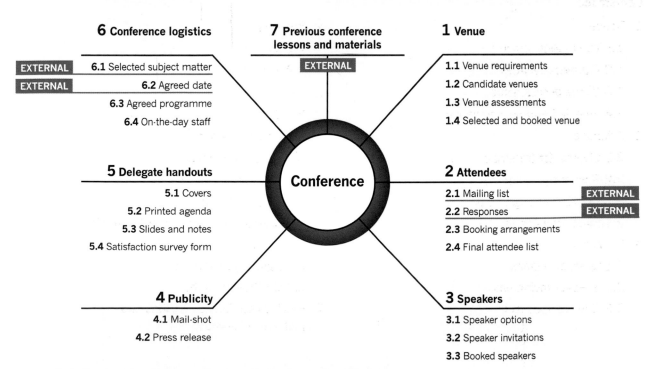

Figure D.2 Product breakdown structure in the form of a mindmap

D.4 EXAMPLE OF A PRODUCT DESCRIPTION

Identifier	Conference/4.1/version 1.0
Title	Mail-shot
Purpose	The mail-shot is the primary means of advertising the conference to potential delegates. It will be mailed to a list of professionals working in the industry.
Composition	• Mailing envelope • Letter giving outline explanation of the conference • Leaflet giving detailed explanation of the conference, the venue and how to make a booking • Booking form • Response envelope
Derivation	• Mailing list • Agreed programme • Booking arrangements • Selected venue
Format and presentation	• Letter to be A4 on standard branded letterhead • Leaflet and booking form to be A5 size • Mailing envelope to be C5
Development skills required	• Marketing, design and copywriting skills required • Knowledge of conference necessary
Quality responsibilities	• **Producer** - Event management company • **Reviewers** - as stated under 'Quality skills required' • **Approver** - Membership secretary

Quality criteria	Quality tolerance	Quality method	Quality skills required
Adheres to corporate identity standards	As defined in corporate identity standards	PRINCE2 quality review	Marketing team
Letter and leaflet accurately reflect all agreed details of the conference	None	Inspection	Conference project manager
No spelling or grammatical errors in any elements of the mail-shot	None	Word processor spell-checker Inspection	Proof reader
The covering letter fits on one side of A4	May extend to reverse of a single sheet of A4	Inspection	Proof reader

D.5 EXAMPLE OF A PRODUCT FLOW DIAGRAM

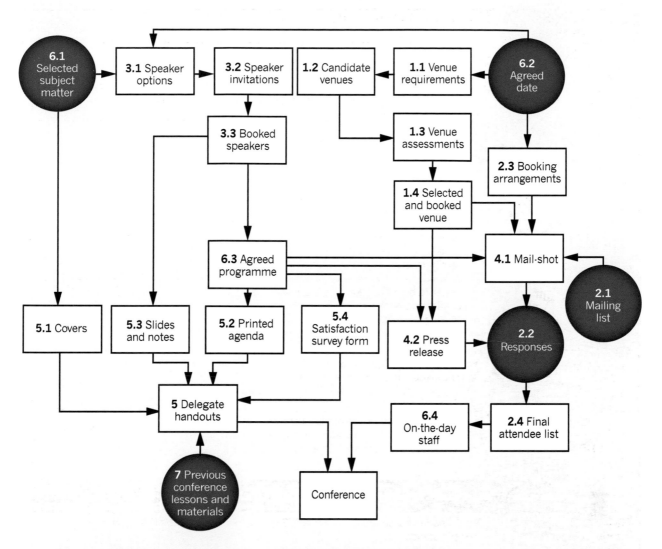

Note: Only the project product, releases and products need to be transferred from the product breakdown structure to the product flow diagram. For example, in this scenario the planner has used 'publicity' in the product breakdown structure but the only publicity products that need to be produced are the mail-shot and press release. 'Publicity' is not a product that requires work but a convenient way to describe the products that provide the publicity for the conference, whereas the delegate handout is a product that is created by bringing together the covers, printed agenda, printouts of the conference slides and notes, and the satisfaction survey form products.

E

The fundamental values and principles of agile (including the Agile Manifesto)

Appendix E The fundamental values and principles of agile (including the Agile Manifesto)

There are a wide variety of agile frameworks, methods and approaches, and many of them give significant prominence to a set of fundamental behaviours. These are referred to using such terms as principles and values. They represent a mind-set and are usually core to the way an approach works, and therefore if they are compromised in any way then so is the approach. The values and principles of some of the agile frameworks, methods and approaches are discussed in this appendix. Some of the approaches below are for software development only.

E.1 THE AGILE MANIFESTO (THE MANIFESTO FOR AGILE SOFTWARE DEVELOPMENT)

We are uncovering better ways of developing software by doing it and helping others do it. Through this work we have come to value:

- **Individuals and interactions** over processes and tools
- **Working software** over comprehensive documentation
- **Customer collaboration** over contract negotiation
- **Responding to change** over following a plan.

That is, while there is value in the items on the right, we value the items on the left more.

The manifesto is a set of values (www.agilemanifesto.org). There are 12 principles behind it:

- Our highest priority is to satisfy the customer through early and continuous delivery of valuable software.
- We welcome changing requirements, even late in development. Agile processes harness change for the customer's competitive advantage.
- We deliver working software frequently, from a couple of weeks to a couple of months, with a preference for the shorter timescale.
- Business people and developers must work together daily throughout the project.
- We build projects around motivated individuals, give them the environment and support they need, and trust them to get the job done.
- The most efficient and effective method of conveying information to and within a development team is face-to-face conversation.
- Working software is the primary measure of progress.
- Agile processes promote sustainable development. The sponsors, developers and users should be able to maintain a constant pace indefinitely.
- Continuous attention to technical excellence and good design enhances agility.
- Simplicity – the art of maximizing the amount of work not done – is essential.
- The best architectures, requirements and designs emerge from self-organizing teams.
- At regular intervals, the team reflects on how to become more effective, then tunes and adjusts its behaviour accordingly.

E.2 SCRUM THEORY

Three pillars uphold every implementation of empirical process control:

- Transparency
- Inspection
- Adaptation.

E.3 THE FIVE VALUES OF eXtreme PROGRAMMING (XP)

- Communication
- Simplicity
- Feedback
- Courage (e.g. being confident, being persistent)
- Respect.

E.4 THE FOUR CORE VALUES OF THE SCALED AGILE FRAMEWORK (SAFe) V3.0

- Alignment (i.e. lining up work to such things as vision and strategy)
- Code quality
- Transparency
- Programme execution (i.e. getting things done).

E.5 THE PROJECT MANAGEMENT DECLARATION OF INTERDEPENDENCE

This was published in 2004/2005 by a group of several agile thought leaders. It was an evolution of the Agile Manifesto and its aim was to address a wider audience such as the project management community and not necessarily just those in the software domain (www.pmdoi.org). To achieve successful results, the declaration commits its proponents to:

- Increase return on investment by making continuous flow of value their focus
- Deliver reliable results by engaging customers in frequent interactions and shared ownership
- Expect uncertainty and manage for it through iterations, anticipation and adaptation
- Unleash creativity and innovation by recognizing that individuals are the ultimate source of value and creating an environment where they can make a difference
- Boost performance through group accountability for results and shared responsibility for team effectiveness
- Improve effectiveness and reliability through situationally specific strategies, processes and practices.

E.6 THE EIGHT PRINCIPLES OF THE DYNAMIC SYSTEMS DEVELOPMENT METHOD

The principles of the **Dynamic Systems Development Method (DSDM)** represent the ethos and culture that need to exist for the successful use of agile. If any of the principles is not being adhered to, this represents a significant risk to the project and therefore the project manager needs to respond accordingly.

- Focus on the business need
- Deliver on time
- Collaborate
- Never compromise quality
- Build incrementally from firm foundations
- Develop iteratively
- Communicate continuously and clearly
- Demonstrate control.

E.7 THE KANBAN METHOD

E.7.1 Foundational principles

- Start with what you do now
- Agree to pursue evolutionary change
- Initially, respect current roles, responsibilities and job titles
- Encourage acts of leadership at all levels.

E.7.2 Core practices

- Visualize
- Limit WIP
- Manage the flow
- Make policies explicit
- Implement feedback loops
- Improve collaboratively, evolve experimentally (using models and the scientific method).

E.8 THE PRINCIPLES OF LEAN THINKING

- Identify customers and specify value
- Identify and map the value stream
- Create flow by eliminating waste
- Respond to customer pull
- Pursue perfection.

E.9 THE FIVE PRINCIPLES OF LEAN STARTUP

- Entrepreneurs are everywhere
- Entrepreneurship is management
- Validated learning
- Build-measure-learn
- Innovation accounting.

F

Transitioning to agile, and what constitutes success?

Appendix F Transitioning to agile, and what constitutes success?

A common mistake made by many organizations is to see working in a more agile way as the goal to be achieved, as opposed to seeing it as an enabler to help the organization achieve its goals. Agile should be seen as a means to an end and not an end in itself.

Organizations and individuals looking to use agile, or improve their agile, should understand the problems they are trying to solve, or the opportunities they are looking to leverage, before commencing on any transition to a new or different way of working.

With respect to 'traditional' projects, there are many common problems that are encountered – such as delivering the final product late, being over budget, the solution containing defects or the solution not being what the customer was expecting.

Therefore, when using PRINCE2 and agile together to solve the aforementioned problems and improve how benefits are delivered to internal or external customers, it is important to create a baseline of where the organization currently is, before starting on a journey of transition. From this baseline the organization can set goals to be achieved and create plans to help to achieve them. This can then be used at a future date to see what impact using agile with PRINCE2 has had.

F.1 DIFFERENT FORMS OF SUCCESS

When using PRINCE2 and agile on a project it is important to distinguish between the following three different types of success:

- The success of the business case in terms of the benefits delivered
- The success of the project and the project management involved
- The success of the agile way of working.

Aside from exceptional or unusual situations, it will always be the benefits that are the most important. Different stakeholders may have their own measures of success depending on whether they are suppliers or customers and what benefits they stand to gain from the project. Even if there are problems using PRINCE2 or agile or there are complications with the project, the customer may still be very happy if the product produced sells well and achieves the benefits that were forecast. Conversely, the customer is unlikely to be happy if PRINCE2 and agile enabled the project to come in ahead of time and under budget, yet the final product didn't sell anything as well as expected.

It is important to understand the relative merits of these three areas as they have a very clear order of priority.

It is important that all of these three areas are measured, and it is a sign of an organization's maturity as to how well this is achieved and how the results are acted upon.

When measuring these three areas, it is important that there are no overlaps or blurring of boundaries between the areas, as they are quite different.

Measuring the success of the project and the success of the business case is already covered by PRINCE2, but measuring the success of how agile has been used is not. The areas to look at when reviewing the success or otherwise are identified by the Agilometer in Chapter 24. The question to ask for each of the sliders is:

- How much did each area help?
- How much did each area hinder?
- Did we assess the slider correctly at the start of the project?

When an organization invests in improving how projects are delivered, it is important to be able to assess the merits of that investment. It is also important to be able to distinguish between the benefits delivered (as a whole) by the appropriate use of PRINCE2 and the benefits delivered by agile (as a whole). It may turn out to be the case that the benefits have been achieved through using the two together, as the whole is greater than the sum of the parts.

PRINCE2, agile and PRINCE2 with agile are all enablers. Their contribution needs to be measured. If it is not being measured, it will not be possible to gauge success.

FURTHER INFORMATION

Organizational maturity and P3M3: https://www.axelos.com/p3m3

G

Advice for a project manager using agile

Appendix G Advice for a project manager using agile

PRINCE2 Agile has been created by a large team of contributors who all share a passion for project management in an agile context. Just for fun, the whole team were asked the following question:

> *What would you say to a relatively inexperienced project manager running a project in an agile context? What advice would you give them?*

They were asked to express this as a user story in the form:

As <a project manager responsible for managing a project using agile>

I would <something you would do>

So that <some kind of benefit>

Their replies were as follows; we hope you find them useful.

G.1 COLLABORATION AND SELF-ORGANIZATION

I would	So that
Trust the team to deliver	I am not getting in their way by checking up on them
Leave the team to get on with it	Their creativity is not stifled by an interfering boss
Trust the people who know best how to deliver the right solution	The (right) solution is delivered right
Ensure that the project board is very clear on what 'empowered' means	Team members will be supported and will not be overruled
Involve the team in release planning	I get an honest view of when we can make releases and what's involved
Focus on having a stable team around me	We can harness the fact that teams are more innovative and effective than individuals
Insist that the customer has cleared their diary to guarantee their involvement (e.g. three days a week)	The risk of the customer not being available is largely removed
Ensure the agile delivery team is satisfied that the customer representative is fully engaged	The output meets the customer's needs

G.2 TRANSPARENCY, COMMUNICATION AND EXPLORATION

I would	So that
Clearly communicate the product vision to my team	They know what they are building and why they are building it
Deliver something that users can use and relate to quickly	We get input from users in order to make sure we are on the right track
Ensure the whole team (customer and supplier) is involved in the process of defining and agreeing the project's vision	The team is engaged and motivated to realize this vision from the start
Make sure that the project team has an MVP that is truly a 'minimum'	The team can learn something useful as soon as possible (and then refine it)
Ensure that the senior stakeholders involved understand very well that some requirements WILL be dropped from the list (MoSCoW)	Their expectations can be managed from the start
Engage with and try to understand the project's stakeholders	Misunderstandings are avoided, and support for the project is increased
Try to understand and communicate the project's planned benefits, and whether anything threatens them	The team doesn't become too product-fixated and understands the ultimate purpose of the project
Ensure that the customer representative on the team is satisfied that their needs are being addressed	The output meets the customer's needs
Ensure that the project team all attend a kick-off meeting to agree how the management approach will be 'configured' to meet the project requirements	The entire team understand how the project will be run and how agile behaviours and techniques will be integrated in order to achieve a successful outcome

G.3 ENVIRONMENT

I would	So that
Work with the team managers to ensure that the delivery team is having fun	People are well bonded, and the commitments that they make to their peers during an iteration are strengthened
Make sure that the team is trained up in Scrum	They have a good grounding in a core agile delivery method
Ensure I understood what flavour of agile is being proposed/used	I can tailor project planning, reporting and control to suit it
Be clear about the delivery process and methodology with stakeholders	I am setting expectations early around the delivery outputs (i.e. we will be working iteratively towards our destination)
Make sure that I have read *The Lean Startup*	I have a viewpoint on how projects running under 'conditions of extreme uncertainty' could be run and how PRINCE2 could support this
Hire a brilliant product owner and get them trained accordingly	The project has more chance of being successful
Ensure that the team is set up to make releases on demand (or as close to that as possible)	The technical infrastructure does not get in the way of delivering business value
Ensure that the entire team works in the same location as much as possible	A true team is formed working towards a common goal
Ensure that the project team is aware and understands the role of a 'servant' project manager	The team knows what to expect throughout the project in terms of the level of control versus coaching and support. This will help to ensure that delivery teams are empowered and collaborate, can be self-organizing (within the agreed tolerances) and are able to make rapid, informed decisions without unnecessary delay

G.4 PLAN, MONITOR AND CONTROL

I would	So that
Touch base with everyone in the project every day	I know whether they are happy
Focus on removing problems hindering the teams	They can get the work done
Make sure we hold frequent retrospectives	The team improves over time
Ensure that the project team understands and has agreed on 'what to fix and what to flex' (i.e. tolerances have been set for the six key aspects of the project)	The project can benefit from agile and thereby maximize the value delivered to the customer
Ensure that I understand the teams' information radiators (visibility boards)	I can track progress without asking for additional reporting from the agile teams
Ensure that the project-level requirements are prioritized ASAP	In the heat of the project, when there are some issues, there is little discussion needed as to what needs to be dropped – everyone should see MoSCoW as a gain more than a pain
Use product-based planning	Expectations are aligned on deliverables
Link products/deliverables to benefits	The right work is prioritized
Ensure that I have agreed reporting metrics and frequency with the agile teams	I am confident that beneficial progress is being made and they understand why I need to know
Ensure I understood how they manage and measure rework	I know how much is 'good' and helps the solution to progress, and how much is due to mistakes, so that I can ensure that sprint plans make sufficient allowances for fixing defects
Synchronize across sprint start and end dates across multiple agile teams	Interfaces between teams' systems can be adjusted in the following sprint
Ensure the agile teams are not continually deferring the 'difficult work' to later sprints	The integrity and benefits of the solution aren't degraded

H

The definitive guide to Scrum

Appendix H The definitive guide to Scrum

This appendix is a copy of the Scrum Guide which is the copyright of Scrum.Org and ScrumInc. It is reproduced here under the Attribution-ShareAlike licence of Creative Commons, which is accessible at:

http://creativecommons.org/licenses/by-sa/4.0/legalcode

and also described in summary form at:

http://creativecommons.org/licenses/by-sa/4.0/

By utilizing this Scrum Guide, AXELOS acknowledges and agrees to be bound by the terms of the Attribution-ShareAlike licence of Creative Commons for the content of this appendix.

The material in this appendix was developed and sustained by Ken Schwaber and Jeff Sutherland and is reproduced here with the original punctuation and spelling.

The original Scrum Guide can be downloaded from www.scrumguides.org

The Scrum Guide™

PURPOSE OF THE SCRUM GUIDE

Scrum is a framework for developing and sustaining complex products. This Guide contains the definition of Scrum. This definition consists of Scrum's roles, events, artifacts, and the rules that bind them together. Ken Schwaber and Jeff Sutherland developed Scrum; the Scrum Guide is written and provided by them. Together, they stand behind the Scrum Guide.

DEFINITION OF SCRUM

Scrum (n): A framework within which people can address complex adaptive problems, while productively and creatively delivering products of the highest possible value.

Scrum is:

- Lightweight
- Simple to understand
- Difficult to master

Scrum is a process framework that has been used to manage complex product development since the early 1990s. Scrum is not a process or a technique for building products; rather, it is a framework within which you can employ various processes and techniques. Scrum makes clear the relative efficacy of your product management and development practices so that you can improve.

The Scrum framework consists of Scrum Teams and their associated roles, events, artifacts, and rules. Each component within the framework serves a specific purpose and is essential to Scrum's success and usage.

The rules of Scrum bind together the events, roles, and artifacts, governing the relationships and interaction between them. The rules of Scrum are described throughout the body of this document.

Specific tactics for using the Scrum framework vary and are described elsewhere.

SCRUM THEORY

Scrum is founded on empirical process control theory, or empiricism. Empiricism asserts that knowledge comes from experience and making decisions based on what is known. Scrum employs an iterative, incremental approach to optimize predictability and control risk.

Three pillars uphold every implementation of empirical process control: transparency, inspection, and adaptation.

Transparency

Significant aspects of the process must be visible to those responsible for the outcome. Transparency requires those aspects be defined by a common standard so observers share a common understanding of what is being seen.

For example:

● A common language referring to the process must be shared by all participants; and,

● Those performing the work and those accepting the work product must share a common definition of "Done".

Inspection

Scrum users must frequently inspect Scrum artifacts and progress toward a Sprint Goal to detect undesirable variances. Their inspection should not be so frequent that inspection gets in the way of the work. Inspections are most beneficial when diligently performed by skilled inspectors at the point of work.

Adaptation

If an inspector determines that one or more aspects of a process deviate outside acceptable limits, and that the resulting product will be unacceptable, the process or the material being processed must be adjusted. An adjustment must be made as soon as possible to minimize further deviation.

Scrum prescribes four formal events for inspection and adaptation, as described in the Scrum Events section of this document:

● Sprint Planning

● Daily Scrum

● Sprint Review

● Sprint Retrospective

THE SCRUM TEAM

The Scrum Team consists of a Product Owner, the Development Team, and a Scrum Master. Scrum Teams are self-organizing and cross-functional. Self-organizing teams choose how best to accomplish their work, rather than being directed by others outside the team. Cross-functional teams have all competencies needed to accomplish the work without depending on others not part of the team. The team model in Scrum is designed to optimize flexibility, creativity, and productivity.

Scrum Teams deliver products iteratively and incrementally, maximizing opportunities for feedback. Incremental deliveries of "Done" product ensure a potentially useful version of working product is always available.

The Product Owner

The Product Owner is responsible for maximizing the value of the product and the work of the Development Team. How this is done may vary widely across organizations, Scrum Teams, and individuals.

The Product Owner is the sole person responsible for managing the Product Backlog. Product Backlog management includes:

● Clearly expressing Product Backlog items;

● Ordering the items in the Product Backlog to best achieve goals and missions;

● Optimizing the value of the work the Development Team performs;

- Ensuring that the Product Backlog is visible, transparent, and clear to all, and shows what the Scrum Team will work on next; and,
- Ensuring the Development Team understands items in the Product Backlog to the level needed.

The Product Owner may do the above work, or have the Development Team do it. However, the Product Owner remains accountable.

The Product Owner is one person, not a committee. The Product Owner may represent the desires of a committee in the Product Backlog, but those wanting to change a Product Backlog item's priority must address the Product Owner.

For the Product Owner to succeed, the entire organization must respect his or her decisions. The Product Owner's decisions are visible in the content and ordering of the Product Backlog. No one is allowed to tell the Development Team to work from a different set of requirements, and the Development Team isn't allowed to act on what anyone else says.

The Development Team

The Development Team consists of professionals who do the work of delivering a potentially releasable Increment of "Done" product at the end of each Sprint. Only members of the Development Team create the Increment.

Development Teams are structured and empowered by the organization to organize and manage their own work. The resulting synergy optimizes the Development Team's overall efficiency and effectiveness.

Development Teams have the following characteristics:

- They are self-organizing. No one (not even the Scrum Master) tells the Development Team how to turn Product Backlog into Increments of potentially releasable functionality;
- Development Teams are cross-functional, with all of the skills as a team necessary to create a product Increment;
- Scrum recognizes no titles for Development Team members other than Developer, regardless of the work being performed by the person; there are no exceptions to this rule;
- Scrum recognizes no sub-teams in the Development Team, regardless of particular domains that need to be addressed like testing or business analysis; there are no exceptions to this rule; and,
- Individual Development Team members may have specialized skills and areas of focus, but accountability belongs to the Development Team as a whole.

Development Team Size

Optimal Development Team size is small enough to remain nimble and large enough to complete significant work within a Sprint. Fewer than three Development Team members decrease interaction and results in smaller productivity gains. Smaller Development Teams may encounter skill constraints during the Sprint, causing the Development Team to be unable to deliver a potentially releasable Increment. Having more than nine members requires too much coordination. Large Development Teams generate too much complexity for an empirical process to manage. The Product Owner and Scrum Master roles are not included in this count unless they are also executing the work of the Sprint Backlog.

The Scrum Master

The Scrum Master is responsible for ensuring Scrum is understood and enacted. Scrum Masters do this by ensuring that the Scrum Team adheres to Scrum theory, practices, and rules.

The Scrum Master is a servant-leader for the Scrum Team. The Scrum Master helps those outside the Scrum Team understand which of their interactions with the Scrum Team are helpful and which aren't. The Scrum Master helps everyone change these interactions to maximize the value created by the Scrum Team.

Scrum Master Service to the Product Owner

The Scrum Master serves the Product Owner in several ways, including:

- Finding techniques for effective Product Backlog management;
- Helping the Scrum Team understand the need for clear and concise Product Backlog items;
- Understanding product planning in an empirical environment;
- Ensuring the Product Owner knows how to arrange the Product Backlog to maximize value;
- Understanding and practicing agility; and,
- Facilitating Scrum events as requested or needed.

Scrum Master Service to the Development Team

The Scrum Master serves the Development Team in several ways, including:

- Coaching the Development Team in self-organization and cross-functionality;
- Helping the Development Team to create high-value products;
- Removing impediments to the Development Team's progress;
- Facilitating Scrum events as requested or needed; and,
- Coaching the Development Team in organizational environments in which Scrum is not yet fully adopted and understood.

Scrum Master Service to the Organization

The Scrum Master serves the organization in several ways, including:

- Leading and coaching the organization in its Scrum adoption;
- Planning Scrum implementations within the organization;
- Helping employees and stakeholders understand and enact Scrum and empirical product development;
- Causing change that increases the productivity of the Scrum Team; and,
- Working with other Scrum Masters to increase the effectiveness of the application of Scrum in the organization.

SCRUM EVENTS

Prescribed events are used in Scrum to create regularity and to minimize the need for meetings not defined in Scrum. All events are time-boxed events, such that every event has a maximum duration. Once a Sprint begins, its duration is fixed and cannot be shortened or lengthened. The remaining events may end whenever the purpose of the event is achieved, ensuring an appropriate amount of time is spent without allowing waste in the process.

Other than the Sprint itself, which is a container for all other events, each event in Scrum is a formal opportunity to inspect and adapt something. These events are specifically designed to enable critical transparency and inspection. Failure to include any of these events results in reduced transparency and is a lost opportunity to inspect and adapt.

The Sprint

The heart of Scrum is a Sprint, a time-box of one month or less during which a "Done", useable, and potentially releasable product Increment is created. Sprints best have consistent durations throughout a development effort. A new Sprint starts immediately after the conclusion of the previous Sprint.

Sprints contain and consist of the Sprint Planning, Daily Scrums, the development work, the Sprint Review, and the Sprint Retrospective.

During the Sprint:

- No changes are made that would endanger the Sprint Goal;
- Quality goals do not decrease; and,
- Scope may be clarified and re-negotiated between the Product Owner and Development Team as more is learned.

Each Sprint may be considered a project with no more than a one-month horizon. Like projects, Sprints are used to accomplish something. Each Sprint has a definition of what is to be built, a design and flexible plan that will guide building it, the work, and the resultant product.

Sprints are limited to one calendar month. When a Sprint's horizon is too long the definition of what is being built may change, complexity may rise, and risk may increase. Sprints enable predictability by ensuring inspection and adaptation of progress toward a Sprint Goal at least every calendar month. Sprints also limit risk to one calendar month of cost.

Cancelling a Sprint

A Sprint can be cancelled before the Sprint time-box is over. Only the Product Owner has the authority to cancel the Sprint, although he or she may do so under influence from the stakeholders, the Development Team, or the Scrum Master.

A Sprint would be cancelled if the Sprint Goal becomes obsolete. This might occur if the company changes direction or if market or technology conditions change. In general, a Sprint should be cancelled if it no longer makes sense given the circumstances. But, due to the short duration of Sprints, cancellation rarely makes sense.

When a Sprint is cancelled, any completed and "Done" Product Backlog items are reviewed. If part of the work is potentially releasable, the Product Owner typically accepts it. All incomplete Product Backlog items are re-estimated and put back on the Product Backlog. The work done on them depreciates quickly and must be frequently re-estimated.

Sprint cancellations consume resources, since everyone has to regroup in another Sprint Planning to start another Sprint. Sprint cancellations are often traumatic to the Scrum Team, and are very uncommon.

Sprint Planning

The work to be performed in the Sprint is planned at the Sprint Planning. This plan is created by the collaborative work of the entire Scrum Team.

Sprint Planning is time-boxed to a maximum of eight hours for a one-month Sprint. For shorter Sprints, the event is usually shorter. The Scrum Master ensures that the event takes place and that attendants understand its purpose. The Scrum Master teaches the Scrum Team to keep it within the time-box.

Sprint Planning answers the following:

- What can be delivered in the Increment resulting from the upcoming Sprint?
- How will the work needed to deliver the Increment be achieved?

Topic One: What can be done this Sprint?

The Development Team works to forecast the functionality that will be developed during the Sprint. The Product Owner discusses the objective that the Sprint should achieve and the Product Backlog items that, if completed in the Sprint, would achieve the Sprint Goal. The entire Scrum Team collaborates on understanding the work of the Sprint.

The input to this meeting is the Product Backlog, the latest product Increment, projected capacity of the Development Team during the Sprint, and past performance of the Development Team. The number of items selected from the Product Backlog for the Sprint is solely up to the Development Team. Only the Development Team can assess what it can accomplish over the upcoming Sprint.

After the Development Team forecasts the Product Backlog items it will deliver in the Sprint, the Scrum Team crafts a Sprint Goal. The Sprint Goal is an objective that will be met within the Sprint through the implementation of the Product Backlog, and it provides guidance to the Development Team on why it is building the Increment.

Topic Two: How will the chosen work get done?

Having set the Sprint Goal and selected the Product Backlog items for the Sprint, the Development Team decides how it will build this functionality into a "Done" product Increment during the Sprint. The Product Backlog items selected for this Sprint plus the plan for delivering them is called the Sprint Backlog.

The Development Team usually starts by designing the system and the work needed to convert the Product Backlog into a working product Increment. Work may be of varying size, or estimated effort. However, enough work is planned during Sprint Planning for the Development Team to forecast what it believes it can do in the upcoming Sprint. Work planned for the first days of the Sprint by the Development Team is decomposed by the end of this meeting, often to units of one day or less. The Development Team self-organizes to undertake the work in the Sprint Backlog, both during Sprint Planning and as needed throughout the Sprint.

The Product Owner can help to clarify the selected Product Backlog items and make trade-offs. If the Development Team determines it has too much or too little work, it may renegotiate the selected Product Backlog items with the Product Owner. The Development Team may also invite other people to attend in order to provide technical or domain advice.

By the end of the Sprint Planning, the Development Team should be able to explain to the Product Owner and Scrum Master how it intends to work as a self-organizing team to accomplish the Sprint Goal and create the anticipated Increment.

Sprint Goal

The Sprint Goal is an objective set for the Sprint that can be met through the implementation of Product Backlog. It provides guidance to the Development Team on why it is building the Increment. It is created during the Sprint Planning meeting. The Sprint Goal gives the Development Team some flexibility regarding the functionality implemented within the Sprint. The selected Product Backlog items deliver one coherent function, which can be the Sprint Goal. The Sprint Goal can be any other coherence that causes the Development Team to work together rather than on separate initiatives.

As the Development Team works, it keeps the Sprint Goal in mind. In order to satisfy the Sprint Goal, it implements the functionality and technology. If the work turns out to be different than the Development Team expected, they collaborate with the Product Owner to negotiate the scope of Sprint Backlog within the Sprint.

Daily Scrum

The Daily Scrum is a 15-minute time-boxed event for the Development Team to synchronize activities and create a plan for the next 24 hours. This is done by inspecting the work since the last Daily Scrum and forecasting the work that could be done before the next one. The Daily Scrum is held at the same time and place each day to reduce complexity. During the meeting, the Development Team members explain:

● What did I do yesterday that helped the Development Team meet the Sprint Goal?

● What will I do today to help the Development Team meet the Sprint Goal?

● Do I see any impediment that prevents me or the Development Team from meeting the Sprint Goal?

The Development Team uses the Daily Scrum to inspect progress toward the Sprint Goal and to inspect how progress is trending toward completing the work in the Sprint Backlog. The Daily Scrum optimizes the probability that the Development Team will meet the Sprint Goal. Every day, the Development Team should understand how it intends to work together as a self-organizing team to accomplish the Sprint Goal and create the anticipated Increment by the end of the Sprint. The Development Team or team members often meet immediately after the Daily Scrum for detailed discussions, or to adapt, or replan, the rest of the Sprint's work.

The Scrum Master ensures that the Development Team has the meeting, but the Development Team is responsible for conducting the Daily Scrum. The Scrum Master teaches the Development Team to keep the Daily Scrum within the 15-minute time-box.

The Scrum Master enforces the rule that only Development Team members participate in the Daily Scrum.

Daily Scrums improve communications, eliminate other meetings, identify impediments to development for removal, highlight and promote quick decision-making, and improve the Development Team's level of knowledge. This is a key inspect and adapt meeting.

Sprint Review

A Sprint Review is held at the end of the Sprint to inspect the Increment and adapt the Product Backlog if needed. During the Sprint Review, the Scrum Team and stakeholders collaborate about what was done in the Sprint. Based on that and any changes to the Product Backlog during the Sprint, attendees collaborate on the next things that could be done to optimize value. This is an informal meeting, not a status meeting, and the presentation of the Increment is intended to elicit feedback and foster collaboration.

This is a four-hour time-boxed meeting for one-month Sprints. For shorter Sprints, the event is usually shorter. The Scrum Master ensures that the event takes place and that attendants understand its purpose. The Scrum Master teaches all to keep it within the time-box. The Sprint Review includes the following elements:

- Attendees include the Scrum Team and key stakeholders invited by the Product Owner;
- The Product Owner explains what Product Backlog items have been "Done" and what has not been "Done";
- The Development Team discusses what went well during the Sprint, what problems it ran into, and how those problems were solved;
- The Development Team demonstrates the work that it has "Done" and answers questions about the Increment;
- The Product Owner discusses the Product Backlog as it stands. He or she projects likely completion dates based on progress to date (if needed);
- The entire group collaborates on what to do next, so that the Sprint Review provides valuable input to subsequent Sprint Planning;
- Review of how the marketplace or potential use of the product might have changed what is the most valuable thing to do next; and,
- Review of the timeline, budget, potential capabilities, and marketplace for the next anticipated release of the product.

The result of the Sprint Review is a revised Product Backlog that defines the probable Product Backlog items for the next Sprint. The Product Backlog may also be adjusted overall to meet new opportunities.

Sprint Retrospective

The Sprint Retrospective is an opportunity for the Scrum Team to inspect itself and create a plan for improvements to be enacted during the next Sprint.

The Sprint Retrospective occurs after the Sprint Review and prior to the next Sprint Planning. This is a three-hour time-boxed meeting for one-month Sprints. For shorter Sprints, the event is usually shorter. The Scrum Master ensures that the event takes place and that attendants understand its purpose. The Scrum Master teaches all to keep it within the time-box. The Scrum Master participates as a peer team member in the meeting from the accountability over the Scrum process.

The purpose of the Sprint Retrospective is to:

- Inspect how the last Sprint went with regards to people, relationships, process, and tools;
- Identify and order the major items that went well and potential improvements; and,
- Create a plan for implementing improvements to the way the Scrum Team does its work.

The Scrum Master encourages the Scrum Team to improve, within the Scrum process framework, its development process and practices to make it more effective and enjoyable for the next Sprint. During each Sprint Retrospective, the Scrum Team plans ways to increase product quality by adapting the definition of "Done" as appropriate.

By the end of the Sprint Retrospective, the Scrum Team should have identified improvements that it will implement in the next Sprint. Implementing these improvements in the next Sprint is the adaptation to the inspection of the Scrum Team itself. Although improvements may be implemented at any time, the Sprint Retrospective provides a formal opportunity to focus on inspection and adaptation.

SCRUM ARTIFACTS

Scrum's artifacts represent work or value to provide transparency and opportunities for inspection and adaptation. Artifacts defined by Scrum are specifically designed to maximize transparency of key information so that everybody has the same understanding of the artifact.

Product Backlog

The Product Backlog is an ordered list of everything that might be needed in the product and is the single source of requirements for any changes to be made to the product. The Product Owner is responsible for the Product Backlog, including its content, availability, and ordering.

A Product Backlog is never complete. The earliest development of it only lays out the initially known and best-understood requirements. The Product Backlog evolves as the product and the environment in which it will be used evolves. The Product Backlog is dynamic; it constantly changes to identify what the product needs to be appropriate, competitive, and useful. As long as a product exists, its Product Backlog also exists.

The Product Backlog lists all features, functions, requirements, enhancements, and fixes that constitute the changes to be made to the product in future releases. Product Backlog items have the attributes of a description, order, estimate and value.

As a product is used and gains value, and the marketplace provides feedback, the Product Backlog becomes a larger and more exhaustive list. Requirements never stop changing, so a Product Backlog is a living artifact. Changes in business requirements, market conditions, or technology may cause changes in the Product Backlog.

Multiple Scrum Teams often work together on the same product. One Product Backlog is used to describe the upcoming work on the product. A Product Backlog attribute that groups items may then be employed.

Product Backlog refinement is the act of adding detail, estimates, and order to items in the Product Backlog. This is an ongoing process in which the Product Owner and the Development Team collaborate on the details of Product Backlog items. During Product Backlog refinement, items are reviewed and revised. The Scrum Team decides how and when refinement is done. Refinement usually consumes no more than 10% of the capacity of the Development Team. However, Product Backlog items can be updated at any time by the Product Owner or at the Product Owner's discretion.

Higher ordered Product Backlog items are usually clearer and more detailed than lower ordered ones. More precise estimates are made based on the greater clarity and increased detail; the lower the order, the less detail. Product Backlog items that will occupy the Development Team for the upcoming Sprint are refined so that any one item can reasonably be "Done" within the Sprint time-box. Product Backlog items that can be "Done" by the Development Team within one Sprint are deemed "Ready" for selection in a Sprint Planning. Product Backlog items usually acquire this degree of transparency through the above described refining activities.

The Development Team is responsible for all estimates. The Product Owner may influence the Development Team by helping it understand and select trade-offs, but the people who will perform the work make the final estimate.

Monitoring Progress Toward a Goal

At any point in time, the total work remaining to reach a goal can be summed. The Product Owner tracks this total work remaining at least every Sprint Review. The Product Owner compares this amount with work remaining at previous Sprint Reviews to assess progress toward completing projected work by the desired time for the goal. This information is made transparent to all stakeholders.

Various projective practices upon trending have been used to forecast progress, like burn-downs, burn-ups, or cumulative flows. These have proven useful. However, these do not replace the importance of empiricism. In complex environments, what will happen is unknown. Only what has happened may be used for forward-looking decision-making.

Sprint Backlog

The Sprint Backlog is the set of Product Backlog items selected for the Sprint, plus a plan for delivering the product Increment and realizing the Sprint Goal. The Sprint Backlog is a forecast by the Development Team about what functionality will be in the next Increment and the work needed to deliver that functionality into a "Done" Increment.

The Sprint Backlog makes visible all of the work that the Development Team identifies as necessary to meet the Sprint Goal.

The Sprint Backlog is a plan with enough detail that changes in progress can be understood in the Daily Scrum. The Development Team modifies the Sprint Backlog throughout the Sprint, and the Sprint Backlog emerges during the Sprint. This emergence occurs as the Development Team works through the plan and learns more about the work needed to achieve the Sprint Goal.

As new work is required, the Development Team adds it to the Sprint Backlog. As work is performed or completed, the estimated remaining work is updated. When elements of the plan are deemed unnecessary, they are removed. Only the Development Team can change its Sprint Backlog during a Sprint. The Sprint Backlog is a highly visible, real-time picture of the work that the Development Team plans to accomplish during the Sprint, and it belongs solely to the Development Team.

Monitoring Sprint Progress

At any point in time in a Sprint, the total work remaining in the Sprint Backlog can be summed. The Development Team tracks this total work remaining at least for every Daily Scrum to project the likelihood of achieving the Sprint Goal. By tracking the remaining work throughout the Sprint, the Development Team can manage its progress.

Increment

The Increment is the sum of all the Product Backlog items completed during a Sprint and the value of the increments of all previous Sprints. At the end of a Sprint, the new Increment must be "Done", which means it must be in useable condition and meet the Scrum Team's definition of "Done". It must be in useable condition regardless of whether the Product Owner decides to actually release it.

ARTIFACT TRANSPARENCY

Scrum relies on transparency. Decisions to optimize value and control risk are made based on the perceived state of the artifacts. To the extent that transparency is complete, these decisions have a sound basis. To the extent that the artifacts are incompletely transparent, these decisions can be flawed, value may diminish and risk may increase.

The Scrum Master must work with the Product Owner, Development Team, and other involved parties to understand if the artifacts are completely transparent. There are practices for coping with incomplete transparency; the Scrum Master must help everyone apply the most appropriate practices in the absence of complete transparency. A Scrum Master can detect incomplete transparency by inspecting the artifacts, sensing patterns, listening closely to what is being said, and detecting differences between expected and real results.

The Scrum Master's job is to work with the Scrum Team and the organization to increase the transparency of the artifacts. This work usually involves learning, convincing, and change. Transparency doesn't occur overnight, but is a path.

Definition of "Done"

When a Product Backlog item or an Increment is described as "Done", everyone must understand what "Done" means. Although this varies significantly per Scrum Team, members must have a shared understanding of what it means for work to be complete, to ensure transparency. This is the definition of "Done" for the Scrum Team and is used to assess when work is complete on the product Increment.

The same definition guides the Development Team in knowing how many Product Backlog items it can select during a Sprint Planning. The purpose of each Sprint is to deliver Increments of potentially releasable functionality that adhere to the Scrum Team's current definition of "Done". Development Teams deliver an Increment of product functionality every Sprint. This Increment is useable, so a Product Owner may choose to immediately release it. If the definition of "done" for an increment is part of the conventions, standards or guidelines of the development organization, all Scrum Teams must follow it as a minimum. If "done" for an increment is not a convention of the development organization, the Development Team of the Scrum Team must define a definition of "done" appropriate for the product. If there are multiple Scrum Teams working on the system or product release, the Development Teams on all of the Scrum Teams must mutually define the definition of "Done".

Each Increment is additive to all prior Increments and thoroughly tested, ensuring that all Increments work together.

As Scrum Teams mature, it is expected that their definitions of "Done" will expand to include more stringent criteria for higher quality. Any one product or system should have a definition of "Done" that is a standard for any work done on it.

END NOTE

Scrum is free and offered in this Guide. Scrum's roles, artifacts, events, and rules are immutable and although implementing only parts of Scrum is possible, the result is not Scrum. Scrum exists only in its entirety and functions well as a container for other techniques, methodologies, and practices.

ACKNOWLEDGEMENTS

People

Of the thousands of people who have contributed to Scrum, we should single out those who were instrumental in its first ten years. First there was Jeff Sutherland working with Jeff McKenna, and Ken Schwaber working with Mike Smith and Chris Martin. Many others contributed in the ensuing years and without their help Scrum would not be refined as it is today.

History

Ken Schwaber and Jeff Sutherland first co-presented Scrum at the OOPSLA conference in 1995. This presentation essentially documented the learning that Ken and Jeff gained over the previous few years applying Scrum.

The history of Scrum is already considered long. To honor the first places where it was tried and refined, we recognize Individual, Inc., Fidelity Investments, and IDX (now GE Medical).

The Scrum Guide documents Scrum as developed and sustained for 20-plus years by Jeff Sutherland and Ken Schwaber. Other sources provide you with patterns, processes, and insights that complement the Scrum framework. These optimize productivity, value, creativity, and pride.

Glossary

Glossary

acceptance criteria

A prioritized list of criteria that the project product must meet before the customer will accept it, i.e. measurable definitions of the attributes required for the set of products to be acceptable to key stakeholders (PRINCE2 definition).

The term is commonly used in agile for assessing whether a user story has been completed.

Agilometer

The Agilometer is a tool that assesses the level of risk associated with using agile in combination with PRINCE2. This allows PRINCE2 to be tailored in such a way that best mitigates the level of risk. The Agilometer should evolve to suit the needs of each organization.

backlog

A list of new features for a product. The list may be made up of user stories which are structured in a way that describes who wants the feature and why.

backlog item

An entry in a backlog. This may be in the form of a user story or task and may be held in many forms such as in a spreadsheet or displayed on a whiteboard.

baseline

A reference level against which an entity is monitored and controlled.

benefit

The measurable improvement resulting from an outcome perceived as an advantage by one or more stakeholders, and which contributes towards one or more organizational objective(s).

benefits review plan

A plan that defines how and when a measurement of the achievement of the project's benefits can be made. If the project is being managed within a programme, this information may be created and maintained at the programme level.

brainstorming

A technique that helps a team to generate ideas. Ideas are not reviewed during the brainstorming session, but at a later stage. Brainstorming is often used by problem management to identify possible causes.

burn chart

A technique for showing progress (e.g. such as with a timebox) where work that is completed and work still to do is shown with one or more lines that are updated regularly/daily.

business ambassador

A role in DSDM that is the pivotal role (but not the only role) in understanding the business view of a project.

business case

The justification for an organizational activity (strategic, programme, project or operational) which typically contains costs, benefits, risks and timescales, and against which continuing viability is tested.

change authority

A person or group to which the project board may delegate responsibility for the consideration of requests for change or off-specifications. The change authority may be given a change budget and can approve changes within that budget.

checkpoint report

A progress report of the information gathered at a checkpoint, which is given by a team to the project manager and which provides reporting data as defined in the work package.

class of service

Broadly defined category for different types of work. The classes influence selection decisions, in that different classes of service are typically associated with qualitatively different risk profiles, especially with regard to schedule risk and the cost of delay. Four generic classes of service are widely recognized: 'standard', 'fixed date', 'expedite' and 'intangible'.

communication management strategy

A description of the means and frequency of communication between the project and the project's stakeholders.

configuration item

An entity (asset) that is subject to configuration management. The entity (asset) may be a component of a product, a product or a set of products in a release.

configuration item record

A record that describes the status, version and variant of a configuration item, and any details of important relationships between them. *See* configuration item.

configuration management

Technical and administrative activities concerned with the creation, maintenance and controlled change of configuration throughout the life of a product.

configuration management strategy

A description of how and by whom the project's products will be controlled and protected.

constraint

A restriction or limitation that a project is bound by. It may be challenged during an MoV study.

contingency

Something that is held in reserve, typically to handle time and cost variances, or risks. PRINCE2 does not advocate the use of contingency because estimating variances is managed by setting tolerances, and risks are managed through appropriate risk responses (including the fallback response that is contingent on the risk occurring).

definition of 'done'

A set of criteria that is used to determine if a piece of work or a collection of work items is completed. Something is either 'done' or it is 'not done'.

definition of 'ready'

A set of criteria that is used to determine if a piece of work is ready to be started.

demo

Short for 'demonstration', this is an event where a product or interim product, in whatever state of readiness, is shown to a person or group (e.g. to a customer) in order to get feedback and show progress. The product being 'demoed' could be static (e.g. a paper design) or dynamic (e.g. a working prototype).

DevOps

A collaborative approach between development and operations aimed at creating a product or service where the two types of work and even the teams merge as much as possible.

discovery (phase)

See sprint zero.

disruptive

A widely used term that has more than one definition but in general terms refers to situations where there are high degrees of uncertainty (e.g. with product innovation) and the product being developed will significantly disrupt (intentionally or accidentally) the existing environment or marketplace (e.g. 3D printing).

Dynamic Systems Development Method (DSDM)

An agile project delivery framework developed and owned by the DSDM consortium.

early adopter

A term given to a customer who is one of the first to buy or use a product. They typically may like innovative products and therefore may expect to pay more for them although these products may not be to a level of quality that later customers will receive. This type of customer is very useful for early feedback on the product.

emergent

A concept in agile that refers to creating solutions and making decisions in a way that gradually converges on an accurate solution and doesn't involve a lot of upfront work. The opposite would be to spend time and try to predict how things will happen. An example would be 'emergent architecture' whereby work could be started on the product and then the best architecture would emerge as the product develops. The alternative would involve doing a lot of work in advance to decide how the product will be built.

empirical/empiricism

Using evidence to make decisions as opposed to reasoning or intuition.

epic

A high-level definition of a requirement that has not been sufficiently refined or understood yet. Eventually, an epic will be refined and be broken down into several user stories/requirements.

exception

A situation where it can be forecast that there will be a deviation beyond the tolerance levels agreed between project manager and project board (or between project board and corporate or programme management).

executive

The single individual with overall responsibility for ensuring that a project meets its objectives and delivers the projected benefits. This individual should ensure that the project maintains its business focus, that it has clear authority and that the work, including risks, is actively managed. The executive is the chair of the project board. He or she represents the customer and is responsible for the business case.

experiment

An investigation into something that is carried out in a series of specific steps (which may involve research) in order to prove or disprove a theory or idea. This can be used to validate an idea or to try to improve something such as the way a team is working.

feature

A generic term that is widely used to describe something a product does, or the way it does something. A feature can be at any level of detail (e.g. it is waterproof, it makes a tone when switched off) and can relate to a specific requirement, user story or epic. Another similar term is 'function'.

flow-based

This avoids the use of partitioning work into timeboxes and manages work by using a queue. Work is then continually pulled into the system (which may itself be a high-level timebox) and moves through various work states until it is done.

Gantt chart

A commonly used technique for planning work activities against time in the form of horizontal lines or bars showing when the activities start and end. This can then be used to schedule dependencies between the activities. This is unlikely to be of use for a timebox or sprint where time is fixed and the work is ordered dynamically by the team.

gap analysis

An activity that compares two sets of data and identifies the differences. Gap analysis is commonly used to compare a set of requirements with actual delivery.

highlight report

A time-driven report from the project manager to the project board on stage progress.

information radiator

A general term used to describe the use of walls or boards containing information that can be readily accessed by people working on the project. It can contain any information, although it would typically show such things as work to do and how work is progressing.

issue

A relevant event that has happened, was not planned and requires management action. It could be a problem, benefit, query, concern, change request or risk that has occurred.

Kaizen

A Japanese philosophy that literally means 'good change' but is widely understood to refer to continual improvement. It involves everyone contributing on a regular basis to make many small beneficial changes that build up over time to improve the efficiency of the way a team or organization works.

Kanban

A way to improve flow and provoke system improvement through visualization and controlling work in progress. Written in kanji (Chinese characters), it means 'sign' or 'large visual board'. Written in hiragana (Japanese characters) it means 'signal cards' (singular or plural). In technical presentations of the mechanics of Kanban systems it usually means the latter. Used informally, it refers to the use of Kanban systems (visual or otherwise) and the Kanban method.

Kanban board

A tool used in Kanban to visually display the work in the system (or timebox). It is usually made up of a series of columns and possibly rows where work items move from left to right as they move through various states in order to be completed.

Kanban method

An evolutionary approach to change described by David J. Anderson in *Six Core Practices and Four Foundational Principles*.

Kanban system

A 'pull system' implemented by limiting the number of Kanban (cards) in circulation.

Kano

A model, developed by Noriaki Kano, which is used to help understand customer preferences. The Kano model considers attributes of an IT service grouped into areas such as basic factors, excitement factors and performance factors.

lead time/cycle time

Interpreted differently by many in the Kanban community (some see these two terms as representing different things) but in simple terms it refers to how long a work item takes to go through the system or timebox.

Lean

An approach that focuses on improving processes by maximizing value through eliminating waste (such as wasted time and wasted effort).

lessons report

A report that documents any lessons that can be usefully applied to other projects. The purpose of the report is to provoke action so that the positive lessons from a project become embedded in the organization's way of working and the organization is able to avoid the negative lessons on future projects.

level of quality

The overall quality level of a product as defined by the project product description (customer's quality expectations and acceptance criteria).

manage by exception

A technique by which variances from plan that exceed a pre-set control limit are escalated for action – for example, where spends exceed budget by 10%.

minimum viable product (MVP)

In a PRINCE2 Agile context the term MVP broadly aligns with the Lean Startup view that it is a 'version of the final product which allows the maximum amount of validated learning with the least effort'. This should not be confused with the viability of the project as a whole. Typically, an MVP would be delivered as early as possible during the project.

It is important to note that an MVP is about learning and may not go into operational use; it may be in the form of a simple experiment or prototype.

Plan-Do-Check-Act (PDCA)

A four-stage cycle for process management, attributed to W. Edwards Deming. Plan-Do-Check-Act is also called the Deming Cycle. Plan – design or revise processes that support the IT services; Do – implement the plan and manage the processes; Check – measure the processes and IT services, compare with objectives and produce reports; Act – plan and implement changes to improve the processes.

planning horizon

The period of time for which it is possible to plan accurately.

product-based planning

A technique leading to a comprehensive plan based on the creation and delivery of required outputs. The technique considers prerequisite products, quality requirements and the dependencies between products.

product description

A description of a product's purpose, composition, derivation and quality criteria. It is produced at planning time, as soon as possible after the need for the product is identified.

product owner

The role assigned to managing the product backlog in order to get the most value from it by ordering and prioritizing it.

product roadmap

A diagram or document that shows the intended development path for a product. This would typically be a long-range plan that may cover several months if not years. It exists outside a project context but could be used to trigger project work.

project

A temporary organization that is created for the purpose of delivering one or more business products according to an agreed business case.

project assurance

The project board's responsibilities to assure itself that the project is being conducted correctly. The project board members each have a specific area of focus for project assurance, namely business assurance for the executive, user assurance for the senior user(s), and supplier assurance for the senior supplier(s).

project brief

Statement that describes the purpose, cost, time and performance requirements, and the constraints for a project. It is created pre-project during the Starting up a Project process and is used during the Initiating a Project process to create the project initiation documentation and its components. It is superseded by the project initiation documentation and not maintained.

project initiation documentation (PID)

A logical set of documents that brings together the key information needed to start the project on a sound basis and conveys the information to all concerned with the project.

project kick-off

Usually, a single event to start off a project where visioning may take place and the team comes together for the first time. These events can be run as workshops and require preparation to ensure that time is used as effectively as possible. See also visioning.

project manager

The person with authority and responsibility to manage a project on a day-to-day basis to deliver the required products within the constraints agreed by the project board.

project plan

A high-level plan showing the major products of the project, when they will be delivered and at what cost. An initial project plan is presented as part of the project initiation documentation. This is revised as information on actual progress appears. It is a major control document for the project board to measure actual progress against expectations.

project product description

A special type of product description used to gain agreement from the user on the project's scope and requirements, to define the customer's quality expectations, and to define the acceptance criteria for the project.

project support

An administrative role in the project management team. Project support can be in the form of advice and help with project management tools, guidance, administrative services such as filing, and the collection of actual data.

prototype

Something created to help prove or disprove an idea, or to help to improve the general understanding of a situation (e.g. the customer's needs). It could be something that evolves into a real product or is thrown away.

pull system

A way of working in which work is started or 'pulled' from upstream, but only as capacity becomes available. Kanban systems are pull systems. The availability of capacity and the ability to pull work is indicated by the gap between current work in progress and the corresponding limit. *See also* push system.

push system

The act of placing work into a system or activity without due regard to its available capacity. *See also* pull system.

quality assurance

The planned systematic process that will be used to provide confidence that outputs match their defined quality criteria.

quality criteria

A description of the quality specification that the product must meet, and the quality measurements that will be applied by those inspecting the finished product.

quality review technique

A quality inspection technique with defined roles and a specific structure. It is designed to assess whether a product that takes the form of a document (or similar, e.g. a presentation) is complete, adheres to standards and meets the quality criteria agreed for it in the relevant product description. The participants are drawn from those with the necessary competence to evaluate its fitness for purpose.

quality tolerance

The tolerance identified for a product for a quality criterion defining an acceptable range of values. Quality tolerance is documented in the project product description (for the project-level quality tolerance) and in the product description for each product to be delivered.

RACI

A widely used technique to define who is responsible for what on a project, or with a process. RACI typically stands for (who is) 'responsible, accountable, consulted and informed' with respect to certain deliverables or steps in a process. There are many variations of RACI that can be used instead.

release

The set of products in a handover. The contents of a release are managed, tested and deployed as a single entity.

requirement

A term to describe what a product does and/or how it will do it. A requirement can be written in the form of a user story if desired and will exist with other requirements in the form of a list.

retrospective

A regular event that looks at how the process of doing work can be improved. In keeping with the agile concept of 'inspect and adapt', these events help teams to continually improve their working practices, little by little, over time.

risk

An uncertain event or set of events that, should it occur, will have an effect on the achievement of objectives. A risk is measured by a combination of the probability of a perceived threat or opportunity occurring, and the magnitude of its impact on objectives.

risk log

See risk register.

risk management strategy

Describes the goals of applying risk management to the activity, the process that will be adopted, the roles and responsibilities, risk thresholds, the timing of risk management interventions, the deliverables, the tools and techniques that will be used, and the reporting requirements. It may also describe how the process will be coordinated with other management activities.

risk register

A record of all identified risks relating to an initiative, including their status and history. Also called a risk log.

safe-to-fail

A safe-to-fail experiment is one that is designed to have only limited impact on the system or the plan in the event of failure.

Scrumban

The application of Kanban or the Kanban method in the context of an existing implementation of Scrum. In simple terms, it is Kanban, when the 'what you do now' is Scrum.

senior user

The project board role accountable for ensuring that user needs are specified correctly and that the solution meets those needs.

sensitivity analysis

A technique for testing the robustness of a calculation or model by assessing the impact of varying the input, to reflect the risk that the calculation or model might not be accurate.

spike/spiking

A temporary piece of work used to understand more about a given situation. It may take the form of a prototype or some research and is often used to reduce uncertainty from a technical or customer viewpoint. Experiments are similar.

sprint

A fixed timeframe (typically of 2–4 weeks) for creating selected features from the backlog.

sprint zero

A specific sprint at the beginning of a piece of work in order to address many upfront activities (e.g. forming a team, visioning, defining the architecture). Also referred to as iteration zero or (the) discovery (phase).

stage (management stage)

A PRINCE2 term that describes a section of the project that a project manager is managing at any one point in time. It is in effect a high-level timebox and will usually contain one or more lower-level timeboxes such as releases or sprints. The concept of a PRINCE2 stage does not have an exact equivalent commonly used in agile.

stage plan

A detailed plan used as the basis for project management control throughout a stage.

stand-up meeting

A short meeting to assess progress. Typically lasting 15 minutes or less, they involve describing work that has been done, will be done and any problems being encountered.

SWOT analysis

Acronym for 'strengths, weaknesses, opportunities and threats'. A technique to determine favourable and unfavourable factors in relation to business change or current state.

team dynamics

The interpersonal interactions between the individuals on a team. This relates to the culture and attitudes of the people in the team and needs to be managed carefully as it can be a very positive and powerful force when it is working well, but it can be destructive when it breaks down.

team manager

The person responsible for the production of those products allocated by the project manager (as defined in a work package) to an appropriate quality, timescale and at a cost acceptable to the project board. This role reports to, and takes direction from, the project manager. If a team manager is not assigned, then the project manager undertakes the responsibilities of the team manager role.

test-driven

The concept of writing tests or quality checks before building the product or sub-product as opposed to after.

timebox

A finite period of time where work is carried out to achieve a goal or meet an objective. The deadline should not be moved, as the method of managing a timebox is to prioritize the work inside it. At a low level a timebox will be a matter of days or weeks (e.g. a sprint). Higher-level timeboxes act as aggregated timeboxes and contain lower-level timeboxes (e.g. stages).

tolerance

The permissible deviation above and below a plan's target for time and cost without escalating the deviation to the next level of management. There may also be tolerance levels for quality, scope, benefit and risk. Tolerance is applied at project, stage and team levels.

trading (or swapping)

The act of handling change by replacing one or more requirements (or features or user stories) with others of a similar size in terms of effort.

transparency

A fundamental agile behaviour which involves making as many things visible as possible in order to help the way people work. This can involve displaying progress on a wall or the frequent delivery of products. Importantly, transparency also covers areas such as openness and honesty.

user story

A tool used to write a requirement in the form of who, what and why.

validated learning

The idea of learning through the use of experiments carried out in a scientific way: i.e. using a series of carefully designed steps and using measures to prove the success or otherwise of the experiment.

value

The benefits delivered in proportion to the resources put into acquiring them.

velocity

A description of the rate of progress a team is making. For example, if a team is completing 20 user stories per week then this is their velocity and it can be used to empirically forecast their future rate of progress (assuming that the conditions remain the same).

vision

The annunciation of a desired future state.

visioning

An exercise or phase that aims to understand the overarching goal of something (e.g. a project). It would try to answer questions such as: Why is this work taking place? Who is it for? What might it look like? *See also* project kick-off.

Waterfall methodology

A development approach that is linear and sequential, with distinct goals for each phase of development. Once a phase of development is completed, the development proceeds to the next phase and earlier phases are not revisited (hence the analogy that water flowing down a mountain cannot go back).

work in progress (WIP)

Work that has been started but not delivered from the system or timebox. It is commonly used as a status for incidents, problems, changes etc.

work-in-progress (WIP) limit

A constraint on the amount of WIP allowed in a given part (or column) of the system at any one time. Typically expressed as a number (i.e. the maximum number of work items allowed), it creates the concept of a pull system.

work package

The set of information relevant to the creation of one or more products. It will contain a description of the work, the product description(s), details of any constraints on production, and confirmation of the agreement between the project manager and the person or team manager who is to implement the work package that the work can be done within the constraints.

workshop

An event where people come together in a room to achieve an objective (e.g. to create a list of requirements or solve a problem) by using interaction and creativity in order to work quickly and accurately. It is not related to light engineering.

Index

Index

ability to work iteratively and deliver incrementally
      slider 215, 217
acceptance criteria 42, 94, 230
acceptance of agile slider 215, 218
actionable metrics 184–5
adaptation (Scrum) 314
Adaptive Software Development (ASD) 12
advantageous environmental conditions slider 215, 218
agile
    history 9–10
    principles 10–13
Agile Manifesto 9–10, 297
Agilometer 213–18
anchoring 106
artefact transparency 321–2
ASD (Adaptive Software Development) 12
aspects, PRINCE2 39–40
assess (risk management) 111

backlogs 11, 30, 314–15, 320–1
baseline changes 119–20, 227
baseline management products 205–7
BAU (business as usual) 5–6, 19
BDD (behaviour-driven development) 96, 97
behaviour dashboards 53
behaviour-driven development (BDD) 96, 97
behaviours, agile 13, 285
benefit aspect 39, 40
benefits 66–8
benefits review plans 205, 257
big visible charts (BVCs) 132
Bono, Edward de, Six Thinking Hats 239
brainstorming 239
build-measure-learn feedback 185–6
burn charts 28, 115, 129–30
business analysts 76, 87–8
business as usual (BAU) 5–6, 19
business case 205, 257–8
Business Case theme 35, 58, 63–9
BVCs (big visible charts) 132

calibration 101
centres of excellence 75
CFDs (cumulative flow diagrams) 180–1
change, embracing 41, 42–3
change authorities 84, 280
Change theme 35, 59, 119–23
chaotic domain 149, 150
charts 132
checkpoint reports 208, 258

classes of service 177
cliffs 149, 151
Closing a Project process 137–8, 197–201
coaches 82
cohorts (groups of users) 186
collaboration behaviour 51, 68, 307
collaborative improvement 179
collaborative planning 103
communicate (risk management) 111–12
communication, rich 51, 235–40, 308
communication management strategy 205, 259
complex domain 149, 150
complexity levels 149–50
complicated domain 149, 150
concepts, agile 13
configuration item records 207, 259–60
configuration management strategy 121, 205, 260–1
continued business justification principle 50
contracts 249–52
control, monitoring and 127–8, 163, 309
Controlling a Stage process 137–8, 161–9
corporate and programme management 84
cost aspect 39, 40
cost of delay 182
Crystal 12
CSMEs (customer subject matter experts) 81–2, 87, 280
cumulative flow diagrams (CFDs) 180–1
customer representatives 281
customer subject matter experts (CSMEs) 81–2, 87, 280
customers
    collaboration with 249–50
    requirements 41, 44, 86–8
cycle time 181
Cynefin framework 149–51

DAD (Disciplined Agile Delivery) 12
daily logs 207, 261
daily scrums 114, 318–19
dashboards, behaviour 53
de Bono, Edward, Six Thinking Hats 239
deadlines, meeting 41
decision-making 121–2
defined roles and responsibilities principle 50
delay, cost of 182
deliveries, time-based 250
delivery team quality assurance role 282
delivery teams 77–9
detail changes 119–20, 227
development teams 315
DevOps 12

Directing a Project process 137–8, 155–7
Disciplined Agile Delivery (DAD) 12
disorder domain 149
disruptive technologies 145–6
'done' 96, 97, 321, 322
dynamic change 227–8
Dynamic Systems Development Method (DSDM)
    12, 298

ease of communication slider 215, 217
email communication 236–7
emergent, definition 105
emoticons 236
empiricism 101–2, 103, 104–5
end dates 103
end project reports 208, 262
end stage reports 208, 262–3
environment, agile 285, 308
epics 27, 229
estimation 106–8
exception reports 208, 263
exceptions 127
executives 84, 279
experiments 52, 115, 179–80
exploration behaviour 52, 308
eXtreme Programming (XP) 12, 298

face-to-face communication 236–7
feature-driven development (FDD) 12
features, definition 26
feedback 168
feedback loops 122–3, 179, 185–6
Fibonacci sequence 106
final delivery stage 29–30
five domains 149
five targets 40–4
five whys 239
flexibility on what is delivered slider 215, 216
flexing 39–43
flow-based working 12, 102–3, 105
flow management 179
focus on products principle 50
frequent releases 243–5
functional requirements 221
funnel metrics 187

Gantt charts 59, 102
gap analysis 239
Glad! Sad! Mad! feedback 167–8
group work 239

highlight reports 208, 264

identify (risk management) 111
impact/effort grids 239
implement (risk management) 111–12
incentive schemes 250–1
increments 162, 321
information radiators 27, 130–3
Initiating a Project process 25–7, 137–8, 143–51
initiation stage 25–7
inspection (Scrum) 314
INVEST mnemonic 229
issue registers 207, 264–5
issue reports 208, 265
iterations 162

just-in-time (JIT) planning 104

Kanban boards 28, 177
Kanban method 12, 176–83, 299
Kanban tickets 177–8
knowledge management (KM) systems 66–8

lead time 181
leadership, and management 85
Lean Startup 12, 122, 146, 184–7, 244, 299
Lean thinking 12, 299
learn from experience principle 50
lessons logs 207, 266
lessons reports 208, 266–7
level of collaboration slider 215, 217
levels of complexity 149–50
levels of uncertainty 146
Little's Law 183

manage by exception principle 50
manage by stages principle 50
management, and leadership 85
management by exception 156
Management of Risk (M_o_R) 115
Management of Value (MoV) 66
management stages *see* stages
Managing a Stage Boundary process 137–8, 191–4
Managing Product Delivery stage 137–8, 173–87
Managing Successful Projects with PRINCE2 21
Manifesto for Agile Software Development 9–10, 297
minimum viable product (MVP) 50, 64, 186, 251
monitoring and control 127–8, 163, 309
M_o_R (*Management of Risk*) 115
MoSCoW 223–4
MoV (*Management of Value*) 66
multi-skilling 79–80
multiple-team projects 81–2

'must' 215
MVP (minimum viable product) 50, 64, 186, 251

non-functional requirements 221

obvious domain 149
ordering (prioritization) 225–6
Organization theme 35, 36, 58, 73–90
outcomes 66, 67, 250, 252
outputs 66, 67, 250

Pastor of Fun 89
penalty clauses 251
phased Waterfall methodology 243
phone communication 236
plan (risk management) 111–12
planning 102–6, 309
planning horizons 104–5
planning poker 59
plans (product) 205, 267–8
Plans theme 35, 59, 101–8
playing cards 106, 107
points estimates 102, 106
pre-project stage 25–7
premature contract termination 250
premature project closure 201
principles, PRINCE2 34, 49–53
prioritization of requirements 223–8
prioritization with dots 239
process, agile 286
product backlogs 11, 314–15, 320–1
product-based planning 105, 222
product breakdown structures 290–1
product descriptions 94–5, 205, 221–2, 257–76, 292
product flow diagrams 293
product owners 63, 75, 86–7, 314–15
product roadmaps 11
product status accounts 208, 269
programmes, definition 33
progress controls 127
Progress theme 35, 59, 127–33
progressive elaboration 104
project assurance 84, 280
project boards 84, 155–6, 279
project briefs 206, 270
project chartering 145
project initiation documentation 206, 270–1
project kick-off 64
project management 17, 33
Project Management Declaration of
    Interdependence 298
project management team 73–4

project managers 27, 76, 77–9, 84, 155–6, 279
project mandates 25
project product descriptions 94, 146, 206, 271–2,
    289–90
project support 84, 280
projects
    characteristics 5–6, 33
    closure 197–201
proof of concepts 115
prototyping 115
pull systems 176

quality, protecting the level of 41–2
quality aspect 39, 40
quality management 95
quality management strategy 206, 272–3
quality planning 95
quality registers 207, 273
Quality theme 35, 58, 93–8

RACI (Responsible, Accountable, Consulted and
    Informed) 80
rationalism 102
'ready' 96, 231
record products 207
refactoring 96
relative estimation 106, 107
releases 11, 162, 163, 243–5
report products 207–8
requirements 221–8
    contractual aspects 251
    decomposition and granularity 222–3
    prioritization 223–8
requirements engineers 76, 87–8
retrospectives 29, 166–8
rich communication behaviour 51, 235–40, 308
rich pictures 239
risk, definition 111
risk aspect 39, 40
risk burn-down charts 115
risk management procedures 111–12
risk management strategy 206, 274
risk registers 113, 207, 275
Risk theme 35, 59, 111–15, 121
rolling-wave planning 104

SAFe (Scaled Agile Framework) 12, 298
safe-to-fail experiments 179
Scaled Agile Framework (SAFe) 12, 298
scope aspect 39, 40
Scrum masters 75, 315–16
Scrum of Scrums 162

Scrum teams 314–16
Scrum theory 297, 313–14
Scrumban 180
Scrums 12, 21, 64, 174, 313–22
self-organization behaviour 52, 76, 77, 307
senior suppliers 84, 279
senior users 84, 279
servant leadership 83–6
single-team projects 80–1
Six Thinking Hats 239
SMART 229
spike (spiking) 52, 115
sprint backlogs 11, 321
sprint planning 105–6, 317
sprint retrospectives 319–20
sprint reviews 319
sprint zero 64, 145
sprints 11, 163, 316–18
stage boundaries 137–8, 191–4
stages 74, 138–9, 162–5
staging areas 244–5
stand-up meetings 28, 113–14, 163
Starting up a Project process 137–8, 143–51
sticky notes 240
success, measuring 303–4
supplier representatives 281
supplier subject matter experts 81, 281
swapping, definition 42
SWOT analysis 239

T-shirt sizing 107
tailor to suit the project environment principle 50
targets, five 40–4
TDD (test-driven development) 96
team-based estimation 107
team dynamics 43
team managers 76, 77–9, 84, 279
teams
    rules 88–9, 179
    stability 41, 43
    see also delivery teams; development teams;
        Scrum teams
technical debt 96
technical stories 231
techniques, agile 13, 286
telephone communication 236
test-driven, definition 95
test-driven development (TDD) 96
testing 95–6
themes, PRINCE2 35–6, 57–60
Thinking Hats 239
Three Cs technique 229

time aspect 39, 40
time-based deliveries 250
timeboxes 6, 102–3
tolerances 39–40, 127
trading, definition 42
transparency behaviour 51, 132, 308, 314, 321–2

uncertainty levels 146
user stories 27, 228–31

validation and verification (V&V) 96
value 65–8
vanity metrics 184–5
velocity, definition 60
visibility (transparency) behaviour 51, 132, 308, 314
vision 11
visioning 64, 145, 239
visualization 130–3, 177–8, 236–7

Waterfall methodology 9–10, 243
work in progress (WIP) 176, 178–9, 181–2
work items 180–2
work packages 162, 163, 174–5, 207, 275–6
working agreements 88–9
workshops 238–40
written communication 236–7

XP (eXtreme Programming) 12, 298